STEVE PIDD

TAKING DOWN GOLIATH

RESOLVING MENTAL DISORDERS THROUGH THE MINISTRY OF THE HOLY SPIRIT

ABOUT THE AUTHOR

Steve and his wife Em first began to deal with people exhibiting, at times, severe mental disorders around 1991-92. It began a journey into finding God's answers for resolving these problems, which continues to develop today. Even from those early beginnings they had been experiencing some level of success. In 1998, they moved to a new place of effectiveness, when they began to experience the ministry that they now describe as, 'Truth Encounters.'

Their Christian service in this area was shared with their work as Senior Pastors until 2018. At that time, they felt that God was encouraging them to prioritize the training aspect of the ministry. They have been involved in Schools revolving around different aspects of healing internationally beginning from 1997. Since 2001 they have been conducting the 'School of Healing and Freedom' that they developed. They have presented this training in various locations, in Australia, and across the World over that time.

More information regarding the 'School of Healing and Freedom' can be accessed on their website. www.418centre.org

STEVE PIDD

TAKING DOWN GOLIATH

RESOLVING MENTAL DISORDERS THROUGH THE MINISTRY OF THE HOLY SPIRIT

EDITION 2

Copyright
Written and compiled by Steve Pidd
Edition 2
June 2022

All enquiries can be directed in writing to:
Steve Pidd
Email: contact@418centre.org

All rights reserved. This book is copyright. Apart from any fair dealing for the purposes of private study, research, criticism or review, as permitted under the Copyright Act, no part may be reproduced in any form (including electronically) without written permission.

THE HOLY BIBLE, NEW INTERNATIONAL VERSION®, NIV®
Copyright © 1973, 1978, 1984 by Biblica, Inc, ™
Used by permission. All rights reserved worldwide

THE NEW KING JAMES VERSION (NKJV)
Copyright © 1975, 1982 Thomas Nelson Publishers
Used by permission. All rights reserved

HOLY BIBLE, NEW LIVING TRANSLATION®, NLT®
Scripture quotations marked (NLT) are taken from the Holy Bible, New Living Translation, copyright ©1996, 2004, 2015 by Tyndale House Foundation. Used by permission of Tyndale House Publishers, Inc., Carol Stream, Illinois 60188. All rights reserved.

endorsements

It is my sincere belief that Steve Pidd and his wife Em would probably be the most experienced, knowledgeable and authoritative people in this area of ministry in this country. I say that without hesitation.
Pastor Lynnette Scholar, CRC Churches International, Mildura, Victoria, Australia

The healing ministry that has occurred in peoples' lives in our community has seen marriages saved and lives changed dramatically for the better. Many of these people now see healing as a normal part of their faith and have helped others with their healing.
Grant Laidlaw, Organic Church, Creswick, Victoria, Australia. Director Log Cabin Camp

Steve Pidd visited our church for 10 days ministry in 2012. The teaching and ministry he brought on personal healing was both thoroughly biblical and effective in its content. It led to transformation in many lives as well as helping greatly in the establishment of a ministry centre that continues today.
Peter Vincent, Community Church Bishops Stortford, UK

Pastor Steve Pidd and his wife Em are international leaders who personify a transformative way of ministry known as 'Truth Encounters'. The purpose and process of a 'Truth Encounter' is in the name. I had no reservation in writing this commendation having experienced this ministry and its release first hand. In addition, I have observed the transformative impact within my wife and friends where broken hearts have been restored.
Dean Emeritus, Professor David Giles, Professor of Educational Leadership Flinders University, Adelaide, South Australia

This is a very special School that has healed so many people. Pastors come from very far away, even other nations to attend the School. People are coming with many burdens struggling with things in their lives...through the School they're being touched, transformed, healed and set free, they will never be the same again. They have a testimony of the amazing things that God is doing inside and out, both spiritually and physically.
There are hundreds of Pastors who are coming together in unity on these Schools. It is a wonderful School, very unique, with many healed and delivered. Pastors are teaching their people what they have learnt, others are being reached with the materials being used in Churches and Bible Schools.
Pastor Wilson Ngando. Kenya

contents

INTRODUCTION   9

PART 1   **THE CHURCH AND MINISTRY TO MENTAL DISORDER**

Chapter 1	A world desperately in need of good news	13
Chapter 2	Beginnings in Ministry to Mental Disorder	23
Chapter 3	Mental Disorder from a Biblical Perspective	29
Chapter 4	Categorizing Mental Disorders	37
Chapter 5	'Heart beliefs' and identity	49
Chapter 6	The Origin of the Problem	57
Chapter 7	The 'heart' and modern Science	67
Chapter 8	The God Solution	83
Chapter 9	Accessing Memory for Healing and Freedom	93
Chapter 10	The Ministry Process	99
Chapter 11	Considering other important factors	117

contents cont.

PART 2   **SPECIFIC MENTAL DISORDERS**

Chapter 12	Healthy perspective on dealing with disorders	127
Chapter 13	Depression	133
Chapter 14	Anxiety and stress related disorders	145
Chapter 15	Common personality disorders	159
Chapter 16	Bipolar disorder	175
Chapter 17	Sleep disorders	183
Chapter 18	Dissociative disorders	189
Chapter 19	ADHD	199
Chapter 20	Eating disorders	209
Chapter 21	Substance misuse related disorders	217
Chapter 22	Schizophrenia	225
Chapter 23	Neurodevelopmental disorders	237
Chapter 24	Conclusion and Summary	245

introduction

You can't send an army into battle without the equipment and resources needed to confront their foe. Many Christians would like to help with the harvest, but simply have never been properly equipped to be bringers of the good news in its entirety.

Perhaps we can offer a story from the natural world to illustrate the need of preparation for taking ground from your enemies. There was a time of training, equipping, and putting together of resources prior to the D-day landing in World War 2. For the Church to fulfill her purpose and be all that she can be, there needs to be provision of equipping and preparation from the Kingdom of God to fuel the push to present a full and complete Gospel.

Those planning the D-day landing knew that on June the 6th 1944, when the troops endeavoured to take ground, they would need backing and supply from beyond the battle front. I love the story of Operation Pluto. The allies had calculated that 60% of the needs of their armies as they began the invasion would be fuel. It was going to be a very important and needed resource for their success. As an example, a Sherman tank would travel only about 250 metres on a litre of fuel....4 litres to the kilometre. (.7 miles on a gallon) Operation Pluto was a series of pipelines laid under the sea from Britain to Normandie.

Altogether there were 17 lines, which totalled more than 800 kilometres of pipeline which were laid. They were able to deliver 4.5 million litres a day, and contributed a massive 180 million litres of fuel to the war effort. The existence and installation of these channels or conduits of resource, were a critical factor for success and victory. The point that I'm trying make is that the supply came from another place, and was delivered onto the battle front where it was most needed. These conduits joined both the place of resource, and the place of need.

For the Church, we could say that there is an unlimited supply of provision from the Kingdom of God. The mission is to get it from heaven to earth where it is needed in a practical way. It must be delivered to the battlefront through supply lines that are connected to both heaven and earth. That's us! Our knowledge of the ways of God in ministry are those access points for supply. Knowing how to release Gods provisions to mankind makes us the delivery mechanism that He has purposed and intended all along. What if the end time revival of the church, so that it can bring in the Harvest, involves equipping the body of Christ to meet every type of need? Things that the World system cannot resolve. What if the harvest happens because people are drawn to the church, because the church is equipped to heal and free people of any kind of problem? In reality, the Bible reveals that this was always Gods redemptive plan for the gospel? What if people come to the Kingdom of God because the body of Christ has practical answers, more than just good music, and not just for religion. And I like, and value good worship music!

Religion at the end of the day involves activities that relate to God, that we can either do without Him, or we include Him in our programs, but we're in control. Unreligious Christianity is when God does things through His Church, that can only be done by His ability. So, when we talk about religion, we're talking about dealing with God on our terms. This could include some institutional repetitive practices, or more obviously supposedly pleasing Him through particular rituals or ways of doing things.

This publication is directed to helping us become a line of supply, addressing one of those areas of human need. Namely, we're presenting how to bring God's provision to the increasing problem of dealing with Mental disorders. Just as the requirement of fuel was 60% of what was needed to take back the ground in World War 2, easily 60% of the work of the Church would be in the area of Mental restoration in some form.

Names, locations and some details are changed at times in this publication in order to preserve confidentiality. The essence and lessons learnt in stories used as illustrations are based on genuine case histories. *

PART 1

THE CHURCH AND MINISTRY TO MENTAL DISORDER

CHAPTER ONE

A world desperately in need of good news

Preamble

Let me note at the beginning of this publication that one of my proof readers commented that it was as though; 'I laboured through the first two chapters, and then it was almost like I was set free.' This is to some degree true. There are some attitudes that I felt needed to be addressed, given the general position on mental disorders that appears to be prevalent in much of the modern church. To me these perspectives have left many unnecessarily suffering who could be set free. The thinking that has invaded the church has prevented a lot of God's children from receiving a permanent and complete healing.

Perhaps 20 years ago Christians were horrified if they thought that anything that was being ministered to them was from the world, or psychiatry. Now much of the modern church encourages you to seek out these methods of help with your mental and emotional issues. It is as if the gospel of man in the form of humanism has taken over. To describe this, it is taking the position that mankind will fix you without God. Surely this is a shadow from the fall of man, where we read the temptation of Satan in Genesis 3:5 claiming that man 'will be like God.' In other words, mankind now having access to new areas of knowledge, will attempt to fix their own problems rather than going to God for his help.

Have grace for me in these early chapters as I am wanting to turn people back to seeking and receiving God's provisions. I am seeking to address what appears to me to be a church that has become spiritually disoriented on this subject, and forgotten that God can set people free through us. It's a little bit like if your car has drifted off the edge of the road on one side, you have to pull the wheel pretty hard to get it back in the middle. Don't miss the ministry model which comes later because of these early chapters which address these positions. I'm reminded of the story of the frog being slowly boiled alive. He would quickly jump out if put in boiling water, but if he is placed in tepid water which is slowly heated up, he may well not notice the increase in temperature, and in the end be boiled alive.

The scope of the problem
According to figures released by the World Health organization, 1 in 4 people are likely to suffer from a mental disorder of some kind. That's around 2 billion people across the earth, and these figures are generally applicable to the modern church as well. In Australia they estimate that half of the population will suffer from a mental health condition at some time in their life. Conservatively we could project that for every person who is identified as having mental disorder, there are just as many who are never diagnosed. In practice it is my opinion that the number who would never even seek help is at least as many as those who do. In many nations that we visit there is virtually no mental health system to begin with. It makes it imperative for mankind that the church is equipped with the good news of the provision of God to minister into these areas.

Let me say, that given the epidemic of mental health issues that the world faces in these times, we should be thankful that there are so many people in the secular world who are dedicated to helping those with needs in this area. Their efforts in research, provision of support networks, and care in training cannot be underrated. The need for the input of mental health professionals is without question. Many people suffer the consequences of brain damage from recreational or other drugs, birth defects, and many other mental health issues. Without these supporting institutions, psychiatric wards, and places of rehabilitation there would be no hope for so many people.

We're not at odds with the mental health professionals. What we're saying is that the Church can certainly do its part in sharing in this work, particularly in supporting those in the Kingdom of God. We have the same goals, we're just dealing with the issues from a Biblical perspective, and have the benefit of the ministry of the Holy Spirit. We're certainly not saying that the mental health profession should be avoided, but rather we are recommending that the church should be equipped, so that Gods provisions can be the first option for those with these problems who choose to seek out the good news.

Over decades of ministry, we've seen multiple thousands of times where God has supernaturally set people free from disordered thinking that they could not change by their own efforts. Often times, at best they could hope to learn how to manage their condition. This is certainly not the good news that God promised. Many of these people have been on some kind of medication, which, in turn, has produced its own problems and side effects. At times we have ministered to people who have not been suicidal until they have begun taking a drug. Medications that can in some people change their chemistry and lessen suicidal tendencies, can at other times, in different people work the other way.

Our chemical body is a finely tuned system that can easily be disrupted. I ministered to a lady recently who was given a drug to treat depression. The result was that she began to have panic attacks. This was something that she'd never in her life experienced before. These attacks were purely the result of the pharmacological effect of the medication on her body. Some of these drugs are designed to mask the symptoms. Others attempt to balance, or reduce, the hormonal imbalances that are the outworking, and end of the line result in the body because of the persons disordered thinking.

In essence they are often attempting to fix the problem by dealing with the fruit and not the root. Sadly, today many consider inappropriate behaviours and mental disorder to be the result of chemical imbalances. Consequently, even children are at times medicated as the first attempt to resolve these behavioural problems. By the time they are teenagers they can have many complications from multiple drugs being used to balance each other out. The evidence is that in fact, the chemical imbalances are usually the result of mental/emotional disorder.

Research on why thinking produces confusion
I saw an article produced recently where some very advanced researchers observed the conflict between two separate but interrelated sources of thought in an individual as being the cause of mental issues. They concluded that these sources needed to be reconciled in order to deal with mental disorder. This research, hailed as the latest insight, is what we've been teaching and experiencing for years.

Obviously working without the benefit of the knowledge of the Bible and its teaching on the *'heart'* as the problem other source of thought, they had to come up with a theory as to why this might be. So, they theorised that we must have a primitive or reptilian brain. This is hailed as the newest discovery! Any Christian can read at any time about the *'heart'* in the word of God, and after we explain what it means, understand it as the root of the problem.

The Church and Ministry to Mental Disorders

Mental disorders are a set or group of disorders that are coming from deeper 'root' issues. If Christians are taught or led to believe that God can't or won't heal you, then you will get help where you can. As previously stated, this will usually lead to the secular world and the mental health professionals. For us this seems strange. For decades we've had people come to those of us who practice this type of ministry, after at times many years of expensive visits to Psychiatrists and Psychologists. Most often these people having experienced little or no change in their condition.

Many times, these people are now presenting with drug related issues from the various prescriptions and medications that they are on. In fact, in part, the motivation for writing this publication is largely because we have had so many people come for help who have not been helped by the methods of the World, and we then see God set them free. He does this just as He said He would by using the Biblical principles that we will be outlining in this book. As we will explain, this comes about through the ministry of the Holy Spirit.

In saying all of this I am in no way minimalizing the good work of the mental health profession. I think that they are a gift from God to mankind in general, and also to Christians who have no access to ministry from the church for their support and healing. I believe them to be a gift from God, but not <u>the</u> gift of God, the Holy Spirit. We understand that His ministry is primarily for believers, or those who will become believers by faith. That is to say that, God's goodness is for those who desire it, and can accept it.

At times we have Psychologists or other mental health professionals who are Christians attend our Seminars or training. On occasions they share the difficulties that they have to deal with through being limited in what types of approaches that they can use. So, I understand the commitment that these great people have to help those hurting or suffering. I can see the frustration that they have dealing with non-believers who aren't open to the gospel.

Statistics indicate that Psychiatrists in the U.S. suicide at a rate of more than 5, and up to 6 times that of the general population. A further article reported that 81% of Psychiatrists and Psychologists suffer from mental illness. A survey conducted in 2009 by the American Psychological Association concluded that of 87% of graduate Psychologists suffered from anxiety, and 68% reported symptoms of depression. Another major American survey found 61% of Psychologists were clinically depressed and 29% suffered from suicidal thoughts. The Psychiatric adviser reported this figure as 62% with depression, and 42% presenting with suicidal ideation or behaviour.

An article from the British Psychological Society, 27th April 2016 cited 46% suffered from depression, and 49.5% reported that they felt that they were failures. This and other readily accessible information is an indication that the methodologies and approaches that these people have been trained in, as a generalization, is not working for them. Clearly there is a need for the good news of the gospel and freedom from God amongst these people as well.

Recently I heard of a Christian carer who asked the psychiatrist that they were dealing with what the next step was for the mentally ill Christian that they were helping. The psychiatrist reportedly stated that they didn't know what to do. Another different man who visited me for ministry reported that his psychologist was more messed up than he was, and that all he did was talk about his own problems.

I understand that if Pastors aren't equipped to minister the gospel to the people and set them free, then giving the pastoral responsibility to the Psychiatrists and Psychologists to help those in need manage their problem may be the only remaining option. In that context we can be very appreciative of their dedication and efforts to help support those suffering in these areas. They are often doing an admirable job, working within the limitations of being without the benefit of the counsel of scripture, and consequently not working with the whole picture.

I'm sure that many people that we never see receive good and beneficial help and support from the mental health professionals. But the fact remains that we have people, (almost exclusively Christians), week in week out, coming for help who still have their problems after sometimes years of various secular treatments and approaches.

Is it possible that we, the Church, need to revisit God's letter of intent regarding the broken and captive? Should we again seek out why the

Holy Spirit and the anointed presence of God is on the Church today. (See Luke 4:18) Personally, I don't understand, why would we even seek to be disciples if we have no intention of being equipped to fulfil the Gospel?

Indeed, the workers are few, and so are those prepared to be trained in this work of the gospel. This means that believers with needs, who can't find or access genuine gifts, need to bridge their faith by trying to meet their needs through the processes offered by the World. The ministry that we are proposing in this book is very simple. Any believer can learn to do it. Some people struggle because it seems 'too' simple, "surely it can't be that easy?"

Hopefully you will see as we have, it is profoundly simple, but simply profound. It does require laying down your life, (that is your time,) to facilitate Gods will being done on Earth, and see people healed and released for His glory. With mental disorders there are often multiple beliefs that compound to create the profile. This can mean that at times a number of sessions are required to resolve the symptoms.

Mental disorders and the modern Church
There seems to be increasing pressure from advancing cultural humanism on many churches, particularly in big cities, to harmonize with the World in this area. In practice the world and the Kingdom of God operate with radically different principles and perspectives. In the end are we seeking to be seen to be doing the 'right thing' in our cultural setting, rather than pursuing the dictates of the gospel? Have we believed that mental disorders are bigger than Goliath, and too difficult for God and His Church to deal with?

Many consider, because this is seemingly such a big intimidating problem, that you have to have the special training and techniques used by people who don't understand the Bible, or believe in God and His promised provisions. Others simply seem to think that helping people in these areas is not their role. This can be a 'cop out' for not wanting to learn to how to help people. Or for not trying to do anything that you can't do in your own ability, because it might require faith, however small.

In a later chapter as we explain the Luke 4:18 passage, hopefully it will become obvious that this ministry is central to the Gospel. I recall a number of years ago visiting a large church in Northern Australia. They moved powerfully in the gifts of the Spirit, but their position was that if you had some kind of problem, you needed to be sent to a Psychiatrist or a Psychologist, or both. Have we now made these people the Pastors, and given them our mission?

Let me reiterate, we are not putting ourselves against these mental health workers. They offer support to a secular World that would otherwise have no hope. We *are* recommending trying God first, before you complicate things with drugs, or learning that your problem can only be managed, but never healed. God normally doesn't seem to heal side effects, so medications usually end up creating additional problems. It also makes our work harder if you've been down that road, because the world may in many instances be teaching you the opposite of what we are. We then have to work through what you've learnt from them before we can be effective in ministry.

It can be like sending a believer to an atheist for advice, and then expecting them to give God's perspective. It also at times means that we have to negotiate the effects of any drugs being used to bring about your healing. Normally this is still possible, but more difficult, depending on the amount and the type of drug that you are using. Either way it makes our work harder. Of course, if there are no trained ministers available, or you have no intention of looking to God for your help, then that may be your only remaining option. (We understand and acknowledge that drugs at times do help and support those suffering with mental disorders.)

Having worked with many who have suffered various treatments, my recommendation would be to; seek healing and freedom first, instead of management. Deal with the root of the problem, rather than learning coping mechanisms, or treating the fruit of the issue with chemicals. Let me repeat, these can at times create further imbalances to a delicate system, creating a myriad of other unwanted complications and side effects. These side effects would still usually need to be worked through even after healing. This means having to deal with sometimes long-term withdrawal symptoms.

It also means that because your brain chemistry and emotions are out of balance because of the drugs, so you don't receive the full benefit of your freedom and receive a sense of wellbeing until they are completely out of your system.

Even so, having said all of this, as Christians it's unfair on the medical profession, even ridiculous to expect them to be able to do what only God can do. Neither can Pastors or ministers heal you. But the Holy Spirit can heal you through them if they are trained in what to do.

Trained ministers

We have to ask the question, is a part of the problem that as the modern church we have had an emphasis on producing leaders, not ministers? We have to be very careful as ministers and leaders to not send the people in our care to World systems where they may be harmed by drug use and systems, that at best help them to manage their problems. God offers healing and freedom, and we have been given the task of ministering to God's children. To God this is a very serious matter. We see very clearly in the book of Ezekiel Chapter 34, that God warns those of us with this responsibility to not prioritize our own wants and careers over the healing of the people in our care.

> *Ezekiel 34:1-2,4 The word of the LORD came to me: [2] "Son of man, prophesy against the shepherds of Israel; prophesy and say to them: 'This is what the Sovereign LORD says: Woe to the shepherds of Israel who only take care of themselves! Should not shepherds take care of the flock? [4] You have not strengthened the weak or healed the sick or bound up the injured. NIV*

(Notably, the word 'shabar' translated here as injured, according to Strong's Concordance means to break up into pieces, or even broken hearted.)
We need to understand that the people in our congregations are not a part of our ministry, they are our ministry. What I mean here is, Church numbers and people following us are not there as a part of our personal success. They are there because God wants us to minister the good news to them. Their personal healing journey is, in part, our responsibility if they are open to the truth and seeking help. Am I taking the body of Christ to task here? Yes! Absolutely. This is a very real and present problem. There are so many suffering with these problems, and so few who can minister, and yet God has the answer.

Our 'interactive' God

This book will not make much sense to you if you do not believe that God interacts with mankind by the Holy Spirit facilitating His word through faith. There were religious people in the time of Jesus such as the Pharisees and the teachers of the law. They talked about God, and put a heavy load on the people, telling them how they should think and behave. But they had no faith or connection with God to help those in need. They just loaded them down with the word, and expected them to resolve their own issues. Perhaps this is what was referred to later in the scriptures.

> *2 Timothy 3: 5 having a form of godliness but denying its power. NKJV*

Does this refer to people who don't actually believe that God can bring change to the situations of His people? Jesus, quoting Isaiah the prophet, stated these people 'honoured Him with their lips, but their hearts were far away.'

> *Mark 7:6 He replied, "Isaiah was right when he prophesied about you hypocrites; as it is written:" 'These people honor me with their lips, but their hearts are far from me. NIV*

In other words, they said all of the right things, and said nice things about God. But they weren't in the type of relationship where they had faith. And as a result, they weren't available for Him to work through to heal and free the people. In any case, I don't think that any of us want to be in that group, and particularly in these times of such great need for the good news of Gods favour, interaction, and provision.

The complication of 'Many voices'

Many Christians that we deal with, especially young people, are confused by 'many voices.' To begin with, they have the viewpoint of religious leaders who have no experience in the ministry of the Holy Spirit to these issues. Next, they have the impression from their religious environments that God does not deal with mental disorders for some reason. When, in fact, it is high on His list of priorities for His church.

Then you have the instruction of the Psychiatrists, Psychologists or counsellors that they have been sent to. These secular people work very hard to help the needy to <u>manage</u> their problems which is admirable. But they are handicapped by not understanding spiritual principles, or the spiritual dynamics that are often involved in mental disorders. They work without the benefit of biblical instruction and insight on these matters. And they are endeavouring to help without the ministry of the Holy Spirit. This group often includes secularly trained Christian counsellors who add in a few prayers or scriptures to what they do, but again work independently of the Holy Spirit.

In addition to these other voices, there are well meaning Christians telling them to memorize scriptures, and, that this will cure them. Or that God will sovereignly set them free in an instant because they declare it or prophesy it. Others propose that perhaps you're being attacked by demons, and once they're cast out, you'll be free. Still more suggest that if you just think about yourself as a New Creation, then all of your problems will go away. These concepts at times hold a part of the truth, but in isolation normally will not resolve your problem.

You have to ask yourself the question; have you ever seen these models resolve mental disorders? So, these many ideas and voices in your head end up creating confusion. It makes it harder to find the Truth about where your help will come from, and what will be the hand of God for you.

Summary

In summary, we acknowledge the great efforts of the medical profession to help those who are suffering in this area. I am sure that many people receive great support in managing their maladies. We are not trying to compare or compete with the efforts of the secular world's attempts to help the afflicted. We also simply want to help, and are offering a Biblical perspective on how to be set free for those who are wanting to accept the freedom that God offers.

In this publication I am not proposing that every Christian should attempt to minister to the broken and hurting who are suffering from mental disorders. I am recommending that many would seek to be trained, and to operate under mature spiritual covering and advice. Jesus was revealed in the Gospels primarily as a minister. He was a leader in the sense that He had people who followed Him in the pattern of ministering to the people. His teaching and example was primarily in training and releasing His disciples into how to minister as He did. Hear, see, do.

The word Christian or Christians combined is used 3 times in the New Testament. There are many people with interesting ideas in the world who would describe themselves as Christian. However, the word disciple or disciples is found almost 300 times. It's fairly simple to find a Christian, they're common, everywhere. In my experience it's not so easy to find a disciple. That is, someone dedicated to following Jesus in the work that He did.

CHAPTER TWO

Beginnings in Ministry to Mental Disorder

As I begin to write on this important subject, I note that it appears that very little resource has been produced about this in Christian circles. Consequently, there is not much material that I'm aware of to give the Church perspective on how the body of Christ should view mental disorder. Nor is there much information on how to approach, and resolve these problems by basing our efforts on Gods plan for dealing with them along Biblical lines. So, before we get into how to set the captives free, let's first set the scene here as we begin. Later in Part 1 we'll present the model for ministry. Part 2 will be diagnostic in regards to the usual 'roots and fruits' of specific disorders.

Let me open by making the statement that people seem to be afraid to step into the area of mental healing, which I would estimate is 95% predictable, and is an easily learnt process. In contrast, the body of Christ leans largely towards physical healing, which is to a certain extent unpredictable, and is typically 95% reliant on faith. Personally, I don't see why this needs to be the case. In my experience mental healing is easier to resolve, (although more labour intensive), and we personally minister in both areas. Have we not understood Gods plan for this area of ministry? Is the body of Christ suffering in the same way as those who don't know God at all. Is this because of a lack of knowledge about God's intentions for mental restoration?

Hosea 4:6 My people are destroyed for lack of knowledge. NKJV

This passage refers to a knowledge of God, what He really wants, and His ways and provisions. In fact, the New Living Translation renders it this way.

> Hosea 4:6 *My people are being destroyed because they don't know me. NLT*

What Qualifies us to write on this subject?
This book is primarily intended to be a practical 'how to,' and diagnostic publication. I think that it's reasonable for the reader to ask what qualifies us to make the authoritative statements that we're going to present. So, I will briefly outline how we've arrived in the place where we can testify of how God works in this area. As with the early disciples we are simply sharing with you 'what we have seen and heard,' and relating to you our experiences of Gods workings in this type of ministry. It's probably all the more necessary to explain where we are coming from, because, as I have already stated, there appears to be very little about dealing with mental disorders in Christian literature.

As the old saying goes; 'there's no shallow end in God's pool.' In other words, God often puts you into a situation where you're way out of your depth. You have no way of dealing with your circumstances without His help. Nothing is too hard for God, but often the things that we're presented with are too hard for us! This is usually because of what we don't yet know about God, His Word, and His ways. In this place you begin to earnestly seek Him for the answers that only He can provide. This was certainly the case for us in 1991-2, where we found ourselves thrust into dealing with extreme mental disorder.

At that time, we were approached to work with and help a 9-year-old male child who I can only describe as the most broken person I had ever seen. We'll call him, 'Bob,' in order to make his story anonymous and protect his identity. To this day I have never seen anyone else who suffered the degree of brokenness that this child suffered from. I will make reference to that case here and there throughout the publication where applicable. Needless to say, we did not have all of the tools that we now have to resolve the problems that we were faced with. So, his ministry was over a protracted period of time as we learnt and applied what the scriptures revealed about dealing with these issues. At that time, we did not understand the underlying issue of corrupted identity that undergirds most mental disorder, as we do today.

Amongst other issues he presented with: Dissociative identity disorder, ADHD, Schizophrenia, ODD, non-verbal autism, OCD, fits, sleep disorders, self-harming behaviour, violence, allergies, along with many other problems. He was quite insane, and he was as close to being completely demonised as I have ever seen anyone. I recall looking back at him as I left his home after the initial assessment. And, as I looked at him, he stopped manifesting for the shortest time, just a brief moment, and looked at me. I remember thinking; "wow, there's a person in there!" It was a glimpse of the trapped and broken person that we were later to draw out and establish. We'll take up the outcome of working with Bob at the conclusion of Part 1.

His ministry was to be the beginning of 30 years, and tens of thousands of hours working in the area of helping restore God's order and wholeness to disordered mental states. Today we can confidently present what God can, and wills to do for those suffering with mental issues. An average week for my wife and I would be to see between ten and twenty healing and freeing moments relating to mental disorder. In these times we witness the Holy Spirit resolve mental and consequent emotional issues in a very practical and user-friendly way. If you take that back to 1998 where we first experienced the ministry model that I will present later in Part 1, you will quickly calculate multiple thousands of healing moments.

Depression resolved

A typical example of this would be our time with a Church where we ministered recently. Over 5 days my wife and I ministered to around 20 people. Amongst other problems which presented, at least 4 of those people had suffered from long term depression. By way of illustration of what we experience, and see God do, I will attach a couple excerpts from some of the testimonies that we have received from those ministered to.

"I have spent over 40 years living with depression. I've been in a psychiatric unit, had lots of counselling both Christian and non-Christian, deliverance ministry, had faith, confessed the word, medications ...tried everything on offer but nothing worked, which is so disheartening, especially as a Christian.I t was easy for me to believe that healing wasn't going to happen to me. After the teaching from Ps Steve and School of Healing and Freedom, I booked in for a ministry session. I'm on a new path living in freedom after ministry from the Holy Spirit working through the 'Truth Encounters' process. I am free from the deceptive beliefs that I held about myself all of those many years."

Another lady that I ministered to, either that day, or the day after had an almost identical testimony of all the things that she had tried. She was also set free. The following is from a lady that my wife ministered to during that same week.

"Prior to having prayer, I was feeling beaten down, depressed. It had become a real effort to go forward. God being God, as always, met me in my need. I had two memories that had pain attached to them, way back in my childhood. After prayer, inviting the Holy Spirit in, the pain attached to the memories is no longer there. Gone!! Thank you, Jesus. All glory to God. Since then, the main difference that I have noticed is that I'm not depressed. Plus, no pain attached to those memories. I have what I need for the journey ahead. Thank-you Jesus, Holy Spirit, all praise to our faithfully healing God."

These are typical of the stories and feedback that we receive week in week out. It's certainly not because we're clever, it's because God is able and committed to setting the captives free. It is also not because we have some special gift that others cannot operate in. We're just like everyone else. If I spent 30 years working as a mechanic fixing cars, even if I was a bad mechanic, I would probably know more about car problems than the average person. So, we're not boasting, and certainly don't consider ourselves anything more than others. It's simply what we have been doing.

Over the years we have refined and developed the process that we're wanting to present in this book and teach to others. Before we go forward, let me explain how we began to work in this particular model. Through the 1990's we mainly worked in the area of deliverance and Biblical counselling. This usually produced some kind of positive results, but most times did not completely resolve people's issues.

First experiences of the Truth Encounters ministry
In 1998 we were ministering to a lady with an anxiety problem. This had begun in an abusive situation when she was a child. The Holy Spirit set her free in a way that we were not expecting, and had not experienced before. It was the beginning of a learning curve which culminated in the 'Truth Encounters' ministry model that I will be describing in this book. Since that time, we've consistently seen God heal beliefs that cause various kinds of mental and emotional distress, disorder and duress.

As I have already described, most weeks over the period since then, we see many of these disruptive beliefs that affect mental order and wholeness resolved as the Holy Spirit sets them free. These are areas of thinking that neither the person, or any other person, or any drug, can change or put back into order. The result has been that God has predictively and consistently brought freedom and healing to the persons suffering.

So, when we say, if you do the maths, that's many thousands and thousands of these healing moments that we've experienced in varying environments across at least five continents, those figures only relate to those worked with by my wife and myself. Along with ministering ourselves, we've had the privilege of training others who also see the same freedom and healing come to those tormented by out of order or unwanted thinking. As you can imagine, the result is that you could not convince us that God does not, cannot, or will not, minister to mental problems.

Anybody whose thinking is not completely in order, has mental disorder to some degree. So, that's everyone on the planet, although, not every out of order thought process is necessarily serious enough to have a name.

Only the Church has been given the whole picture that is necessary to minister to mental disorder. I believe that in these times God is wanting us to return to His priorities.

CHAPTER THREE
Mental Disorder from a Biblical Perspective

Revival

In church environments we often talk about 'revival,' but miss the passages that describe what revival is to God. Personally, I think that it's unlikely that we'll ever see 'revival' until we prioritize what God prioritizes.... until what He wants for mankind becomes the central objective of the Church.

> *Isaiah 57:15 For this is what the high and lofty One says-- he who lives forever, whose name is holy: "I live in a high and holy place, but also with him who is contrite and lowly in spirit, <u>to revive</u> the spirit of the lowly and <u>to revive</u> the <u>**heart**</u> of the contrite. NIV (emphasis mine)*

From this text we can readily deduce that God wants His people revived. We take note from Strong's Concordance that amongst the meanings of the word translated as 'revive,' are the elements of recovering from our condition, being repaired, restored, and made whole. If our thinking is not ordered, or our mental state is disordered, it's fair to say that we're not whole or complete. We are to some extent, broken.

> *Strong's Concordance: 2421. chayah, khaw-yaw'; <u>quicken</u>, <u>recover</u>, <u>repair</u>, <u>restore</u> (to life), <u>revive</u>, (X God) save (alive, life, lives), X surely, <u>be whole</u>.*

Importantly, pay attention to the fact that a part of what requires revival, repair and wholeness, is what the Bible terms the '*heart.*' When the Bible refers to the '*heart*' it has a very practical and important application that is often missed. The word, mind or minds, appears in the New King James version of the Bible just over 100 times. However, the word, *heart* or *hearts*, is translated almost 1,000 times. Have we as the Church spent all of our time ministering to the mind, but dedicated little of our effort on the area of working with the '*heart?*'

What then is the '*heart?*' And why does it have such a prominent place in the Bible? Most people seem to think of '*the heart*' as some sort of non-descript emotional or spiritual romantic idea. It is in fact an incredibly practical and vital element of our being. It is also fundamental to the ministry process that we're going to present in a later chapter. Because it is such a neglected and untaught area of Christian ministry, I am going to deliberately endeavour to normalize it by <u>repetitively emphasising</u> and <u>referring to it</u> throughout this publication.

The practical meaning of the 'heart'

It's vital to understand what the Bible means when it refers to the '*heart*' in order to be able to comprehend God's intention and plan for us. And why ministering to the '*broken heart*' had such a central place in the ministry of Jesus. Again, referencing Strong's concordance, we can see in the Old Testament Hebrew that the '*heart*' in fact notably means; 'the thoughts and feelings proceeding from our centre which influences our will:

> 3820. leb, labe; a form of H3824; the heart; also used (fig.) very widely for the feelings, the will and even the intellect; likewise, for the centre of anything: (emphasis mine)

It is generally accepted that the 'soul' part of our being, means the mind, will, and emotions. Let me propose then that the '*heart*' is the central part of our souls, affecting our thinking, emotions and decisions. Once we accept this to be so, many scriptures begin to make sense in a very practical way.

> *Proverbs 12:25 Anxiety in the heart of man causes depression, NKJV*

This passage indicates that depression stems from anxiety in the '*heart*.' From what we have just explained, we now understand this to be specific anxious beliefs in the central part of our being. This then influences the thinking in our minds and creates conflict. Later I will explain more on how the '*heart*' has its own beliefs, and how to minister to these broken thoughts. The New Testament is also consistent with its understanding and breakdown of the practical aspects of what the Bible terms the '*heart*.'

Again, we'll use the very reputable Strong's Concordance to ascertain our meaning from the Greek language. Consistent with the Old Testament Hebrew, we see that it means thoughts that are elaborated as feelings from the middle of your being.

> 2588. kardia, kar-dee'-ah; the heart, i.e. (fig.) the thoughts or feelings (mind); also (by anal.) the middle:-- (+ broken-) heart (-ed).

The writer of the book of Hebrews clearly understood this concept, indicating that God was looking and discerning the thoughts and motives that proceed from the 'heart,' and not the mind. Failing to comprehend this leaves us ministering to the mind, which will not resolve, for example, depression. At best, a person can be taught how to use their mind to manage the problem. But it won't produce healing, order, and wholeness, because the mind isn't where the problem lies.

I will explain this more fully when we begin to look at the practical ministry. I will also include some recent science on the subject to support what the Bible has always said in regards to this concept. Suffice to say; once we comprehend the 'heart' in this way, that which scripture is saying about this area takes on a whole new meaning. We can see how the following passage indicates that the 'heart' has its own thoughts, motives, and intentions.

> Hebrews 4: 12 *For the word of God is living and powerful, and sharper than any two-edged sword, piercing even to the division of soul and spirit, and of joints and marrow, and is a discerner of the thoughts and intents of the heart.* NKJV (emphasis mine)

Perhaps we've unconsciously thought; "God mustn't have been as well educated as we are when He used the term 'heart' in the Bible! He seemingly didn't know that it's just a blood pump!" As usual, it turns out that God knows exactly what He's saying, and we, along with science are trying to catch up. We'll discuss the findings of modern research in more detail in chapter 7. For now, let's examine the ministry of the Holy Spirit through Jesus, and how He intends for it to continue through His Church, of which He is the head.

The Holy Spirit, the anointing, and the 'heart'
In Luke 4:18 Jesus unrolls the Scroll of Isaiah at what we now identify, with the inclusion of chapters and verses into the Bible, as Chapter 61, and announces God intentions for restoring mankind. This passage lists God's priorities and plans for the ministry of Jesus, and consequently His

Church. The Luke 4:18 passage is one of two places in the New Testament which details what the Holy Spirit was on Jesus for. It explains what He was anointed to do, and it describes the Fathers mission for Him on the Earth.

> *Luke 4: 18-19 "The Spirit of the LORD is upon Me, Because He has anointed Me To preach the gospel to the poor; He has sent Me to heal the brokenhearted, To proclaim liberty to the captives And recovery of sight to the blind, To set at liberty those who are oppressed; ¹⁹ To proclaim the acceptable year of the LORD." NKJV (emphasis mine)**

*Note: for some reason various other translations have omitted 'to heal the brokenhearted.' This is difficult to understand, when it is clearly present in the Greek language that it is translated from.

To break this down, we can plainly see that the Spirit of the Lord is upon Him firstly to preach the good news. The word translated here as preach also means to declare, or 'bring' the good news, which is incidentally how it is rendered in the New Living Translation. To amplify this then, our observation is that the Holy Spirit was on Him, and anointing Him, to declare and 'bring' the good news or gospel. People studying the scriptures often use what is known as the law of first reference. In other words, things are listed in order of importance.

So, when Jesus reads out what the good news was going to be, and lists Gods purposes and intentions for His ministry on Earth, we observe that the very first thing that he states is that He has been sent to heal the broken hearted. As we've just explained, the '*heart*' means thoughts and feelings coming from your centre or middle. In fact, feelings are an elaboration or extension of a thought that is felt in the body. So, they are one and the same. We've now come to understand that the '*heart*' holds beliefs that produce these thoughts and feelings. They affect how we perceive life, ourselves, and consequently influence our decisions. As we saw in Hebrews 4:12 they even shape our motivations towards doing what we do.

The Ministry of Jesus and mental disorder
We could then sum this up as Jesus announcing that He's going to heal or central thinking that is broken and not in the order that God intended. This thinking is distorted and influenced by the beliefs of the '*heart*.' In the modern world this is described, if it is sufficiently distorted, as mental disorder. So, it could be interpreted that Jesus was announcing that the Spirit of the LORD was on Him to resolve mental disorder, and that this was the number one priority of His mission.

The word translated 'heal' in this passage is the Greek word, iaomai, which means to cure, heal, and importantly, make whole. There are various different Greek words translated as 'heal' in the New Testament. Many times, when we use the term 'heal,' it is interchangeable with concepts such as, repair, put back in order, restore. These are consistent with the meaning bring to wholeness in an area, such as mind or even body. In fact, healing of the body often results from bringing the thinking back into order. Healing here then, is used in reference to fixing something that is broken.

Healing is the remedy, or way to deal with something that has lost its integrity, (wholeness), and is now broken down out of created order. According to Websters dictionary, to be whole means to be entire; complete; unimpaired; not defective; healthy; sound. In other words, nothing is out of order. In regards to healing the brokenhearted, we could then justifiably paraphrase this announcement of Jesus as; 'I have come to bring wholeness to the disordered thinking that people hold at the core of their being.'

It is worth noting that God's Spirit works to bring us a disciplined, in order, or sound mind, as it is described. Clearly from the following passage the antithesis, or opposite state, of mental soundness is anxiety. Fear described as anxiety is normally present in some form in virtually every mental disorder observed by man. It has not come from God, but from another source which we'll explain in a later chapter.

> 2 Timothy 1: 7 *For God has not given us a spirit of <u>fear</u>, but of power and of love and of <u>a sound mind</u>. NKJV (emphasis mine)*

A sound, ordered, disciplined or self-controlled mind is translated here from the Greek word; sophronismos.

This then, rounds out our introduction of Luke 4:18 as the basis for understanding God's position and priority on healing mental disorder. In fact, it shows us that it is a central part of the good news. It's bad news if God can't or won't help you with mental disorder. But it's good news to hear that He both wants to, and is able and committed to resolving these issues. The passage goes on to relate how Jesus would announce freedom from captivity and release the oppressed. Most often this bondage that He's referring to exists because of deceptive beliefs that are held at '*heart*' level. The old saying is that if the devil has your mind, he has you! We'll take up this theme, and Gods plan to deal with it, as we continue to unfold God's priorities in this area.

The anointing of the Holy Spirit and the Church

As we've already indicated, Luke 4:18 describes what the ministry of Jesus was to be. To announce and bring the good news of Gods favour and grace, and then demonstrate it by ministering God's goodness and provision to those in need. We then see Him performing these tasks throughout the gospels. It was in fact the reason that the anointing and presence of the Holy Spirt was upon Him, specifically to perform these tasks. The other reference to the Holy Spirit empowering Him for ministry is found in the book of Acts. Let me point out that the power of the devil is deception. If our thinking is broken down in regards to ourselves, others, and even God, then we can expect that the devil is behind it. It is how he gains power <u>over</u> us, and fulfills his goals for us.

> *Acts 10:38 how God anointed Jesus of Nazareth with the Holy Spirit and power, and how he went around doing good and healing all who were <u>under</u> the <u>power of the devil</u>, because God was with him. NIV (emphasis mine)*

So then, why is the anointing of the Holy Spirit on the Church that Christ Jesus is the head of? Naturally it follows that our ministry and work co-labouring with Him will be to outwork the same Gospel instructions that He operated under. In other words, the presence and anointing of the Holy Spirit is on us, the Church, for exactly the same reason that it was on Jesus. To heal the brokenhearted, to set the captives free, and to heal the sick.

> *John 20:21-22 So Jesus said to them again, "Peace to you! As the Father has sent Me, I also send you." ²² And when He had said this, He breathed on them, and said to them, "Receive the Holy Spirit." NKJV*

The good news is that as we set ourselves to learn how to perform this mission, the result, which we can testify to personally, is our own healing and restoration. This includes a closer walk with God, partially because we're involved in what He's all about, which is helping and restoring people. And also, because we come into a greater understanding of His nature as we see Him ministering to the hurting through us. We place ourselves in a position of faith and reliance on His ability and provision.

> *Isaiah 58: 6,8 "Is this not the fast that I have chosen: To loose the bonds of wickedness, To undo the heavy burdens, To let the oppressed go free, And that you break every yoke? ⁸ Then your light shall break forth like the morning, Your healing shall spring forth speedily, And your righteousness shall go before you; The glory of the LORD shall be your rear guard. NKJV*

Taking on the mission
I observe many areas of the modern church today encouraging Pastors to the put off the responsibility of ministering to mental disorder through healing the broken hearted. Is it possible that we've been deceived into sending them to the world for their help? Again, have we expected the mental health professionals to do the work that the Holy Spirit is meant to do through us, and given them our mission? What I am saying, is that God, through believers, is more capable than anyone working in their own abilities, no matter how well trained.

Could we be expecting many souls to be saved, but our focus is mainly on offering them a good church service? Certainly this is important, but what if we have no good news about God resolving the person's problems? Tell someone who is depressed that they'll be going to heaven in 50 years from now when they die. It's good news, but much less than God the Father intended, and Jesus paid for.

The masterplan of discipleship
There were limitations in how many people Jesus could reach personally. In part this was because He limited Himself to being the Son of man, walking the Earth in a physical body as we do. He announced that making disciples who would do what He has been doing was the answer to the needs of so many. God has not moved in the notification of His plan for the Church. As the Father sent Jesus, so He is sending us. The challenge seems to be to get the modern Church back on mission, prioritising what God prioritises.

Our observation is that often there is a great deal of activity around churches, but very few people fulfilling the job description provided for us in Luke 4:18. When we set ourselves to pursue the commission that we have been given to continue the work of Jesus in our times, if you are like us, you will find that 95% of the work that you do will be ministering to the *brokenhearted*. That doesn't mean that you won't heal the sick or cast out demons. It means, in my experience, most of your work will be in this area. I think that is because this is the greatest area of need, and perhaps that's why God has listed it as His priority.

> *Mathew 9:37-38 He said to his disciples, "The harvest is so great, but the workers are so few.* [38] *So pray to the Lord who is in charge of the harvest; ask him to send out more workers for his fields." NLT*

CHAPTER FOUR
Categorising Mental Disorders

Collating symptoms
What are termed 'mental Illnesses' or 'mental disorders,' are names given to a grouping of symptoms, problem responses, behaviours or feelings. For example, anxiety or depressive disorders. So, these titles are identifying tags used when people present with the same general list of problems as another person. As a rule, they identify the 'fruit' of the issues and not the 'root' of the problems. Later when we get into specific mental problems, we will endeavour to give you both the 'fruit,' and what we have found to be the common 'roots' to these issues.

Most articles that you can study on these disorders will instruct you that that these problems often share common elements with other mental illnesses. And that the identifying traits for these problems varies slightly from one case to another. This may well be because of the attempt to partition and label these illnesses for the sake of identification and treatment. Even though there is an attempt to categorize and 'box off' disorders, in reality many of them come from the same 'root' problems and '*heart*' beliefs. The 'fruit' then is often a collection of different responses and ways of coping, or compensating for these inner beliefs, which predictably produces the different 'fruit' that presents.

Having the same 'root' beliefs is why the conditions so often overlap. But it also points to the fact that if there can be a variety of 'fruit,' that there may be extra elements to the disorder that are other times absent with other problems. This can indicate that you might be looking at a sometimes larger, and sometimes smaller 'root' base of '*heart*' beliefs. To put this another way, mental disorders can have the same 'root' beliefs, along with additional beliefs that compound the problems and can produce either additional, worse, or more complex disorders. This in turn attracts new titles and descriptions for the symptomatology that the person fits into. It's also why people are at times diagnosed with multiple disorders and illnesses because of the 'fruit' that they present with.

What we can tell you after many years of ministry, is that over and over you repetitively minister to people with the same causative inner beliefs as others carry.

So, as we begin, we must bear in mind that many of what are termed 'mental illnesses' or 'mental disorders' share characteristics and traits with other disorders. This is because the people with the problems have similar distorted inner beliefs about their identities that produce these imbalances. They may manifest differently because of the degree of damage, the depth of the identity trauma and abuse that has been received, and/or the personality of the individual. Along with these influences are items such as the general environment that they grew up in, and may still live in today.

We can summarize then, by reiterating that the names of mental disorders are basically the collation of the particular symptoms, results, or 'fruits' of 'deeper inner beliefs' learnt in previous historical situations. They are observations of the consequent reactions, responses and behaviour as evidence of these beliefs. So, they are in essence, a collection of 'fruit' that is categorized and named.

Many of the studies and articles on these problems list the symptoms, *fruit*, or outcome of the disorder. It is, however, difficult to find information on the *roots* of the problem, with most articles stating that that don't know where the mental disorders come from. So, they suggest multiple possibilities. They usually propose environmental factors, possible genetic influences, or an upset in biological factors of some kind.

In practice we have not found any genetic interference in healing ministry ever. Although we acknowledge generational spiritual influences that can affect gene expression. As a principle, in general the majority of the time your chemical state follows your thinking, and not the other way around. In not understanding the genesis (origin or mode of formation of something) of the problem they generally set about to manage the symptoms. As we've said, because this list of identifying traits, symptoms, behaviour and responses to stressors are common, they are often found in other disorders as well.

So, naming disorders, and listing the 'fruits' of problems can be a massive over complication. We've spent many years simply asking; "what is your problem?" Later we would find out that there had been some kind of diagnosed disorder resolved. So why write the book? There is value as a diagnostic tool in what we are going to work through. We're going to list and suggest, along with the symptom's, the typical roots of the problems. So, if you see the 'fruit,' you will know what kind of 'root' that you're generally dealing with. Before we get to the diagnostic section in Part 2, we're going to give you tools to be set free.

Let me make it clear here that we rarely ask people the secular name of the issues that they're presenting with. At times we do know, because they have up until the time of ministry been receiving treatment from a Psychologist, Psychiatrist or counsellor of some kind. We normally just begin with; 'what is your problem?'

Putting into perspective the stigma of Mental disorder
By definition nobody on the planet has perfect order in their thinking. Therefore, all of us have some measure of mental 'dis-order,' and exhibit characteristics that at times fit into these categories, although we may never be diagnosed. In fact, almost everyone's thinking is out of order in some way in regards to how they see or perceive their identity, although they may not be aware of it, and have convinced themselves that they don't have issues. Labels can be cruel, and sadly people can make these labels their identity, that is who we believe that we are, like *Blind* Bartimaeus in the Bible. If I have a cold or influenza, then it's not who I am, it's a condition that I find myself in because of something that I've been exposed to.

It can be identified by the symptoms that I'm dealing with. I would not identify myself as influenza Steve, I've got influenza, because after a while I won't have it. In much the same way you might be Steve who has Bipolar, but it's not who you are, it's what you've got. This condition is a result of programming and influences that have come to you through situations and circumstances. These troublesome '*heart beliefs*' can be removed, and your current condition can pass away, and you will recover completely. This happens through the ministry of the Holy Spirit, as He facilitates the intentions of God for you.

When my wife and I first began to go out together, we were, like most people presenting to each other our best version of ourselves. We suppressed all of the hurts and negative issues that we carried. Later, when we married, we began to see all of the other side of each other that hadn't been evident when we were courting. The good news is that the negative things that now surfaced were not the true us. They were the result of the distorted identity beliefs that we both carried. Later, when these were resolved, we ended up getting the best version of each other. That is, the version of us that we saw when we used to go out together at the beginning of the romance…. us without the junk!

In a church environment it is best to avoid using secular terms and tags where possible. Otherwise, we are perhaps adding to the belief of unworthiness that the person often already carries. With that in mind this book is intended to be a diagnostic tool for the use of ministers or people who have already been diagnosed and categorized by the world system. This is increasingly something that the modern church has to deal with for reasons that we've already described.

So then, what is Mental Disorder?

A Mental Disorder then, by definition, is when something in your thinking process is not functioning in a healthy orderly way. In much the same way as a physical disorder is when one or more of your bodily systems are out of order. The prefix 'dis' means 'not' or 'none.' So, when we add 'dis' to the beginning of a word it now takes on an opposite meaning. In this case then we can say that a mental disorder is when your thinking is not in order, or there is no order in some area. This means a lack of wholeness, peace and harmony in your thinking. Your mental processes are impaired, disordered, corrupted, disrupted, not whole…. or we could say that they are; broken, or unsound, because they are not working as the designer intended.

Diagram 1

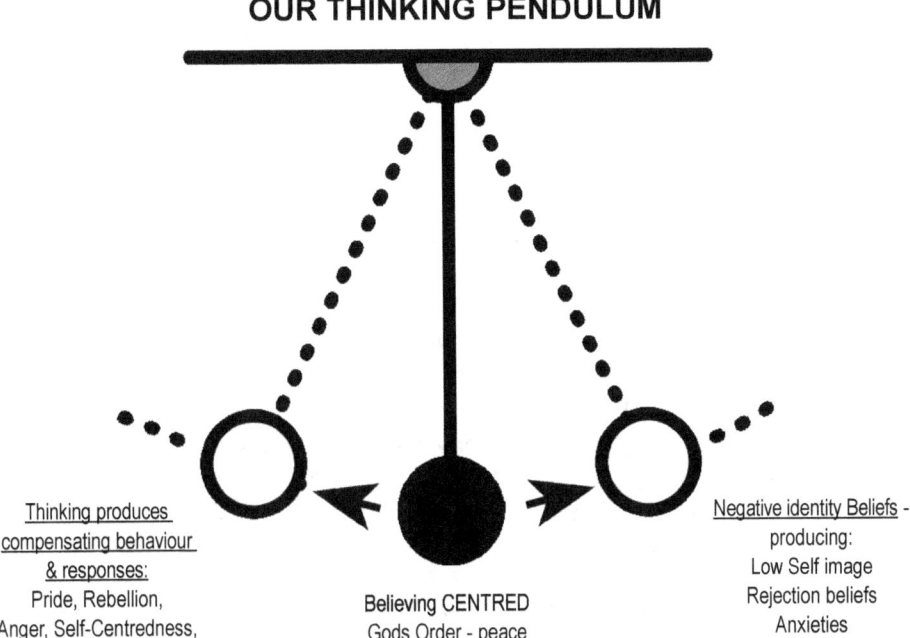

Mental order and spirituality

This lack of wholeness in our thinking lowers our defences against the possibility of being deceived by spiritual entities. It opens us to the probability of trying to solve our problems ourselves, and these solutions are often the basis of sin. Therefore, as with every other area of our person, mental disorder also has a spiritual dynamic. Jesus, referring to His own state of wholeness, points out that because He has no wrong beliefs in Himself, the devil has no way of leveraging Him or manipulating Him. His thinking was whole and healthy, and in the order that God the Father intended. Jesus had a correct picture of His identity, how the Father saw Him, what the Father really is like, and what His mission on Earth was. He also had perfect discernment of the deception in others that caused them to be vulnerable to the devils' schemes.

> John 14:30 *"I will no longer talk much with you, for the ruler of this world is coming, and he has nothing in Me. NKJV (emphasis mine)*

We take 'nothing in me' to mean, no wrong thinking or areas of deception. The New International version words it as; 'He has no hold on me,' and The New Living version renders it; 'He has no power over me.' In other words, because Jesus had no wrong areas of believing, the result is that the devil has no power or hold on Him. This is the place that we as believers are aiming for through the process of receiving truth in sanctification. Very much this is the journey of conforming to the likeness of Christ, and coming to the fulness of His stature. This happens through being established in truth about God, and about one's own identity. References: Romans 8:29, Ephesians 4:13

Mental disorder produces emotional imbalances
What are termed mental disorders also produce related emotional issues, and most often have a relational and physical outworking. For example, anxiety is a negative feeling or emotion that is, in the first instance a thought or belief about your circumstances. Anxiety is made a chemical reality in your body through the release of stress hormones. When these are imbalanced long term, your physical body is also imbalanced. So, disordered thinking becomes negative emotion, which in turn results in physical problems. This is why with many mental problems there are co-occurring emotional and eventual bodily disease issues.

We could say that if your mind is not at ease, then your body may flag that dis-ease. If your mind is not in order then eventually your physical state will be out of order as well. It can be a bit like a jigsaw puzzle in the sense that if there are parts missing that should be there, then the picture is not whole and complete. If there are areas of our thinking, such as positive thoughts absent, then the picture of our person and identity can also be not whole.

Let me reiterate, there are a number of different words in the New Testament that are translated as heal. For example, the Greek words, *Iaomai*, or *Sozo*. Both of these words for heal, include wholeness as a part of the meaning. When we use the term healing: we mean 'make whole' through some means. We have already presented that healing a *broken heart* literally means to make whole the broken thoughts coming from the beliefs held in the centre of your being. The result of this is balanced emotional states, and results in physical wellbeing. Perhaps in the following passage John was referring to the outworking of your soul functioning well will be being in good health. Science certainly undergirds this concept.

> 3 John 2 *Dear friend, I pray that you may enjoy good health and that all may go well with you, even as your soul is getting along well.* NIV

Certainly, the Bible is all about resolving disordered, unbiblical thinking. At times this is through renewing your mind in regards to God's instructions on what our thoughts and attitudes should be. We do this through voluntarily learning about the ways of God, and basing our thinking on biblical precepts. Importantly, it happens also through dealing with the influences of involuntary thinking and believing that is the result of *heart beliefs*. We'll begin to deal with this ministry of the Holy Spirit shortly.

Healthy mind, healthy body

Illness or disorder then, whether mind or body, relates to some area that lacks wholeness and proper functionality. The lack of peace in your thinking progresses from not being at 'ease' in your thought processes, to not being at 'ease' in your body and health. Hence the term for physical disorders of dis-'ease.' When there is a lack of balance or peace in your thinking, it is played out in your body by an organ in your brain known as the hypothalamus? The hypothalamus elaborates thought into your body mainly through your electrical system, (Central nervous system,) and your hormonal system, (Endocrine system, chemical messengers.)

By way of simple example, if you begin to think about your favourite food, your hypothalamus will instigate the release a hormone called ghrelin. This hormone will begin to make you feel hungry. The intake of food was initially a thought, but now your hypothalamus has translated it, and elaborated it into a physical state. If you have, for example, bitterness, anger, anxiety or self-rejection, this thinking, whether conscious or unconscious will be outworked in your body hormonally through the action of the hypothalamus. If our thinking hasn't become Gods thinking, it will have a negative impact on mind, emotion and finally body.

> Proverbs 4:20-23 Pay attention, my child, to what I say. Listen carefully. [21] Don't lose sight of my words. Let them penetrate deep within your heart, [22] for they bring life and radiant health to anyone who discovers their meaning. [23] Above all else, guard your heart, for it affects everything you do. NLT (emphasis mine)

Again, we note in this passage that the 'heart,' is inner thoughts and beliefs that influence your thinking.

Within our chemical bodies is what is known as the 'hormone cascade.' Implicated in this cascade are hormones that balance each other out. Physically, when these are in balance, this is known as 'homeostasis.' This word means that your physiological processes are balanced, and you are in health. As a well-known doctor once said to me; "as far as your body goes, hormones make the world go around." Mental order, resulting in emotional and relational wholeness then are the basis for physical health.

Disorder or not at ease in your thinking often means <u>dis</u> - ease in your body

We have found that almost exclusively the problem thinking behind many mental disorders is related to your identity. So, theoretically if you have a mental disorder and lack of wholeness in how you see yourself, nine times out of ten you will have a co-existing chronic health problem. Or at the very least a predisposition for a physical disease or syndrome which may not yet be realized because you are young. The experts tell us that nearly 90% of diseases are caused by negative emotions of some kind.

As we've just illustrated, emotions are a chemical and electrical elaboration of a thought or belief. So, the reason that physical conditions and mental disorders run together is most often because the roots of the complaint are one and the same. (Just as mental and emotional states are one and the same, stemming from the same source.) Possibly the other 10% of diseases that people suffer are indirectly caused by mental and corresponding issues. These can occur through other disorders such as eating disorders, poor nutrition, lack of exercise as the result of your condition, substance abuse, or even prescription medications.

There are multiple studies easily accessible on the internet to confirm that mental and physical illnesses are often co-occurring. One study concluded that 74% of people with a mental disorder had been given a diagnosis of at least one chronic health problem, and 50% having two or more chronic health issues. I would imagine that the age of the person would have a part to play in this. The study went on to report that persons with serious mental illness tend to be in poorer health than persons without mental disorders.

Another article from the Canadian Mental Health Association stated that 'mental health and physical health are fundamentally linked.' The article went on to point out that people with mental disorders are at a higher risk of experiencing a wide range of chronic physical conditions, and conversely people with chronic health conditions can be diagnosed twice as often as presenting with anxiety and depression as the general population. Indeed, anxiety of various kinds is implicated in some form in more than half of the diseases' that we deal with. It is almost always present in some form with mental disorders.

As I've already stated, there are a great many scholarly and internet articles and studies that confirm this as factual, so I will not labour the point. A couple of further thoughts: Firstly, not everyone is diagnosed as having a disordered mental and emotional state. Secondly, any negative mental and emotional issues, even if not severe enough to be categorized as a mental disorder, will have a negative impact on health and wellbeing.

The old saying is that it begins in the mind but ends in the body. Actually, in practice, it most often begins with the influence of 'heart beliefs' on the mind, which then corrupt your thought processes, and these play out in emotions and health.

The most common source of conflicted thought

Why is your mental state challenged to begin with? What does the Bible say about this conflicted, anxious, or confused thinking that is not working together in an orderly way? Why does it almost seem as if your mind is working against itself. What is the reason for your thinking not lining up, and you being double minded and having contention in your thoughts?

I've already proposed that in order to understand all of this you need to understand what the Bible calls the 'heart' from a Biblical perspective. I've also offered that most people think it's simply some warm fuzzy emotional or ethereal part of a human being. As we examine this important key to healing mental disorders, in a very practical way you will see that it means much more than this, and has implications for every area of life. To fit all of the pieces together properly, let's briefly look at what is biblically meant in regards to the mind.

> Mathew 22: 37 Jesus said to him, " 'You shall love the LORD your God with all your <u>heart</u>, with all your soul, and with all your <u>mind</u>.' NKJV (emphasis mine)

We note in the previous passage that the 'heart' and the 'mind' are distinct from each other, and though they are linked in function, they are treated as different parts. Your mind means your thinker, reasoner, your computer.

> dianoia, from G1223 and G3563; deep thought, prop. the faculty (mind or its disposition), by impl. its exercise:--imagination, mind, understanding. Strong's Concordance

We could say that your mind uses information that is available to it to think things through, work them out, and come to decisions. It has the capacity to voluntarily learn and store information. This is deliberately learnt information processed by the mind and considered important. This knowledge is reportedly stored in a part of the brain that the scientists term the limbic system. So, on one hand we have memory and things that we've decided that are important to remember, and are now stored in our cranial-brain. Then on the other side we have the 'heart,' which by now we understand to be thoughts and feelings coming from our centre or middle.

This is where we've found the conflict to come from. If you can imagine that your mind is in the middle, and it's trying to settle matters such as how you should perceive yourself, and how you can interact with the world in life. The problem is the conflict between these two sources or streams of information that cannot be reconciled. There's what you would like to think, and decide that you should think, based on information that you've learnt and stored in your brain. For example, that you're acceptable and good enough. But then there's conflict with what you really believe that has been programmed involuntarily into your '*heart*' about who you are when you were growing up. Now there is disorder and confusion as you try to solve this contrary thinking with your mind!

Diagram 2

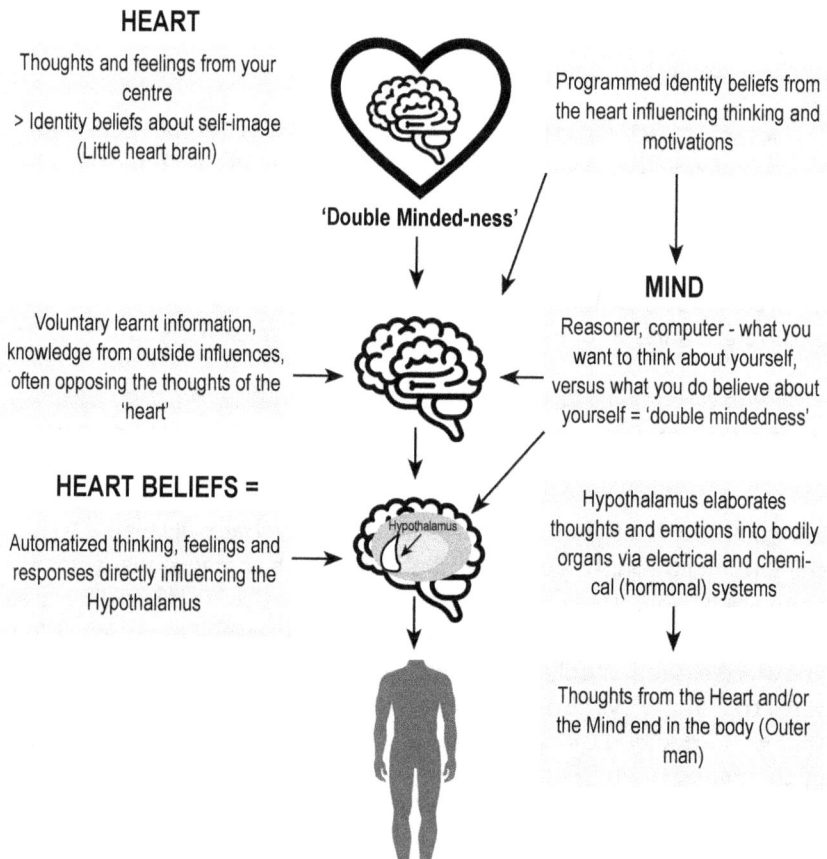

Diagram 3

THE BASIS OF MENTAL CONFLICT

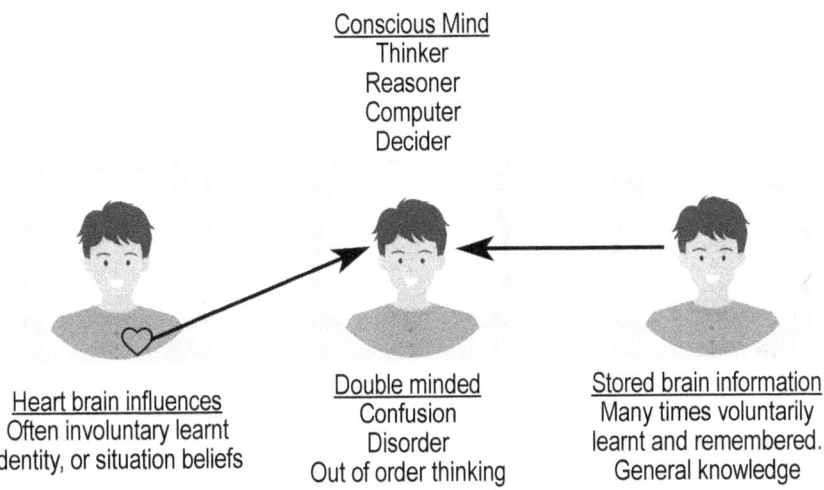

The Apostle Paul floated this crisis between these two factions working against each other in himself in Romans Chapter 7. There was what He knew was right, which he wanted to do. But then there was something else working against that, which worked against producing the behaviour that he wanted. Am I suggesting that he had sufficient conflict for it to be termed mental disorder? No, but I am proposing that there was enough tension to cause him anguish in his attempts to bring his thinking and activities into harmony. As I've pointed out, nobody on Earth has perfect order in their thinking. So, in reality, the degree of disorder is on a sliding scale.

> Romans 7: 15 *I don't understand myself at all, for I really want to do what is right, but I don't do it. Instead, I do the very thing I hate. NLT*

In verse 15 we first glimpse the mental anguish that Paul is going through. Trying to work out these seemingly uncomprehend able inner conflicts are often a feature of mental disorder. It was two streams of thought in one person. He describes both of these influences as; 'I.'

> Romans 7:23-24 *But there is another law at work within me that is at war with my mind. This law wins the fight and makes me a slave to the sin that is still within me. 24 Oh, what a miserable person I am! Who will free me from this life that is dominated by sin?*

The word translated as 'law' here figuratively means another principle. Paul acknowledges that his sin choices are the result of this other, unwanted influence. Jesus clearly stated that sin came from the 'heart.' That is;

the inner thoughts and feelings from your centre. Jesus understood and explained that this was the source of the sin problem. '*Heart*' belief issues. In fact, as we will soon see, the state of our '*heart*' thinking and believing affects everything that we do.

> *Mathew 15:19 For out of the* **heart** *come <u>evil thoughts</u>, murder, adultery, sexual immorality, theft, false testimony, slander. NIV (emphasis mine)*

Once again, we can note that the '*heart*' has its own thoughts. These are just examples of some sins that proceed from efforts to compensate for corrupted thinking and believing at '*heart*' level. There are other lists in the gospels.

> *Romans 7:25 Thank God! The answer is in Jesus Christ our Lord. So you see how it is: <u>In my mind</u> I really want to obey God's law, but because of my sinful nature I am a slave to sin. NLT (emphasis mine)*

In summary, we could say that the power of the sinful nature, or flesh as it is sometimes termed, is the old programming of the '*heart*.' The Bible reveals that it is in fact the root of all other issues.

Proverbs 4:23

As a result, the Bible indicates that the most important thing that we can do, is to be careful to make sure that we end up with the right kind of beliefs in our '*hearts*.' Because of the powerful implications of this for every area of life, I've taken this prime scripture on the '*heart*,' and combined various translations of the passage to amplify, and give proper credence to its meaning. When you remember that the men and women who lead our World have motivations and influences on their decisions that come from their '*heart beliefs*' as well, you begin to see why the '*heart*' holds such a prominent place in God's word. It shapes our paths and condition personally, and our world corporately.

> *Proverbs 4:23 (Composite - Steve Pidd version) <u>Above all else</u>, (in other words it is the most important thing to do!) guard your <u>heart</u>, be careful what <u>conclusions</u> that you come to in your thinking, because they will become '<u>heart beliefs</u>' and programming which <u>will affect everything that you do</u>, and create all of the issues that you will now have to deal with, because <u>those beliefs will influence your thinking</u>, and your thoughts run your life!*

From years of experience ministering to people's issues, I would consider this to be a very accurate picture and understanding of this passage. These inner '*heart*' beliefs have implications for every area of life.

CHAPTER FIVE

'Heart beliefs' and identity

As a man thinks in his 'heart'
Proverbs 23:7 For as he <u>thinks</u> in his <u>heart</u>, so is he. "Eat and drink!" he says to you, but his <u>heart</u> is not with you. NKJV (emphasis mine)

*Authors note. The statement in this verse is a literal translation, and is clearly present in the Hebrew text. I note this, because that which I'm about to propose needs to be based on an accurate scriptural reference. For some reason some other translations have omitted these important components.

Proverbs 23:7 Instructs us that 'as a man thinks in his *heart*, <u>so is he</u>.' '<u>So is he</u>' tells us that the perception of his identity, the state of his values, and what is important to him, will decide the characteristics of his being. That is, who he perceives himself to be...identity.... where he fits into the world, how he considers himself, and what is appropriate in regards to interacting with other human beings.

As we read the full scripture passage, we can see that his state of being is that of a man who doesn't believe that he can be generous for some reason, even though seemingly he would like to be, or considers it the right thing to do. This '*heart thinking*' coming from his '*heart believing*' could relate to a historical situation. We term this a 'situation belief.' So, he may be 'reserved' with what he has because of what he has learnt through past experiences. Perhaps he grew up in a household where there was not enough, or where there was poverty. Or a situation where there was no one there to provide. Perhaps inwardly he now fears that there is no one to look after him and meet his needs, so as a result of this insecurity he feels that he has to look after his own needs and be protective of his resources... hence, he becomes miserly.

In this historical place he experienced anxiety about lack of provision being there.... now he's worried about what will happen if there is not enough? Fear then projects expectantly into the future, and he's now on guard against there not being enough again. Generally, these beliefs are taken in involuntarily, and learnt through some kind of emotionally charged, fearful, traumatic or repetitive experience. So, they are beliefs learnt through experiences, rather than deliberately computed, reasoned out, and deliberately decided and remembered. They are usually taken in through childhood when you're learning about life.

Identity

To go a little deeper, we find in practice that more commonly there is some kind of belief about a person's identity that is at the root of the thinking in their '*heart*.' Your thinking about your identity depicts who you believe yourself to be – so, who you think you are, largely comes out of the thinking and beliefs of the '*heart*.' This is such a vitally important concept to comprehend in resolving all kinds of complaints including mental disorder. So, let's continue to expand this idea.

Your identity is the image of *self* that you hold; or your *self-image*, as it is more often referred to. Self-image dictates how you identify yourself. In other words, what you believe about your *identity* and who you are.... your traits, perception of your characteristics, who you believe yourself to be. When that image of self, or how you see yourself is distorted, is where in our experience almost all problems come from. Your thinking about your SELF is out of order. How you think about your SELF is of prime importance in terms of who you think you are: As the late American Psychologist William James put it: "You're not what you think you are, but what you think, **you are**!"

If you think in your '*heart*,' that you're worthless, stupid, weak, not important, not loveable, not enough, not what you should be, and so on; these become your self-perception, self-image, or identity as we call it, whether it's true or not. Then the conclusion of that thinking in your *heart*, (Proverbs 23:7) might well be that you're not worth providing for, and consequently you need to look after yourself, and make sure that there is enough.

*(Remember that most often you now don't know what you believe in your *'heart,'* because you learnt it a long time ago. Now you know it as emotions, behaviour, responses, attitudes, reactions, anxiety, as disorder, or even illness. This is KEY to understanding the basis of ministry and freedom. For the most part, people are no longer aware of what they believe in their *'hearts.'* They're trying to think what they learnt later in life, and 'know' that they should think in their minds, but it's conflicted.)

The vast majority of what are termed mental disorders come down to a distorted image of SELF at *'heart level.'* In other words, your picture of your identity is corrupted in some way. So, what is termed mental illness, is most often actually broken heartedness.

Remember as he thinks in his *'heart'* so is he, or we could say, **so is** that man, or woman. In other words, how that person is, their state of being, is the direct result of their *'heart'* thinking. This means their spiritual condition, (either in deception or truth about self), their mental and emotional state, their physical condition, and their status in relationships all comes from the thinking of the *heart*. It produces how he or she is!

Psychologists, or well-meaning Pastors may tell you that all you need to do is think this way, or that way, and that will resolve your issues. The problem is that beliefs from the *heart* influence your thinking in another direction, away from what you want to obediently think or believe about yourself. Now you are what the Bible calls *'double minded,'* confused that you can't think and believe the way that you want to. You are conflicted between what you want to think, based on information that you've learnt through life, and what you really think and believe about your identity underneath in your *'heart,'* having been pre-programmed by experiences or repetitive themes.

Conflicted thinking, as 'Double mindedness'

Where there are disordered mental processes, you will generally find confusion, contention, and conflict in the mind. Your reasoning and logic are convoluted, which unsettles your thinking, and produces what can be described as, anxiety, distress, anguish or even torment. You are not at peace and harmony in your thought processes, and cannot resolve this problem. The Bible refers to this state of not being able to get your thoughts to agree with your believing as double mindedness. This condition of conflicted thinking is considered to make you unstable or unbalanced in all of your ways.

Clearly, this does not always mean that your thinking is out of order sufficiently to have a name attached to it. However, it does reveal a principle, that if you are in two minds in your thinking, you are unstable in regards to that which you are trying to resolve, think through, work out, and come to peace about. A part of your thinking is not sanctified, that is, made whole, and in God's order.

James 1: 8 he is a double-minded man, unstable in all his ways. NKJV

Stable means to be firmly fixed, established, or steady. For example, the foundation of a house has to be firmly fixed in the right way to be stable. Everything has to be in the right place, and built in the right order for it to be balanced and able to withstand external pressures. In the case of having faith in God, these external pressures may be in conflict with the word of God.

It is interesting to note, that this passage is referring to coming to wholeness in your thinking. In particular it is in regards to having a correct picture about the true identity of God. Faith in essence comes from knowing who God really is, that He can be trusted, and that His word can be relied on. The double minded man is conflicted between the mental knowledge of God that he has acquired voluntarily through learning, and the involuntary '*heart*' knowledge of God that is founded on his previous experiences of authority figures. In an unfallen world these figures, usually parents, would have modelled the nature of God experientially to their children.

So, retained voluntary head knowledge, and involuntary experientially learnt *heart* knowledge, create instability and contention in the mind, or thinker, which is caught in the middle. You'll find that this principle is consistent throughout scripture. For example, on this subject of faith in God, Jesus pointed out that you can have whatever you believe in your '*heart*,' not what you want to believe in your mind. As we now know, in part, He's referring to having conflicted beliefs in regards to what you believe about who God really is, and what He's prepared to do for you. In my opinion and experience, importantly, this more often this relates to how you believe that He sees you.

Usually how you expect God to see you, and feel towards you, is seen through the lens, or filter, of what you believe in the centre of your being about yourself. If you believe that for example, you're not good enough, not acceptable, not loveable, not important, not worth noticing, and so on...... then even though you choose to believe in your mind that He wants to give you good things, in your 'heart,' you really believe that you're not worthy. Consequently, the practical reality of our faith is based mainly on our own perception of our identity and worthiness for God to help us.

> Mark 11:23 "I tell you the truth, if anyone says to this mountain, 'Go, throw yourself into the sea,' and does <u>not doubt</u> in his <u>heart</u> but <u>believes</u> that what he says will happen, it will be done for him. NIV (emphasis mine)

The Greek word translated *doubt* in this passage means; to hesitate, contend, stagger, waver or be partial. In other words, the person is still trying to work it out and be settled about it. There's contention between two opposing views. There is not order and agreement between his inner believing, and what he would like to think would happen based on learnt information. This includes head knowledge and mental agreement with things taught to you about God, or read in the Bible. This leads only to mental agreement or assent to the information deliberately and consciously taken in. These do not produce beliefs that produce faith in the heart. In our experience this is mostly resolved through dealing with the distorted identity beliefs at *heart* level.

Of course, additionally, in part, this mental conflict could be in regards to how you understand the identity and characteristics of God.

Dealing with conflicted identity
As we've said, most times we can apply this principle to how you perceive your own unstable picture of your identity and characteristics. This gives us powerful insight into mental disorder. In the case of double-mindedness and conflict about God, what you are unstable about there is that what we would like to believe about Him, is in conflict with what we actually believe about Him. In this instance the mental conflict is in regards to the identity and characteristics of God. But it is based on and shaped by how we would expect Him to view us because of how we see ourselves.

So, our own distorted view of our identity is by far the more common faith blocker. There is conflict about what we would like to think about ourselves, and what we really do think about ourselves. In reality, we've found that often the reason that people cannot believe God for their provision, is mostly to do with their impression of their own acceptability. This then comes back to how we perceive our own identities. God appears to be leaving us without a way of dealing with this double-minded, conflicted believing and thinking in James Chapter 1. However, as we move forward to James chapter 4, we see Him giving us the KEY to how to deal with the problem.

James 4:8 Draw near to God and He will draw near to you. Cleanse your hands, you sinners; and <u>purify</u> your <u>hearts</u>, you <u>double-minded</u>. NKJV (emphasis mine)

This passage summarizes the ministry process that we're going to propose as we go along. The passage states that you need to 'cleanse your hands.' In other words, deal with the deeds that may make you feel like you don't deserve God's abundance. As we have just read, it goes on to say that the reason for your double-minded unstable thinking is that your '*hearts*' have not been purified. By now we understand '*hearts*' as beliefs, thoughts and feelings coming from your centre. The Greek word here translated as purify, means; to make clean, or to sanctify. In other words, to deal with the corrupted thinking in the centre of your being which is having a negative influence on, and destabilising effect on your mind.

To sanctify your '*heart*' thinking means to remove the distorted fallen world influenced beliefs that you hold, and bring them into God's order. The way that He tells us to do this is to draw near to Him. We can, therefore summarize this process as identifying our corrupted inner beliefs, and then bringing them to Him to be rectified. These are beliefs that only He can restore. No amount of counselling can heal broken '*heart beliefs*.' It's something that only God can do.

Our work in the ministry process is to help people come to see what their '*heart*' beliefs are. And then God's part is to bring healing and wholeness through the Spirit of Truth. It's simple and we'll explain how it works shortly. More information will not bring about much change, because the problem is not in your mind. Most people have enough knowledge about what they should think, but it has not set them free. The vast majority of mental disorder is rooted here, in the *heart*. There are of course other reasons for mental problems.

Additional reasons for mental disorder
*Some of the main exceptions to '*heart*' beliefs when discussing mental illnesses, are firstly birth defects of some kind. For example; brain damage, or an extremely low IQ, or lack of intelligence. Secondly, damage to chemical brain function. This could come from either recreational or some prescription drugs, medications or treatments. These chemicals produce altered states which can affect your mental condition. Some potent drugs, such as LSD or cocaine, can literally 'fry' the wiring in your brain, destroying brain cells, and producing permanent damage. Virtually all substances of this kind will in the very least chemically alter the functioning of your brain.

Electroconvulsive therapy treatment such as ECT can also reportedly damage your brain function and alter your mental state. There may be additional reasons for mental disorders, such as mechanical brain damage from an accident. However, in my opinion, by far, the majority of mental disorders that have been given names in modern society are the result of the types of sources relating to *identity* or *heart* beliefs that we've been describing. These other exceptions that I've listed would usually need to be healed through the prayer of faith.

CHAPTER SIX

The Origin of the Problem

Before we move into discussing the solution to resolving many mental disorders, we need to identify where the issues began, and how things got out of God's order to begin with. From there we can understand why we're dealing with these disorders, and why restoring God's order is so relevant. To do this properly we have to go back to the beginning. We know that God does not make things that are faulty, dysfunctional, or don't work properly. So, what happened? When God created mankind and placed them on the Earth to rule and reign, they were initially whole and complete.

The genesis or beginning of this problem for mankind was when Adam and Eve sinned. Now with knowledge of good and evil, they formed a different picture of their worth, which I would propose, resulted in a distortion of how they saw themselves. Now, based on this new *self-picture*, instead of expecting God to be there for them they hid. How they saw themselves in their '*hearts*' had changed when they submitted to another nature. They now perceived themselves as unworthy and possibly even evil. This fall came after previously not even being aware of good and evil, and it changed their perception of their characteristics and identity. It also affected their expectation of God being accepting of them. What is known as the old nature, the flesh, adamic, or sinful nature was now established.

The Fall of Man

> *Genesis 3:1 Now the serpent was the shrewdest of all the creatures the LORD God had made. "Really?" he asked the woman. "<u>Did God really say</u> you must not eat any of the fruit in the garden?" NLT (emphasis mine)*

What just happened? The devil sought to bring Adam & Eve <u>UNDER</u> his counsel by deception. This deception came about by creating a perception. What the devil was in fact proposing is that God was keeping something good from them. Implying; "really, He's keeping that from you. Wow, He's not being very fair!" In other words, suggesting that God did not have their best interests at heart. That God is not in fact a good, loving, caring God. The old fallen nature which rules over unredeemed mankind actually has this default position and imprint. Through their eventual decision Adam and Eve displayed that they received as truth and submitted to this idea that God is not fair.

It's worth noting here that the root to rebellious behaviour or attitudes is always a perception of injustice or unfairness. So, the devil was casting doubt over the character and nature of God. By suggesting that God was the 'bad guy' in keeping the tree of knowledge from them, he was also promoting that he, Satan, was the good guy. "Did He 'really' say no? Wow, I would let you eat from it! In fact, I encourage it!"

This temptation is behind virtually every sinful choice made today. Fundamentally proposing; 'This is what you need, this will make you happy.' 'God is keeping the good stuff from you, so you need to take what the world offers, even if it's forbidden and you know that it's wrong!' Sin in either the Old Testament or the New Testament means *to offend, an offense*. So, this first sin was an offense, because they doubted God's character and goodness. God did not reject man, man rejected God as a person who can be trusted and submitted to. It's not surprising then that having submitted to wrong belief, or unbelief about God being the cause of the fall, that the way back to God is through faith.

In fact, access to all of God's provisions are now through faith alone. God has limited Himself to working through faith. We can define true faith then, as having a correct picture of God that causes us to trust in Him. As a result, when the Bible reveals that without faith it is impossible to please Him, we can now understand that He is only pleased when we have a correct picture of Him which is based on truth. It is accepting that He wants good things for us.

> *Hebrews 11:6 So, you see, it is impossible to please God without faith. Anyone who wants to come to him <u>must believe</u> that there is a God and that <u>he rewards</u> those who sincerely seek him. NLT (emphasis mine)*

For Adam and Eve, the perception now created led to a misinterpretation of the situation, and why God in love had protectively forbidden the tree of knowledge of good and evil. Having now concluded that the devil was a better person to take advice from, they made a decision, which led to an action. The action was disobedience, rebellion against the *perception created about* the nature of God. Sin then, comes through being <u>deceived</u> into misinterpreting the truth of a situation…including who we are…and what is actually good for us! In choosing to submit to another spiritual being, the consequence of that choice was that mankind came under the influence and imprint of the nature of that being.

The devil calls God a 'liar'

> *Genesis 3:2-4 "Of course we may eat it," the woman told him. ³ "It's only the fruit from the tree at the center of the garden that we are not allowed to eat. God says we must not eat it or even touch it, or we will die." ⁴ "<u>You won't die</u>!" the serpent hissed. NLT (emphasis mine)*

The devil now proposes an even more direct challenge to God's integrity and trustworthiness! He directly calls God a liar, that is, someone who is deceptive. In saying that 'you won't die,' the devil is proposing that he is the authority that should be trusted in. As we know they submitted to this deception of Satan, thus empowering him and making him the authority over their lives. (Romans 6:16, 2 Peter 2:19)

> *Genesis 3:5 "God knows that your eyes will be opened when you eat it. You will become just like God, <u>knowing everything</u>, both good and evil." NLT (emphasis mine)*

Satan's own problem was wanting to lift himself up to be like God. This led to his own downfall. It's fairly easy to discern in the modern world that mankind is working hard to resolve his problems with his own solutions, apart from God. This includes setting his own standards of morality, and what is acceptable in every area of life, often in the face of the counsel of God found in the scriptures. It is a part of the imprint of Satan who they followed and submitted to. It was a part of his nature, which now became a part of the nature of fallen mankind. In the church, possibly the biggest enemy of revival is that many are 'wise in their own eyes' 'knowing everything'- it's an imprint of the old fallen nature.

Satan's own two problems that brought about his fall, were that He wanted to lift himself up in pride, and to be his own god. And as a result, he no longer wanted to submit to the authority of God and come under him. Pride is where you make yourself above others, and rebellion, where you set your own limits and rules. What was the reason for his fall? We need to make careful note.

> Ezekiel 28:17 Your <u>HEART was filled with pride</u> because of all your beauty. You <u>corrupted your wisdom</u> for the sake of your splendor. So I threw you to the earth and exposed you to the curious gaze of kings. NLT (emphasis mine)

The Pride in his '*heart*' distorted his wisdom. His own pride and desire for *self-realization* led him to fall from his privileged place. When we are in pride we seek to ascend in our *self-esteem* and see ourselves above others. This fallen nature does not want to submit to others. We could describe this as behaviour that is trying to compensate for the loss of identity that we suffered at the fall. We try unconsciously to resolve this corrupted low self-image where we perceive that we are not enough, by becoming, in our own eyes, more than others. This is a manifestation of the old nature that we are trying to destroy as Christians. In my opinion the power of the old nature is the distortion of our identities. This low self-image is how Satan instigates our following and serving his nature.

> Isaiah 14:13-14 For you have said in your <u>heart</u>: 'I will <u>ascend</u> into heaven, I will exalt my throne <u>above</u> the stars of God; I will also sit on the mount of the congregation On the farthest sides of the north; 14 I will ascend above the heights of the clouds, <u>I will be like the Most High</u>.' NKJV (emphasis mine)

We can see that Adam and Eve were now accepting of the counsel of Satan. They were being appealed to through the lust of the eyes, the lust of the flesh, and the pride of life. The very temptations that still seek to bring us into submission. (1 John 2:16)

> Genesis 3:6 The woman was convinced. The fruit <u>looked</u> so fresh and <u>delicious</u>, and it would <u>make her so wise</u>! So she ate some of the fruit. She also gave some to her husband, who was with her. Then he ate it, too. NLT (emphasis mine)

The fallen nature
Before we talk about how this affected identity and impacts on mental disorder, let me just point out some other aspects of this satanic imprint

on humanity. Satan was and is all about 'self.' Self-gratifying, self-serving, self-realization, self-pleasing or pleasuring, self-exalting, and so on. So, as a consequence I often translate the old nature as the 'self-life in a fallen state,' or the 'fallen self-life.' Personally, I'm fairly convinced that when Jesus said things like die to 'self,' and lose your life to gain it, this is what He was referring to. The abundant life is for those living in the new nature, or the new 'self,' spiritually renewed, and seeking to conform to the likeness of Christ, as opposed to the desires of the old nature.

If you die to the old self-centred nature, losing that life, then you are living in the new, Spirit led, God- centred nature. The Bible reveals that these 2 natures are opposed to each other. What is translated as the sinful nature, or the flesh in the Greek language is 'Sarx.' It means the old fallen nature that is conformed to selfish worldly thinking. We can see that as with double mindedness, there is conflict in the thinking and desires. Sarx = the Satan <u>influenced and programmed</u> version of you! We are imprinted with his characteristics and nature, which produces the resultant behaviour; pride, rebellion, control, SELF seeking. Sin began with him. His 'heart' was corrupted and it distorted his own created identity.

> *Galatians 5:17 The <u>sinful nature</u> wants to do evil, which is just the opposite of what the Spirit wants. And the Spirit gives us desires that are the opposite of what the sinful nature desires. <u>These two forces are constantly fighting each other</u>, so that you are not free to carry out your good intentions. NLT (emphasis mine)*

Further evidence that the old sinful nature is all about 'self' can be found in the following passage that describes its activities. You can see that all of the fruit of the fallen sinful nature relates to what you can get for your<u>self</u> to make you feel better about you. Whether it's sensual pleasure, control, or having to be right and win an argument.

> *Galatians 5:19-21 The acts of the sinful nature are obvious: sexual immorality, impurity and debauchery; [20] idolatry and witchcraft; hatred, discord, jealousy, fits of rage, selfish ambition, dissensions, factions [21] and envy; drunkenness, orgies, and the like. I warn you, as I did before, that those who live like this will not inherit the kingdom of God. NIV*

As we've said the power of the Old fallen nature is the corruption of identity that we've suffered. Sin then, such as pride, rebellion, control, bitterness or lusts are often our bad solutions to resolve the perceived needs of this broken inner self. In practice what we find is that when people's *broken hearts* (distorted identities) are made whole through the ministry of the Holy Spirit, they effortlessly become less concerned about meeting these perceived needs, and automatically are more occupied with helping others. So, the fruit of the Spirit in this context, is often the fruit of Him directly ministering into the 'heart' and setting you free. The fruit of the Spirit is clearly caring more about how you deal with others, rather than what you can get for yourself.

> *Galatians 5:22-23 But the fruit of the Spirit is love, joy, peace, patience, kindness, goodness, faithfulness, [23] gentleness and self-control. Against such things there is no law. NIV*

The implications of the fall for the human identity

For Adam and Eve, the issue was in regards to who they were submitting to. It was about who they were allowing to influence them, shape them and their thinking, and imprint them. It was who they were following, and co-operating with. It was the initial introduction of another nature and likeness for mankind, who originally were whole and created in the image of God. This is the KEY to every problem on Earth! Satan does his work through those who are conformed to his likeness. Deceived into serving him and submitting to him by serving themselves. This is how he has his expression and controls the world.

The 'state of being' and characteristics of humanity had changed. The fundamental qualities of who we were meant to be was altered, because our priorities, choices and what we decided that we wanted, and who we followed changed. Our priority and choice now became; the lust of the eyes, the lust of the flesh, and the pride of life. Now what we were all about as people became living for these things, for SELF. Rather than living to be in relationship with God, *pleasing, serving* and obeying Him, now it was about pleasing SELF. We could say; You align yourself with whatever you decide to follow.

We all carry the effects of our fathers. Their characteristics and behaviour have influenced and shaped us because we looked to them for how we should act. Even if they were absentee, we have physical characteristics from them, and our identities and self-worth have been impacted and formed even by them not being there for us.

Let me reiterate, mankind was formerly made in the image and likeness of our true Father, God. In submitting to the devil, and conforming to his image and likeness he gave birth to this new fallen nature in us. Because man made Satan the god of this age, he automatically became the spiritual father of the characteristics that he imparted to all born from that time on. So, we were all born under the influence of this fallen nature.

Nobody was ever born already having received spiritual rebirth. We all had to choose it, just as mankind had chosen to follow another. As we will soon illustrate, because the deception of mankind by the devil to emulate him is the problem, then receiving the truth of God, and being conformed and restored to His likeness is the solution.

> John 8:44 "You are of _your father the devil_, and _the desires of your father you want to do_. He was a murderer from the beginning, and does not stand in the truth, because _there is no truth in him_. When he speaks a lie, he speaks from his own resources, for _he is a liar and the father of it_." NKJV (emphasis mine)

These fallen propensities are why, as children, we misinterpret life in a negative way, and imbibe incorrect beliefs about our identities. We were all born under the power of these spiritual influences. When we choose to follow God, our true Father in heaven, we begin the process of being remade and reshaped to His likeness. These fallen tendencies distorted the identity that God had intended and given to mankind as unique individuals.

Let's just recap here, another way that we could describe your identity is the characteristics that identify you. This relates particularly to your perception of SELF and self-worth, and your consequent image of your identity. That is, who you are, or who you believe that you are, leading to this image of self. In summary, we could say that we're all born under the influence of the fall. Under the shadow of a father that is not our true father.

Distortion of our identity
If then, the perception of your identity depicts how you are, and a person's state of being is based on how that person sees themselves in their _hearts_, then if you are wrong about what you see perceive and believe, then you are deceived. And your picture of self is corrupted and distorted from that which God intended and desires for you.

When we are discussing mental disorders, this is the usual root of the problem. You do not see yourself as God sees you. Your truth about yourself is not God's truth. So, you are conflicted about accepting who God really created you to be. Freedom and wholeness come as God reveals His truth and perspective to your heart in this regard.

> *Proverbs 23:7 "For as he thinks in his heart, so is he. NKJV*

We previously presented that Proverbs 23:7 instructs us that you are who you think you are – your image of self becomes your state of being! In other words, you will live your life according to what you believe about your *identity* in your *heart*. For example, if you believe that you're stupid or dumb, and won't be able to learn as others do, you will not attempt to study or qualify for anything. If you believe that you're not good enough to be acceptable, you may avoid relationships, because you now fear that people will reject your worth. If you believe that you are weak, you will transmit this from the core of your being, and possibly attract being pushed around or even be the recipient of bullying.

The flip side is that if your *heart* has been programmed with positive self-beliefs, then you will be confident, and unstoppable. You will exude value, and worth, because this is what you *think in your heart* about your SELF. Once a person's identity is established and taken to heart, you or anyone else cannot convince them otherwise. For example, once someone believes that they are worthless for some reason, later you will not be able to change that thinking about their identity. But this also goes the other way. If someone learns that they are valuable and significant in their formative years, later you will not be able to convince them that they are not.

It's well documented that the programming of our identity occurs before 10 years old, while our brains are malleable and in a state of plasticity. It is the time where we are deciding our state of being, that is, who we are, and how we are. This includes encoding what we think our characteristics are, and how we believe that others see us. Jesus clearly understood the significance of this. He considered it a priority to show little children that they are valuable, and worthy of time and attention. He rebuked His disciples for not treating them in this way.

> *Luke 18:15-16 Then they also brought infants to Him that He might touch them; but when the disciples saw it, they rebuked them. [16] But Jesus called them to Him and said, "Let the little children come to Me, and do not forbid them; for of such is the kingdom of God. NKJV*

The powerful and permanent influences of key people
Most of these influences on identity occur through the authority figures in our lives, namely our primary care givers. That is Dad and Mum, and other influential authority figures in those early formative years, such as teachers. These are the ones who are meant to be helping us to see ourselves in a positive way. These key figures were, in God's order, to represent Him and His nature, and were intended to protect and guard our *hearts*. Sadly, because of their own brokenness and falleness, they often shape our identities in a negative way. We have no knowledge as small children, so we accept however they deal with us as being a correct assessment of our person. Through this process, falleness and brokenness transfers from generation to generation, right back to Adam and Eve.

In fact, sin began with the spiritual influence or instruction of Satan, and entered the human race through his own falleness and corruptness. Am I saying that mental disorders are sin? No. I'm proposing that they are the result of sin. If people reject you, don't show you love, don't build you up, abuse you, fail to protect you, neglect you, then that is the sin of the fathers. It is sin, because it is offensive to God, because it is manifesting the nature of Satan to your children, rather than the loving, accepting and caring nature of God.

However, knowing that we have all begun under the outworking of the fall, He is gracious and redemptive to us all. I recall teaching one of our Schools to a group of ministers around the turn of the century. As I finished presenting these and other concepts regarding how children are imprinted early in life, one well known minister said to me; "I wish we knew all of that before we brought up our children." I responded with, "me too!" Some of the programming or training in regards to self-perception could be things that we do or say that we shouldn't, negative talk or expectations on our children.

Other negative programming comes from a child coming to fallen conclusions and misinterpretations themselves through things that were never done that should have been. This could be the absence of a hug, or not telling them that they're a great kid, or they're doing ok. It's all a part of the training of the *human identity* that they will carry for life. Only God Himself can change that heart programming once the inner thinking has been concluded and established.

In regards to the importance of this developmental stage of life remaining a shaping force for life, the Bible makes the following statement in

Proverbs Chapter 22:6. Significantly, the word translated child here, refers to someone from the age of infancy to adolescence. This means up until the age of 10 years old. So, before science identified this as the critical time for shaping future pathways, the Bible had already stated it to be so long ago.

> *Proverbs 22:6 Train a child in the way he should go, and when he is old he will not turn from it. NIV*

* Important: Behind most mental disorders, many broken relationships, emotional issues, a high percentage of physical diseases and problems, you will find the <u>distortion</u> and <u>corruption</u> of our identities. This is so important, even critical, for the modern church to understand. When Proverbs 4:23 tells us that our 'heart,' that is, our thoughts, beliefs, feelings and resultant decisions from our middle, affect every area of life, it really means it.

> *Proverbs 4:23 Above all else, guard your heart, for it affects everything you do. NLT*

Having established the root reason and most common cause for mental disorder, let's now move on to the solution. But first, let's make a brief diversion and examine if there is any supportive physical evidence in regards to the role and influence of the 'heart' on the state of our thinking and mental condition.

CHAPTER SEVEN

The 'heart' and modern Science

As a generalization, the Bible says what it means, and means what it says. In our times we regularly find that mankind comes up with things that are 'new,' or 'the latest research.' It often turns out that these 'new' findings were described in the Bible already. The *'heart'* is no exception. Areas of science now appear to confirm that your physical heart has its own little brain and thoughts. Given that we are primarily spiritual beings who have a host body for Earth, it's virtually like a physical manifestation of a spiritual reality.

It's not essential to the teaching, or to receiving your freedom for you to embrace that this little brain of the heart is the resting place of troubling identity beliefs. We are not trying to prove this here, and as I write I acknowledge that I'm not a scientist, and am working outside of my area of expertise....it is simply interesting to explore in the context of the Biblical presentation of the function of the *heart*.

I'm including this chapter because of my constant amazement at the things that God has created. And how research so often eventually reinforces how the Bible is perfect in all of its knowledge and counsel. When the Bible termed the *'heart'* as the source of our problems did God get it wrong? Did we think, "God didn't you know that the *'heart'* is just an organ for pumping blood around the body!" Is God watching us, smiling knowingly, as we begin to discover that the *'heart'* is more than just Bible talk or Christian jargon?

Research on the 'heart-brain' or 'intracardial brain'

Some of the first researchers in the field of psychophysiology to examine the interactions between the heart-brain and cranial-brain were John and Beatrice Lacey.* They invested 20 years into studying the workings of the heart-brain. Their rigorous experimentation and insights are considered pivotal in understanding the heart-brain and cranial-brain connection. As they initiated their studies they determined to follow where the data took them.

> *"Their research played an important role in elucidating the basic physiological and psychological processes that connect the heart and brain and the mind and body..... they observed that the heart communicates with the brain in ways that **significantly** affect how we **perceive** and **react** to the world." (emphasis mine)*

In other words, their studies revealed that the heart-brain shaped how the cranial brain worked out and interpreted the World around them. As we have been stating, our perception of self, and our consequent thinking about how people regard and are dealing with us, will depict how we will react and respond to our circumstances.

> *"As their research evolved, they found that the heart in particular seemed to have its own logic that frequently diverged from the direction of autonomic nervous system activity. The heart was behaving as though it had **a mind of its own**. Furthermore, the heart appeared to be sending meaningful messages to the brain that the brain not only understood, **but also obeyed**. Even more intriguing was that it looked as though these messages could affect **a person's perceptions**, **behavior** and **performance**." (emphasis mine)*

This concept of the 'heart' having its own logic is powerful, and Biblical. In other words, it has its own information. As we have said this information is usually learnt involuntarily through experience, and relates to identity or lessons learnt in significant situations early in life. It is often in conflict with the voluntarily imbibed knowledge that is stored in the brain. So, this knowledge that it holds, produces its own reasoning, which in turn creates its own motivations. This *heart thinking* and believing then influences the mind in the decisions it makes, the perceptions that it holds, and finally the behaviour that ensues.

The research suggests that the 'heart' seemingly has a mind of its own. We have already proposed that these two sources of thinking and desiring were behind the conflicted state of biblical examples such as that which the Apostle Paul detailed in Romans chapter 7:15-23. Not only does the research suggest that there is independent thinking and reasoning going on at 'heart' level, but that the result of this thinking has sufficient sway on the cranial-brain to cause it to obey. This was an important factor for the Apostle Paul who stated that with his mind he wanted to do one thing, but let me suggest that his 'heart' reasoning, motivation and influence depicted what his behaviour would finally be.

> Romans 7:23 But there is another law at work within me that is at war with my mind. This law wins the fight and makes me a slave to the sin that is still within me. NLT (emphasis mine)

In essence, 'heart' beliefs often have the deciding vote on actions, reactions, and behaviour, whether you want them to or not. As we've pointed out, our attempts or solutions to meet the perceived needs of shoring up or compensating for our damaged identities, opens us up to being influenced towards sinful behaviour. If we have low self-image, and think we're less than others, we might compensate for these inner beliefs by becoming prideful, and convincing ourselves that we're more than others. This is how this inner thinking shapes a person's state of being, or put in other terms, how they are. As a man thinks in his 'heart,' so is he.

> "There has since been a growing body of research indicating that afferent information (inward information) processed by the intrinsic cardiac nervous system (heart-brain) can influence activity in the frontocortical areas and motor cortex, affecting psychological factors such as attention level, motivation, perceptual sensitivity and emotional processing." (emphasis mine)

We have previously cited Hebrews 4:12 which states that God is examining the thoughts and motives of the 'heart.' So, this research is consistent with the counsel of scripture, that the thinking of the *heart* has an impact on our motivation for doing what we do. For example, lets conject that as a child a person learns that they are not as good as others, and this becomes a *heart belief* regarding their identity. The result of this *heart belief* could be that they compensate by spending their whole life studying to advance themselves. In reality, the motivation for their efforts could be to prove that they are as good as others, if not better.

We have also already discussed _emotional processing_ and the elaboration of thought via the brain organ the hypothalamus. So, again this research is consistent with other concepts that we've been proposing. Anxious thoughts, for an example, are made a reality in our bodies neurologically, that is, electrically, through our nervous systems, and biochemically, through the release of chemical messengers such as hormones and neurotransmitters.

Heart thoughts shape cranial brain thinking, feelings, emotions, and responses. Then they have their final outworking in the body, or outer man as it is described in the Old Testament. Your body is the end of the line for your thoughts in regards to yourself. Your thinking and resultant behaviour and reactions may go beyond your own person in terms of how it affects others.

Information Source: HeartMath Institute – Article: Heart-Brain -Disclaimer: The author credits the Heart Math Institute for posting these findings from the Lacey's research, and recognizes the Lacey's contribution to this area of study. Articles by John and Beatrice Lacey can be accessed through researchgate.net. Other comments on the research papers from the Lacey's can be referenced on accredited scientific sites such as the American Psychological Association (APA), or PubMed, https://pubmed.ncbi.nlm.nih.gov

With no personal scientific background, or knowledge of the Heart Math Institute's standing in the research community, the author does not acknowledge or endorse any conclusions, interpretations, implementation, training or subsequent methods that the Heart Math Institute may have produced as a result of their investigations of the Lacey's studies.

*PubMed is a free resource supporting the search and retrieval of biomedical and life sciences literature with the aim of improving health–globally and is one of the most widely accessible resources in the world.

The Lacey's findings were considered by some of their peers as controversial at the time of publication. As with most scientific research papers, and indeed theological interpretations, there are always those who for their own reasons hold conflicting or alternate opinions on the results and findings of the studies of others. It's not my position here to defend the conclusions that the Lacey's came to as they examined the data that they collected.

We cannot say for certain that the findings of the Lacey's research are 100% correct from a scientific standpoint - given that we have no qualifications on the subject. The conclusions of their studies do however fit with what we learn from the Bible in regards to the heart having thoughts and feelings of its own. Perhaps some scientific weight and merit, to at least some extent, is added to their research and conclusions when we view other scientific articles relating to the heart holding behaviour and belief influencing information. For example, this excerpt quoted from an abstract of an article by Dr. Mitchell Liester,* titled 'Personality Changes Following Heart Transplantation: The Role of Cellular Memory.'

Personality changes *following heart transplantation, which have been reported for decades, include accounts of recipients **acquiring the personality characteristics of their donor**. Four categories of personality changes are discussed in this article: (1) changes in preferences, (2) alterations in emotions/temperament, (3) modifications of identity, and (4) memories from the donor's life. The acquisition of donor personality characteristics by recipients following heart transplantation is hypothesized to occur via the transfer of cellular memory, and four types of cellular memory are presented: (1) epigenetic memory, (2) DNA memory, (3) RNA memory, and (4) protein memory. Other possibilities, such as the transfer of memory via intracardiac neurological memory and energetic memory, are discussed as well. (emphasis mine)*

Let me briefly expand on how these four categories of changes in personality characteristics are significant and support what we have been proposing.

1. Changes in preferences:

Preferences meaning: 'a greater liking for one alternative over another or others.' The definition includes 'a choosing or special liking for one person or thing rather than another, or others.' So, your preferences are how you make your choices. Normally this would be based on previous learning, history and experiences. It is therefore significant that your choices and decisions are altered when you receive a heart that we assume has been previously programmed by life in another person.

2. Alterations in emotions/temperament:

As we have already pointed out emotions are an elaboration of thought that you feel in your body. It follows then that there are thought influencing communications, thoughts and beliefs originating in the heart. The encyclopedia Britannica describes temperament in psychology to mean; 'an aspect of personality concerned with emotional dispositions and their speed and intensity.' We can conclude then that changes in temperament equate to heart- belief initiated changes in a person's personality.

3. Modifications of identity:

In this book we are presenting that the majority of ministry to the heart that we undertake in the process of healing the 'broken' heart relates to a corruption of the identity in the human personality, and that the problem is largely sourced in the heart. This observation of altered identity and self-perception is therefore what we would expect to find, to at least some degree, with a transplant, if the physical body is going to match the spiritual implications of the soul being influenced by a previously programmed heart.

4. Memories from the donor's life:

Our whole proposition is that the source of the hearts programming will almost always be found in memories of some kind. It is not surprising then, that along with encoded beliefs and conclusions from significant memories you will at times find some measure of recollection of the actual events stored in the donor's heart.

Articles relating to heart transplant recipients such as these, and many others with the same findings are further compelling evidence that appears to strongly indicate that how the Lacey's interpreted the results of their research should be seriously entertained as being very possibly correct, and afforded some further additional credibility as a result.

In any case we're basing our studies here on the Bible as the source of truth, as opposed to science which is fluid and continually changing, adjusting, and being developed.

*Dr. **Mitchell Liester**, MD of the University of Colorado is a Psychiatry Specialist in Monument, CO and has over 37 years of experience in the medical field, and specializes in Neurology and Psychiatry. His full article is under Copyright but can be purchased via various research and science sites. (PubMed, ScienceDirect, ResearchGate, etc.)

I think by now we've established a scientifically proposed interaction between the 'heart-brain' and the 'cranial-brain,' and its consequent interaction and effect on the mind and body. This by implication means that if the heart-brain is faulty or not whole in its beliefs and thought processes, then it will in fact have a significant bearing on the wholeness, health and order of the mind and thinking. This further reinforces the basis of double mindedness, or being in two minds. This means that we can be holding two streams of thought, having recorded different information in different parts of our being, that can hold views that are at times opposing each other.

There is what you want to think, or know that you should logically think in your mind, particularly about your identity and perception of value, significance, and worth in the World. And then there is what you do in fact think in your 'heart,' that causes you problems and keeps you captive. This *Broken heartedness* clearly effects physical health as well, through the resultant chemical and electrical imbalances that outwork in the body.

The heart-brain can learn and remembers

Another research article posted in 2019 that can be accessed on the PubMed site indicated the existence of a heart-brain, with the following excerpts being of particular interest.

Dr. Armour, in 1991, discovered that the heart has its "little brain" or "intrinsic cardiac nervous system." This "heart brain" is composed of approximately 40,000 neurons that are alike neurons in the brain, meaning that the heart has its own nervous system. In addition, the heart communicates with the brain in many methods: neurologically, biochemically, biophysically, and energetically.

Signals from the "heart brain" redirect to the medulla, hypothalamus, thalamus, and amygdala and the cerebral cortex. Thus, the heart sends more signals to the brain than vice versa.

The heart is not just a pump. It has its neural network or "little brain."

Neurons are information messengers that transmit information between different areas of the brain. They are responsible for receiving sensory input, and for sending commands to different areas of the body. They are considered to be the fundamental units of a brain and nervous system. We can observe from these articles that the actual physical heart-brain has the capacity to sense things, to learn, and to remember what was learnt. We've already repetitively proposed that much of this learning and storing information as memory relates to identity, or to situations that experientially teach or train us in some significant way about life. This research is consistent with previous articles that we've quoted already in regards to how this effects perceptions, and even motivations.

We used to have a dog, who as a pup chased cars, and also liked to get out of the yard and go roaming about the countryside. So, I took a piece of rope and tied one end to the dogs' collar, and the other end to a post. It wasn't long and the young dog had learned through the experience of trying to get away, that it was in fact not strong enough, was powerless, and was captive to the situation. After a time, accepting what was learnt through experience, and now believed as fact, the dog no longer tried to break loose. As time went by, I began to only tie the rope to the collar, and not the post, because the dog was now captive to the perception of its state of being. Even though the truth was that it could have moved off, it no longer believed that it was possible because of what it had learnt in its formative years.

When we're teaching these principles on our training schools, I often use some very real looking rubber eggs as an illustration. I will usually have someone stand way back in the audience who is expected to catch these eggs when I throw them. Normally I will keep them waiting quite a long time while I discuss the emotions that they are likely to be experiencing. Invariably, even people who seem confident are actually feeling very nervous. What is happening is that what they now feel as anxiety is not coming from conscious thought, or that which they're trying to think with their mind. Their anxious state and condition is coming from something that they already believe in their *heart* that they have learnt growing up.

Perhaps it is that they are not as good as others. Dropping the egg will prove that this is true. Maybe they've been embarrassed in the past, and made to feel stupid or dumb. Dropping the egg will confirm that belief about their identity. Possibly they grew up in a critical and disapproving environment full of expectations and acceptance conditioned on you being able to perform. Now your identity belief is that you're not good enough, or not acceptable unless you get everything right. Dropping the egg will prove that you are not up to standard. The point is, what you are feeling is probably not conscious thought. It's just a response to an *identity belief in your heart*.

What we're trying to illustrate is that the eggs are not real, even though they appear to be. It is a deception. But your feelings and reactions are the same as if it were true, and they were real. Your heart-brain is interpreting the situation based on your pre-existing identity beliefs, and producing an emotional response based on those perceptions. If you have enough ongoing deceptions that trigger a response relating to your identity or a situation, you will have an anxiety disorder. This is key in understanding the mechanism behind how the research concludes that the heart-brain has the capacity to feel or is implicated in what we feel.

An article posted in February 2022 on neuroscience news.com, and multiple other sites, cited investigations pointing to influences from the heart being implicated in GAD. (Generalized Anxiety Disorder. GAD is listed as a Mental Disorder)

Researchers at the Laureate Institute for Brain Research (LIBR) in Tulsa, Okla., have identified an abnormal link between the autonomic and central nervous systems, specifically via communication between the heart and part of the brain's frontal cortex, in women with generalized anxiety disorder (GAD).

These findings, based on studies conducted on women, suggest very strong mental and emotional responses to influences and communications from the heart. Yet again, we point to the Biblical meaning of 'heart' as thoughts and feelings coming from your centre or middle.

We observe here that information and signals pass from the heart to the brain, and from the brain to the heart. In practice this is an important practical point. Many of the beliefs that we hold about our identity, or specific types of situations in our *hearts* may have at times come from conclusions or interpretations of events made in our brains or minds at critical stages of life. The things that we learnt from these events are stored as programming in our *hearts*. Is this the part of the body where this information is stored? It adds up. Let's move on.

Now as adults this programming, that may at times initially have come in through the door of the mind, now affects and influences our thinking and perspective on self, how others perceive us and consequently our will and decisions. Hopefully we can see how important it is for us to understand that the reason for our heart-brain being in conflict with our cranial-brain, or mind, is that it has its own set of beliefs and thoughts <u>that act independently</u>. As we've pointed out these are often contradictory to what we choose to think, want to believe, and how we consequently act.

Heart science and emotional processing

Firstly, let's remember that the heart perceives and shapes thinking and feeling by interpreting events through pre-existing knowledge. If someone treats you in a caring or appreciative way this will touch these 'heart' beliefs and produce a response in some way. So, if you believe in your *heart* that you're not important, and someone treats you as though you are, then this is <u>processed</u> through the *heart* beliefs that you already hold. The response or reaction then may well be a flood of positive emotion and happiness. The practical reality is that even though your pain and hurt may have been touched and ministered to in that moment, inevitably you will default to the entrenched belief that you're not important.

The flip side of this is, that we may experience people treating us in this positive way, but because it is contrary to what we believe in our *hearts* about ourselves we may not be able to receive it. In this case the heart-brain processes what has happened as not matching inner beliefs, and reframes it as unacceptable and as not being truth. Consequently, your heart-brain beliefs about your identity can work like a forcefield, reframing people's good intentions or encouragement in a negative light.

For example, imagine if I were doing a PowerPoint presentation. After I had completed the work, someone came up to me and said; 'that was really great, but the fonts on the text could be a little larger for those sitting towards the back.' The person most likely is attempting to encourage me, and make my good work even better. But if I have a self-belief that I am not good enough, then rather than accepting the praise and helpful suggestion to take it to the next level, I reframe it as an attack on my worth. Then rather than being grateful I react aggressively or sulk.

At one time I decided to help my wife by washing the dishes. I could see that she was becoming agitated by my attempt to help. What I meant as a good deed was interpreted by her that I was inferring that she was not doing a good enough job. On investigation we found that as a small child her father had berated her repetitively for being untidy. Once she processed the belief, and it was resolved as an issue producing a response, she no longer felt attacked and, unfortunately for me, proceeded to generate a list of other potential things that I could help with.

Remember that an emotion is the outworking of a belief. So, in the preceding research statements, note that the emotional information generated by the 'heart belief' is sent TO the brain, not FROM it. Also note, it affects the mental state, and finally the body. This is significant and consistent with scripture.

> *Proverbs 14:30 A heart at peace gives life to the body, but envy rots the bones. NIV*

If the condition of your *heart* is in good order you can expect health. But if you don't feel good and content about your own identity, you will probably envy others who seem to be doing better, or appear acceptable, and this can lead to physical problems.

> Proverbs 17:22 *A cheerful heart is good medicine, but a crushed spirit dries up the bones.* NIV

In the book of Romans 14:17 we see righteousness, peace and joy are symbols of the Kingdom of God being established in us through the work of the Holy Spirit. We can realistically expect that the outcome of these restored positions in our *hearts* will inevitably produce health and order in our minds and bodies.

Two-way dialogue
"Typically, the study of communication structures between the brain and heart have been approached from a one-sided perspective, with scientists concentrating primarily on the heart's responses to the brain's commands. Recent studies however indicate that communication between the heart and brain actually is a continuous two-way dialogue, with each organ having an influence on the other."

We are one person, with different parts and functions that have to be brought into harmony for mental, emotional, physical and relational wholeness and health. The mission then is to bring together what we know to be true in our renewed minds, and what we perceive to be true in our *hearts*.

Our performance and activity in life is affected by our beliefs. If we think, for example that we'll never be able to be what is expected, then to avoid proving the inadequacy that we perceive that we have, rather than trying and failing, we don't try at all. We're captive to our identity beliefs, and it impacts our outcomes and productivity. God wants us confident in the abilities and identity as a person that He gave us.

The amazing heart
Some people have pointed out that historically through the ages the heart has been considered to be the seat of emotion and thought, hence it's application in literature, and continued use in music and romantic themes. Some time ago I had come to the personal opinion that the heart is the centre of your soul. Recently I read that religious text and philosophers from the past believed also that your heart was the centre of your soul or

being, and additionally they believed that this was where thought came from. So, interestingly mankind historically appears to have not included the brain as a source of thought, and modern thinking until recently excluded the heart as a part of the equation.

All of the modern research articles that I've quoted here fit with what we have been suggesting in terms of science proving what the Bible has said about the *heart* in this regard all along. There are many other articles that could be quoted seemingly confirming the science of the heart-brain. We are indeed fearfully and wonderfully made! Scientifically, as well as Biblically, the *heart* clearly is powerful in its affect, as we can see in the following additional information, which can be found and confirmed through multiple sources.

- *"The heart is the first organ to appear and starts pumping before you have blood."*

- *"The heart has over 40,000 independent neurons."*

- *"The heart also manufactures and secretes hormone blends, one of which is oxytocin; This hormone has been termed the Love Hormone, and is implicated in feelings of love and in bonding, trust, romantic attachment and other human behaviours, along with various physical processes. It is mainly produced in the hypothalamus, and notably, low oxytocin levels have been linked to symptoms of depression."*

Let me propose here that often the good feeling that we interpret as love, is actually emotion coming from acceptance, connection, and being valued. What we're feeling is that we are wanted and significant to another person. It feels good. And we also accept and value them, which in turn ministers to their identity, and makes them feel good. We now have the relational synergy that we describe as love. We love God as a response to His love, acceptance, wanting us, and valuing us in relationship.

> *1 John 4:19 We love each other as a result of his loving us first. NLT*

Through the years when we've ministered to people who have been caught in adultery, the cause is usually that someone has made them feel wanted, attractive and significant. They mistake the good feeling that comes from this experience as love. As they continue to crave the ensuing positive emotional feeling of acceptance it leads them into other problems.

Emotional needs predict behaviour

We've found over time that meeting the emotional needs of a damaged perception of identity is the greatest predictor of behaviour. Meeting those needs motivates us to make life choices to resolve these self-perception issues. Perhaps we need business or ministerial success, because inside we believe that we are a failure, or not good enough. At times, the moral programming of the mind is put aside and justified as the broken *heart* seeks to deal with the self-perception coming from the hidden beliefs that it holds. Because we want to resolve the negative feelings from our corrupted 'heart' beliefs, we can deceive ourselves that our actions and motives are reasonable.

> *Jeremiah 17:9-10 The <u>heart</u> is deceitful above all things and beyond cure. Who can understand it?* [10] *"I the LORD search <u>the heart</u> and examine <u>the mind</u>, to reward a man according to his conduct, according to what his deeds deserve." NIV (emphasis mine)*

In this passage, we yet again see a Biblical distinction between the *heart* and *mind*. It appears from the text that God is searching out the beliefs that produce the behaviour. And then He examines how we respond and deal with these inner-belief inspired tendencies. He's assessing how we think through and reason these out with our minds, and then how we choose to react to these deceits based on His word. Are we seeking truth and accepting our deeds as sinful? Are we repentant in the sense of seeing by the word of God that something is out of order? And do we want to change our thinking? Are we going to Him for help to resolve these beliefs?

Is the heart much more powerful in implication than we first thought? Is this why scripture gives it such a place of prominence?

Once we begin to embrace these ideas many scriptures begin to open up to us. For instance, the Bible at times uses terminology such as where Jesus perceived the 'thinking in their *hearts*?'

> *Mark 2:5-8 When Jesus saw their faith, He said to the paralytic, "Son, your sins are forgiven you."* [6] *And some of the scribes were sitting there and <u>reasoning in their hearts</u>,* [7] *"Why does this Man speak blasphemies like this? Who can forgive sins but God alone?"* [8] *But immediately, when Jesus perceived in His spirit that they reasoned thus within themselves, He said to them, "Why do you reason about these things <u>in your hearts</u>? NKJV (emphasis mine)*

I was listening to a preacher recently, who was preaching about Ananias and Sapphira. He quoted that Satan had 'filled the *heart*' of Ananias, and went on to say; "whatever that means." Viewed through the lens of what we have been proposing, it would be reasonable to deduce that this means that Satan had gotten involved in the inner beliefs that they held, and manipulated them to behave in a particular way. In this instance, they wanted to appear as if they were fully committed in order to have the affirmation of the church.

> *Acts 5:3-4 But Peter said, "Ananias, why has Satan filled your <u>heart</u> to lie to the Holy Spirit and keep back part of the price of the land for yourself?* [4] *"While it remained, was it not your own? And after it was sold, was it not in your own control? Why have you <u>conceived this thing in your heart</u>? You have not lied to men but to God." NKJV (emphasis mine)*

Earlier we see Judas Iscariot being motivated by greed, that is, a perception that he needed more than he had. This led to his decision to betray Jesus for thirty pieces of silver. It was said in that instance that Satan entered his *heart*. In other words, Satan invaded the weak areas of his believing. Seemingly he had more doubt than faith in regards to being dealt with fairly and being provided for, otherwise he would not have attempted to become his own source of provision. As we know he had already been stealing from the purse of the disciples.

Evidently his need and desire to have money and meet his own perceived needs, was greater than his love for Jesus. The outcome of his actions produced remorse in him. That is, he experienced deep regret and guilt. Let me suggest that this shame affected how he regarded his person, and depressed his mental state. Because the betrayal could not be taken back, his possibility of restoring his identity and previous status with Jesus and the others was hopeless. In this depressed, conflicted mental state he concluded that suicide was the only option. But the whole sequence of events began with deception in his *heart*.

Restoring our corrupted heart thinking

This leads us to looking at Gods remedy for dealing with our corrupted *hearts*, and a process that we can follow where He begins by putting in us a 'new heart.' King David also sinned with Bathsheba. His response however was to run back to God for help for his condition. He, like Paul, knew that there was something that he didn't understand that was the cause of his sin. His desire was to work with God to see it resolved. His request was for God to have grace for his sin, but also to resolve the reason that he sinned. He wanted these *inner heart beliefs* to be put back in order. This is the very thing that God wants for all of us, and prioritises in the New Testament.

> *Psalm 51:9-10 Hide Your face from my sins, And blot out all my iniquities.* [10] *Create in me <u>a clean heart</u>, O God, And renew a steadfast spirit within me. NKJV (emphasis mine)*

As you read your Bible you will begin to see that it indicates consistently that this is the source of where many of our problems begin from. King David in Psalm 51 acknowledged that the reason for his wayward behaviour and sin was a lack of pure thoughts and feelings from his 'heart,' or centre. According to Hebrew scholars 'the inner parts' could also be translated as the 'heart,' which, as I've suggested to you is the centre or middle of your soul.

> *Psalm 51:5-6 Surely I was sinful at birth, sinful from the time my mother conceived me.* [6] *Surely you desire <u>truth in the inner parts</u>; you teach me wisdom in the inmost place. NIV (emphasis mine)*

> *Psalm 51: 5-6 For I was born a sinner-- yes, from the moment my mother conceived me.* [6] *But you desire honesty from <u>the heart</u>, so you can teach me to be wise in my inmost being. NLT (emphasis mine)*

It's interesting to note that he stated that God wanted truth in the inner parts, or the 'heart' as it's rendered in the New Living Translation. This desire of God for us to have truth that sets us free in our 'hearts' is foundational to the ministry model that we're going to unfold. In cooperation with what he realized God wants for us, David also developed the desire for a purifying of his *heart thinking*, leading him to invite God to examine this area of his being. It's as if, in modern parlance, he was asking God to run the Holy Spirit anti-virus program across his operating system, and remove the fallen corrupted files. Consequently, he requested that God show him what was there.

> *Psalm 139:23-24 Search me, O God, and know my heart; test me and know my anxious thoughts.* [24] *See if there is any offensive way in me, and lead me in the way everlasting. NIV*

This is a great prayer to pray as a basis for our ministry model. The truth is that it's the same with any Christian ministry; we can 'help you' get healed and free, ... but we can't 'make you' get healed and free. You have to want it, and accept and receive God's ways of providing. Most do. Even God seemingly will not go against the free will that He has given you. Remember His promise in Luke 4:18 to heal, that is bring to wholeness the brokenhearted.

CHAPTER EIGHT
The God Solution

I have endeavoured to explain as thoroughly as possible that the power that Satan has over mankind comes through eliciting cooperation and submission through deception. Additionally, we have now ascertained that the root of the problem is often specifically deception and corruption of one's identity at *'heart'* level. Hopefully we now understand, at least in part, why we see ourselves as we do. Why none of us are 'whole' and completely ordered in our thinking and possession of truth as a result of the fall. And why deception at the root of our beings, is the basis directly or indirectly for virtually all of mankind's problems.

If then, we accept that distorted perceptions and thinking about our *'self'* leads us into following the world is the problem, then the solution that produces a new, renewed, reprogrammed *'heart,'* is God's truth in the inner parts. Truth at *heart* level is therefore vital for our freedom. We can now understand clearly why Jesus said that when we know God's truth, it will make us free.

> John 8:32 *"And you shall know the truth, and the truth shall make you free."* NKJV

This truth needs to be partly through the renewing of the knowledge of God and His ways in the mind. However, many people know the truth in their minds, and in their voluntarily learnt knowledge, but it has not set them free. As I've previously stated, we have found that we also need truth in the 'heart.' This comes through the healing, (bringing to wholeness and repair), of the broken 'heart.' That is, your inner thoughts and feelings in regards to your identity, which are coming from your middle or centre. This wholeness is in our believing, and the thinking that proceeds from it. So, the way back to wholeness is too un-corrupt the distortion and deception that we have received in regards to how we perceive 'self.'

Let me reinforce that your perceived identity is who you think that you are, or how you think that you are. It's <u>your truth</u> about your SELF. By way of a simple example, self-beliefs such as; I'm dumb, useless, worthless, not important, bad, a nothing, unlovable, not good enough, and so on. This *heart* thinking is usually contrary to what you want to think in your mind, and hence the conflict and disorder. Receiving Gods truth then, IS the process of sanctification.

> *John 17:17 "Sanctify them by Your truth. Your word is truth. NKJV*

The Greek word translated 'Sanctify' here is 'hagiazo.' This word means to purify. In this case purify you from deception by means of receiving God's truth. It is sometimes translated as 'to make holy.' It is all the same thing. To be sanctified and purified makes you Holy and separated from the deception that produces corruption and misalignment in your being. God's instrument for dealing with this deception in the process of sanctification is the Spirit of truth. We'll cover this function of His ministry more fully in a later chapter. A part of His work, as this title suggests, is to lead us into all truth, both mentally and at *heart* level.

> *John 16:13 But when he, the Spirit of truth, comes, he will guide you into all truth. NIV*

Practical results of receiving truth
Self-conflict in regards to what we would like to think, and what we actually do think about ourselves, is based on not having God's absolute and unequivocal truth. Perhaps our pendulum is a good illustration of how we become mentally imbalanced through our thinking being out of order. If the pendulum is at dead centre and not swinging backwards and forwards, we could describe its position as at rest, in peace. The further it swings one way or the other the more out of balance and away from wholeness that we are. We could perhaps suggest that small movements away from centre are normal and acceptable, but mentally, the greater the fluctuations the more serious the mental disorder would be.

Diagram 4

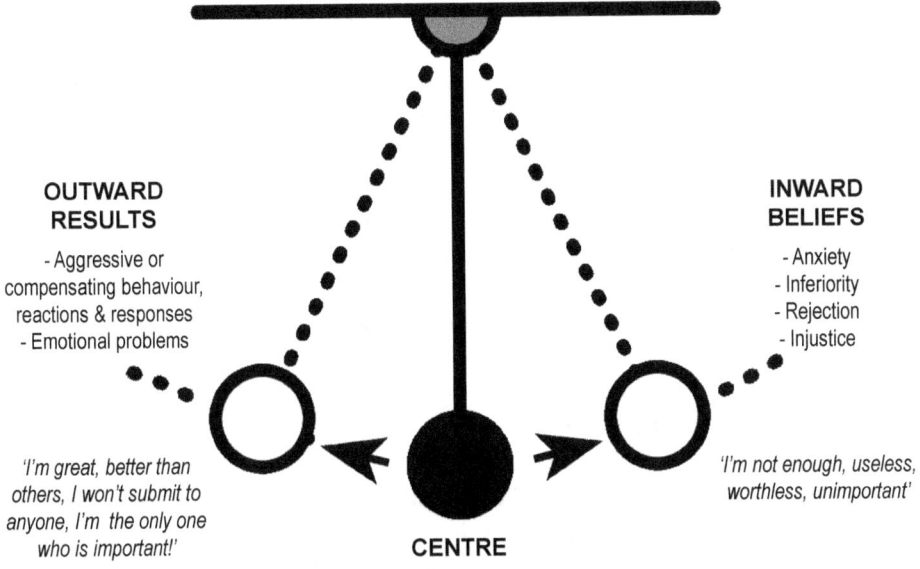

So, our thinking is conflicted and disordered, swinging out of balance between what you want to think, and what you do think.... 'I'm great, I'm not...?' Peace, order and balance comes when the contention is resolved. This means, acceptance of self, and having an identity and purpose that are mediated by God imputing His truth, which is the truth.

God initiates His solution to the problem
What I explain from here until the end of this chapter does not directly relate to the ministry process that we're presenting for resolving mental disorders. However, it is relevant for helping us to understand and comprehend a more complete picture, laying a foundation for perceiving the intentions of God for our restoration. He promises the introduction of a new nature through spiritual rebirth, which means new possibilities, and new life in Him.

> *Ezekiel 36:26-27* "*I will give you <u>a new heart</u> and put <u>a new spirit</u> within you; I will take the heart of stone out of your flesh and give you a heart of flesh.* ²⁷ *"I will put <u>My Spirit</u> within you and cause you*

to walk in My statutes, and you will keep My judgments and do them.
NKJV (emphasis mine)

The introduction of this <u>new human spirit</u> is very exciting, bringing dramatic change through now being born again and in a renewed relationship with God. When we add in the <u>Baptism of the Holy Spirit</u>, where God puts His Spirit within us, joining His Spirit to our spirit, we find ourselves on a very different footing. Now spiritually one with God, if we seek to relate to Him, He has much greater influence and power over your being and faculties! It is interesting that the Greek word '*Charis*,' which is translated as 'grace,' includes the idea of a divine influence on the *heart*. That is, a positive inner drawing towards seeking and following God.

> *1 Corinthians 6:17 But the person who is joined to the Lord becomes one spirit with him. NLT*

The 'honeymoon' dynamic

Our human spirit now witnesses with the Holy Spirit that we are loved and accepted by God. Our spiritual dynamics have changed. We have been translated from one spiritual kingdom to another. The euphoria of this initial dynamic has been described as 'the honeymoon period.' Now being alive to God, and aware of Him and His desire for us at the spiritual level is somewhat like the romance phase of a human relationship. One obvious difference, is that it is relationship with a person that we cannot see. Also, it is primarily spiritual, with implications for affecting the thinking and emotions, rather than completely emotional. It impacts us by enlivening our spiritual senses, which in turn affects mind, feeling and body.

In a natural human relationship this overwhelming sense of romance, acceptance, and love is so much larger for a time than our awareness of our own identity. It's almost as if our personal issues disappear in the blinding light of being ministered to by being valued, wanted, loved and accepted. When the relationship moves past this initial phase and you are subject to the pressures of doing life together, the tendency is to default to the programmed settings. The 'honeymoon' feelings are now being impinged upon by the re-emergence of '*heart beliefs*,' and becoming aware again of our pre-set inner thinking.

In much the same way, with the incoming of the new God aware nature, and the knowledge of the truth of God's love and acceptance in your human spirit, your corrupted sense of identity is overwhelmed. Previously there was little or no contention in your person, as you simply did what you wanted to please yourself according to the old fallen nature. Now as scripture reveals, there are 2 natures which are in conflict with each other. We have to accept that the incoming of the newly created nature does not automatically remove the old fallen, Adamic nature. Now we have a choice which nature we want to live according to. If we choose to walk after the Spirit in the new nature, then we will have opposition from the desires, tendencies, and programming of the old nature.

We deal with this, in part, by the renewing of our minds to the ways of God, and becoming hearers and doers of His word. So, how we now behave is transformed by knowing and aligning with God's ways, as opposed to following the ways of a Satan influenced world. This superior information leads to a deliberate act of our will to follow what is now our learnt knowledge of God.

> Romans 12:2 *Don't copy the behavior and customs of this world, but let God transform you into a new person by changing the way you think. Then you will know what God wants you to do, and you will know how good and pleasing and perfect his will really is.* NLT

Remember though that our reasoning and mental activity are still shaped and influenced by our *heart* beliefs, specifically in regards to our *identities*. In the Ezekiel 36 passage that we have recently quoted, we note that along with a recreated spirit, we have now also been imputed a new soft heart that is open to God's workings, and is prepared to seek Him for change.... but we have a problem! Permit me to reiterate, the introduction of this new nature doesn't automatically delete the old nature....so now we have 2 natures in one person...conflict!

This means that we can, and generally do, default to the old identity beliefs that we hold after the 'honeymoon' period is over. This problem of contradictory, disordered thinking, will continue if it's not resolved through the ministry of the Holy Spirit.

> Galatians 5: 17 *The <u>sinful nature</u> wants to do evil, which is just the opposite of what the Spirit wants. And the Spirit gives us desires that are the opposite of what the sinful nature desires. <u>These two forces are constantly fighting each other</u>, so that you are not free to carry out your good intentions.* NLT (emphasis mine)

The power of the old nature

The power of the old nature then, is largely, being trained to think the way the world thinks. But it is also, most importantly, the programming of the '*heart*' and <u>identity</u> along fallen lines. You may recall, we described the *'heart'* as the centre of your soul. A large amount of the power of the old creation is based on the programming of this area of our being. So, the newly created nature thrives when the old creation is dismantled through healing the *broken heart* by the ministry of the Holy Spirit. In the Ezekiel 36 passage we can see that our stony, hard, unreceptive *heart* has been replaced with a soft *heart* that is capable of receiving freeing truth from God. This opens for us the possibility of healing and restoration for our *hearts*, through the Spirit of Truth dealing with the deception that empowers the fallen self-life.

An illustration of the re-creation process from nature

As a brief diversion, let's contemplate this re-creation from being fallen creatures. Under the old nature we had minimal potential for the life of wholeness and abundant possibilities that God promises. By way of example, I would like to present the process of an earthbound caterpillar crawling on its belly like a small serpent. It then transitions to the re-created ascendant beauty of a butterfly, whose world is so much bigger, and full of potential and destiny. The action of this metamorphosis is amazing, and is such a great illustration of a spiritual principle from a natural source.

> *Romans 1:20 For since the creation of the world God's invisible qualities--his eternal power and divine nature--have been clearly seen, being understood from what has been made, so that men are without excuse. NIV*

Prior to conversion, we are limited earthbound creatures, and through spiritual rebirth we become creatures who can access the higher spiritual dimension. We are now positionally seated in heavenly places in Christ. The imputing of this new nature, re-created human spirit, and pliable heart, places us in a dimension of limitless possibilities. This new nature brings us potential for fullness. It is the beginning of the process, but not the end.

The beginning for our caterpillar is entering the chrysalis, (for a moth a cocoon) which is the place where this transformation will take place. For us, with our renewed spirit we have entered the Kingdom of God. This exposure for us cannot result in anything other than change. In the chrysalis the caterpillar's structure begins to be disintegrated from the inside out. For us, our old nature comes under attack and begins to be challenged from our new spirit, which is situated in Old Testament terminology in our 'innermost being.' So, again, the change comes from the inside out.

What was once the structure of the caterpillar proceeds to dissolve into soupy goo. This is the time when inactivated cells known as 'imaginal cells' come out of dormancy. As we can see by the name, these cells have instruction inherently placed in them in regard to the potential new re-creation of the life, and already see through the imagination the sense of what can be. In our case it is God's imaginings for us, as He knows the good plans and purposes that He has for us. God sets up a 'beachhead' for His Spirit led invasion of our personality in this innermost, or human spirit, part of our being. From there He leads us to possess the land of our personality.

Diagram 5

BIBLICAL PERSPECTIVE OF THE FUNDAMENTAL COMPONENTS OF A HUMAN BEING

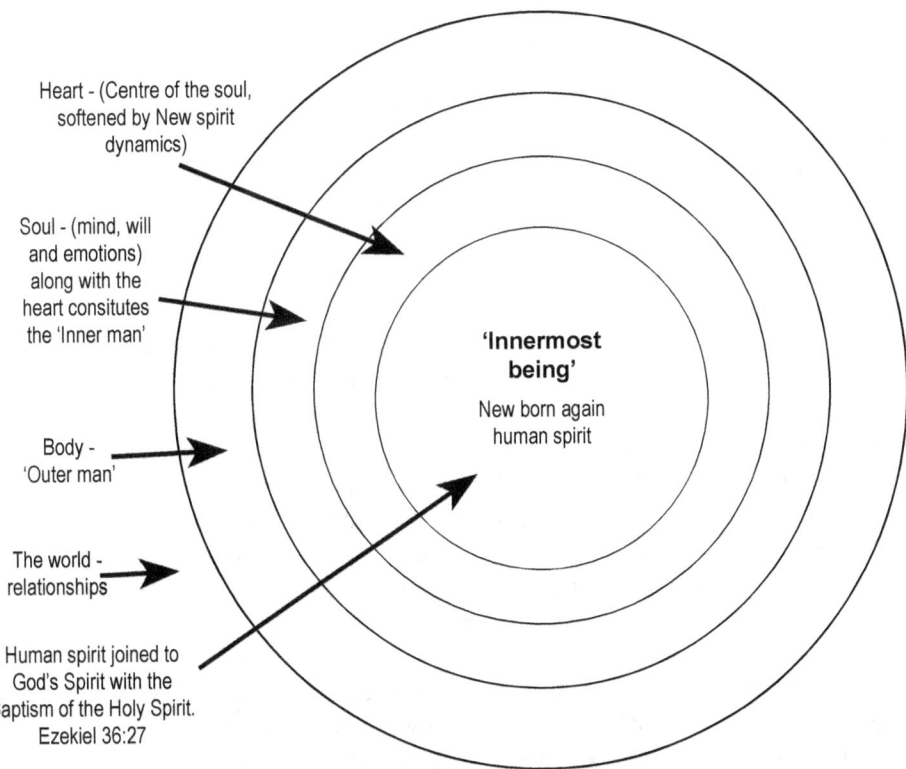

In the chrysalis these 'imaginal cells' begin to work on the construction of the re-created ascendant being. They imagine what can potentially become of the creature, and relentlessly work towards that goal. I think any born again person has a sense of possibilities beyond anything that they could have imagined before their spiritual rebirth. So, for the caterpillar, and us, its messy. As a result of the activation of the 'imaginal cells' the caterpillars immune system produces a response and tries to destroy them. As we have quoted previously, with the imputation of the spirit nature in us, there is now opposition from the old fallen nature, or 'Sarx.' In much the same way as for the caterpillar, these 'imaginal cells' are a threat to the old creatures' existence.

As we know, it is necessary for the caterpillar to be deconstructed for these 'imaginal cells' to complete the task of forming the butterfly. It is to be a completely new being, still retaining the life, but taking on a new and beautiful form as a butterfly. The final outcome of the process instigated by these 'imaginal cells' is to create an incredible new being, vastly superior to the old one. This is the purpose of God. To take our limited fallen life, and to re-create and restore us into His image for a full and abundant life. The promises of God are for those who imagine and pursue this new life, cooperating with him in the process of taking down the old nature. The caterpillar and the butterfly, amazingly, still have the same DNA. They are the same being remade. Now with a new future, and a new ability to experience life in a positive way, with completely new potential.

Making the journey, knowing the destination

There is a butterfly known as a Monarch which is found in North America. These butterflies make a journey of up to 3,000 miles to their winter home in Mexico. How do they know where their destination is? How is it that they're able to get there? Researchers are still working on how they know to make this incredible migration, and how they end up at the right place. We know that it's built in by their creator. It's more than knowledge. For us a new destination is programmed in with the re-creation of our human spirit, we are now travellers on a journey. The journey for us is not distance, it's the process of walking in the new life. God helps us in this growth and metamorphous. (Transformation)

To dismantle the old nature, it is necessary to overcome and dissolve the deceptive 'cells' that it is built on. Destroying and replacing them with truth 'cells' as the building blocks to establish and complete the New creation. So, the incoming of the new nature means that the old situation has passed away, and all things are now possible. It cannot be assumed that this new potential means that the journey is finished, or that there would be no mental conflict or disorder without first receiving ministry. No emotional, physical or relation problems. No sin issues. This position is simply not reality.

Dispossessing our enemies and taking the ground from the inside out

In scripture we find what is known as typology. This is where something is used to explain something else. These 'types' have characteristics that make them identifiable. For example; a sedan is a 'type' of car, identifiable by its characteristics. Jesus referred to His body as; 'this temple.' The temple in Israel had outer courts, the Holy place, and the Holy of Holies which was the innermost place. This, notably, was inhabited by the presence of God. In the Old Testament we see the outer man, the inner man, and the innermost being. In the New Testament we have the body, the soul, and the human spirit. So, we can see the likeness as a 'type' of the temple structure, and our human being.

We are the temple of the Holy Spirit. Where we see temples and cities in scripture as types, they generally refer to the human personality. In the following passage 'a city,' is used as a 'type' to illustrate the condition of a man who has lowered his defences. Perhaps this could come through drug use, alcohol abuse, disordered thinking, or a general lack of self-discipline.

> Proverbs 25:28 Like a city whose walls are broken down is a man who lacks self-control. NIV

If we were to continue to use a 'city' as a 'type,' or as a picture of the human condition, the passage from 2 Samuel 5:6-8 becomes very interesting and possibly instructional. As I understand it, the Jebusites had never been defeated from an attack from outside the city of Jebus. (Later to be called Jerusalem.) King David came in through the water shaft in the centre of the city and dislodged the enemy from the inside out. In like manner, this simple ministry to the 'heart' goes to the core of your person, and takes the ground removing the fortifications of your enemies from the inside out.

I find it fascinating that this could possibly be an Old Testament picture of a strategy for taking over and inhabiting the personality. In a practical sense this is very much what we witness over and over through the ministry process that we're about to describe.

CHAPTER NINE

Accessing Memory for Healing and Freedom

Dismantling Deception

Before we begin to look at specific disorders and their origins, we're going to present in summary the simple ministry model that we use to restore order to the mental condition. Once we understand this process, we can apply this model to the beliefs behind each separate problem. We have proposed that the lack of Gods truth, particularly regarding '*heart beliefs*' about our identities is the root of the problem. As we have previously established, we're personally convinced of this being the basic issue.

This has come through having repetitively witnessed many thousands of times where the Spirit of Truth has resolved the mental issues emanating from these beliefs. This deception which creates our difficulties, and moves us out of Gods intended order, was learnt in historical events that we now term as memories. We commonly have people report; "It's as if I'm discovering who I really am!" This is true, we're being restored to seeing ourselves how God sees us.

At times these historical places include pre-natal imprints on our person before we were even born.* If it has been imbibed and encoded in memory sourced from events or projections from the parents on to them prior to birth, a person grows up with a sense of what they believe. As they grow up and have words, they can now describe what they feel. They also tend to interpret early childhood events based on these pre-existing pre-natal

(In the Womb) beliefs. On occasion when ministering to people we find that there is no initial memory where they took in the belief that we're working with. In that case we may minister to the sense and feeling that possibly began before they were born.

In either case dealing with memory where a belief is learnt is the beginning point, and the first key for understanding this ministry process. Jesus said things such as; "how long have they been like this?" In other words; "does anyone know where this began, what happened to them?" (Mark 9:21) The lady bent over with the Spirit of infirmity 18 years was different 19 years ago. There was something that led to her eventual condition. (Luke 13:11)

The issue is how we have interpreted the contents of memories, and how our conclusions became the '*heart beliefs*' that we now live out of. Let me reinforce, no one was born, born again. Like King David we were all conceived in sin under the negative influences of the fall of man. We therefore, all were under the tendency to misinterpret our identity because that imprint.

More information on prenatal influences can be studied in 'Healing And Freedom Through Truth Encounters,' or the SOHAF (School of Healing and Freedom) Comprehensive Manual by the same author.

The role of memory

As a child when we began to try to interpret our state of being, and conceptualize our identities, the first impressions and experiences in significant events were instrumental in the formation and establishment of our beliefs. Once these beliefs were decided upon in the initial memories, they are then used to interpret what happens later in life. For example, if you aren't picked for the football team when you're 12 years old, you will see that through what you have already previously decided is your identity and characteristics. If your parents never gave you attention when you were growing up, you may have come to the conclusion that you're not significant or worthy of being noticed.

Now, you conclude that this is the reason you have been overlooked for the team. It's an automatized response. Not necessarily a logical calculation. All you know is that you feel sad and unworthy, just as you did when you were a small child deciding who you were. In fact, a later event such as not being picked for the team may be interpreted based on a number of pre-existing beliefs. I ministered to a lady one day whose husband made her feel like she was dumb. He was unwittingly triggering a pre-existing identity belief that she'd learnt at school. He now was the recipient of an unpleasant reaction from her whenever he caused this belief to be touched.

The importance of the Initial memory and context
So, this is our second key. The initial or first memory where the belief was learnt is the place that we need. This is the memory that holds the context and details for why we believe what we believe. It's the '*because*' place. Once we find this memory and search out the identity belief, we want to attach to it a qualifying statement. In the case of the initial memory for the lady who thought she was 'dumb,' this was; "I must be dumb, '*because*,' I can't keep up with the other kids."

Another case was a lady who believed that she was 'stupid.' She had been deliberately made fun of and embarrassed by her teacher because she'd made a mistake when asked to write something on the blackboard. In that embarrassing and emotionally charged moment she believed that she was stupid, '*because*' she couldn't do it properly.

So, our third key is to give the belief that is learnt and stored in the *heart* as memory context. We do this through a statement that qualifies why the person believes what they believe about themselves. In summary, a qualifying statement contains how and why we have believed what we have believed, and why we have come to the conclusions that we have come to. It is why we have interpreted an event the way that we have; how it has shaped our identities, or caused us to perceive situations in particular ways.

Predictive memory
Memory doesn't just relate to events in the past, it has implications for much more than this. What we have learnt and believed in previous situations forms our expectations of what is likely to take place in the future. If no one ever noticed us before when we were forming, and we have taken on the belief that we don't matter and are unimportant, then that belief predicts that this will remain the case in the future. We may just accept that as the truth, and go through life with low self-image and/or depression. Or we may try to compensate and resolve the problem by becoming, in our own thinking, not only important, but the most important, and the only one who matters. This is a doorway to potential issues such as a narcissistic personality profile.

Likewise, if our encoded perception of our characteristics is that we aren't as good as others, we may become high achievers in order to prove that it's not true. Projecting off memory we're trying to resolve the *heart beliefs* that have become our truth. We do this by building an image that fits with what we want to believe. But even though we change the apparent evidence, the inner belief that creates the conflict remains. The source is always the memory.

Memory is also predictive in terms of behaviour and life choices. If we are, for example, anxious about people seeing our perceived weaknesses and shortcomings, we may hide away, or not try anything. If we have been rejected, we now are on guard against it happening again. We are vigilant, watching out for potential rejection, avoiding relationships, or we become independent so that we cannot be hurt again. We can see how memory is much more than a past event. It holds the key to every issue of life, and everything that we do. (Proverbs 4:23) It is a predictor of why we do what we do, and what motivates our thoughts and activities. (Hebrews 4:12)

Memory holds why we believe what we believe about who we are. It interprets how we see our position and place in life in the present. It creates our expectations in regards to how we see our potential in the future. In the event that the content of these memories corrupts a person's self-perception significantly, then you can expect all kinds of mental conflict and anguish. This can come from very deep-rooted painful beliefs, or the collective power of many less intense negative beliefs.

Memory is very much implicated as the source of most mental disorders. Indeed, it's difficult to find a mental disorder that does not include some component of anxiety in regards to a person's state of being and identity. These have been learnt and have their roots in a past event.

Icons, screens and accessing memory
In my other books I have used the analogy of a smart phone screen to help us understand viewing stored information that we hold. As I write this book on my laptop computer, I can only view around two thirds of a page at any one time. I am unable to, and don't see the whole picture of what I have written all at once. I have to search back through previous information that I have recorded to see what is there. The point is, that it IS there, recorded, even though I have to search for it to view it.

In fact, if I have had to stop working on the publication for a while, I have to review what I've written because I no longer remember what I have included, or even at times what conclusions that I have written as I have unpacked the subject matter. This is all stored in this plastic brain that we call a computer. These pre-existing files have to be found and investigated.

And when I do find them and consider them, those thought processes are renewed and come alive to me again.

In much the same way, in memory, we've concluded and recorded things about ourselves that are now stored information. They are not accessed and viewed on the screen of our minds all of the time. They must be deliberately brought up into our conscious mind to be inspected, examined and accepted as something that we believe.

If I asked you to think about a sunset, then your memory and imagination can readily put a picture on the screen of your conscious thinking. Computers, or mini computers such as smart phones have the capacity to store a great deal of information. This downloaded data includes the possibility of corrupted files, or viruses that can affect the operations of the device. In regards to examining information, you can however, normally only view a limited amount of content on your screen at a time. To go on Facebook or TikTok, for example, you will have to go off WhatsApp, or move your emails to the side. Conscious thought is much like this. Normally there will be a main item of thought on the 'screen' of your mind.

Why is this significant? It's relevant because unless we deliberately connect to memory it will remain in storage. In fact, often if we don't like what has been learnt in memory, so we will avoid viewing it as much as possible. The point is though, that unless we voluntarily choose to examine the contents of our memories, we will never see them, or accept them as what we hold to be true. Our fourth key then, is to choose to examine our '*heart beliefs*' by bringing the memories where we concluded them onto the 'screen' of our conscious minds.

Laptops, or perhaps more commonly smart phones, have what are known as 'icons' on the screen when you power up your device. Each of these 'icons,' or little pictures, is representative of a program of some kind that has a function and gives you access to information. Unless we click or tap on them, they remain closed. When we are ministering, we are deliberately clicking or tapping what we see presenting in the story of your problems. We're wanting to open up the whole program or 'app,' (application) relating to your issue. So, we're wanting to connect with memories where '*heart beliefs*' were learnt and bring them up onto the screen of your conscious mind to process.

You now let yourself be fully aware of those beliefs and inner thoughts. The components that we want to access are the memory, beliefs, emotions and context. Even though we often don't know where to go without ministry help, we are aware that we have, for example, an icon behind which we find; fear, anxiety, stress, rebellious feelings, insecurity, injustice, inferiority, anger, bitterness, sadness, confusion, rejection, and so on. Behind each of these icons is the real program that produces these responses to life. All of these negative feelings are produced by a negative belief. These beliefs are the basis of our disordered mental states. Freedom comes by dismantling our deception through encountering God's truth. Because this occurs through the ministry of the Spirit of truth, we call this ministry process; 'truth encounters.'

The fifth key, and foundational to the 'truth encounters' ministry is identifying and accepting what you believe, or hold as true in your '*heart*,' in regards to your identity, or sometimes a situation. It's important to know that because of the aforementioned reasons, that we mostly don't consciously know what these inner beliefs are. This could be because we have learnt and accepted these as our personality traits at a young age. Or it could, as we've suggested, be because we've rejected these beliefs for some reason, such as because we don't want it to be true about ourselves. These beliefs can be painful, or traumatic.

We endeavour to deny, negotiate, cope with, mask, or compensate for these beliefs in some way in order to not have to accept or embrace them. This produces some of the conflicted thinking which disorders our mental states. This phenomenon occurs on a sliding scale which is contingent on what we have been exposed to in life. All of us have begun with some kind of issues. Some are diagnosed, many are not. For freedom, we have to visit these places and allow the Holy Spirit to resolve them.

CHAPTER TEN

The Ministry Process

Preparation for ministry

For any kind of healing or freedom ministry the most important thing is positioning a person to receive. Jesus always taught the people first. Then they knew what was on offer from the Kingdom of God, saw that it was near enough to access, and understood how the provision would come. Before people come for this type of ministry, we usually have them read one of my books, or manuals, that explain the 'Truth Encounters' process.*

Minimally, knowing that not everyone likes to read, we have produced what we term a 'work up' book. This smaller body of material is purposed as a basic introduction to the ministry. It is titled; 'Receiving Truth That Will Set You Free.' We have people read this before they come for a ministry session so that they will understand what is involved, and can then decide if it is for them.

Clearly the more detailed publications on this subject are better suited for 'how to,' and a fuller understanding of the ministry for potential ministers. We also encourage people to prepare by viewing the explanatory clip titled, 4-23. This can be found on the resource page of our website.* For a more complete study, you can access our You Tube Channel. By using the link on the resource page, the clips will come up in order. These clips were mainly produced for download and training in developing nations. They offer some useful instruction for understanding the ministry. Unit 4 is devoted to explaining this ministry.

Remember, the most important KEY to the ministry is to know what you are trying to find. What we are looking for mainly is beliefs about our identity. That is, how we see our characteristics, who we are......in other words beliefs about SELF held at the very centre or core of our being. Additionally, at times we may be looking for beliefs about certain situations, which I'll explain shortly.

*These materials can be investigated on the www.418centre.org website resource page, and ordered through most major book retailers. They can also be viewed in the book index at the rear of this publication.

How a ministry session may be initiated

When a person comes for ministry, we're assuming that they understand the ministry through having read the material, or viewed a clip. The next step is to hear what troubles them, and note things that would produce a distortion of a person's identity, namely, '*heart beliefs.*' With experience we will discern '*heart beliefs*' as they relate their story. Jesus said; 'out of the overflow of the '*heart*' the mouth speaks. So, words are often an indicator of what people believe, locating them in terms of their perspective of self in regards to the world.

> *Matthew 12:34b "...for out of the overflow of the* **heart** *the* **mouth** *speaks." NIV (emphasis mine)*

For example, in the course of telling their story someone may say something such as; 'why bother trying, I would mess it up anyway!' You would note this as an indicator that somewhere in their history they've failed, and most probably imbibed a belief such as; 'I'm a failure, a hopeless case, useless,' or something similar. Remember, we want the qualifying statement. 'I'm a failure, *because..........*' This will give context to why they interpreted the initial event the way that they did, and come to the conclusion about their identity that they have.

Normally a person will need the help of someone who understands the ministry to help them find the root of their problem. They usually require somebody 'outside of their issues' to lead them through. Ideally this will be a person with experience or knowledge of '*what you are looking for.*' Knowing this is the main KEY. Anyone who plays Golf will know that everyone around them will give them tips on how to improve their game. This is because they can see your swing at the ball from outside. You cannot see what it looks like, and what you are doing wrong is not obvious to you because you are in the middle of it. So, knowledgeable direction from an outside perspective, through someone who is not influenced by your thinking can be invaluable.

Another consideration is, that if you're just beginning to receive ministry through the 'Truth Encounters' process, you may have, for instance, deep pain, or intense anxiety. In this case it's best to have someone experienced with you to help with the process. An additional practical reason to have someone with you, is that if you don't have the commitment of being with another person, you will probably keep putting off connecting with your beliefs and memories.

There are 2 main types or kinds of beliefs that are behind mental disorders. We call them 'identity beliefs,' and for the sake of simplicity, 'situation beliefs.'

Identity beliefs
We have covered these continually throughout the book up until this point, so I'll just do a brief summary to reinforce what an identity belief is. Your perceived identity is who you really think that you are, and consequently how you are, in your *heart*. What you really believe about SELF inside. Rather than a lengthy discourse let me suggest some common beliefs reflecting how one's identity is seen: "I'm not loveable, I'm unacceptable, not enough, less than others, stupid, a nothing, dumb, ugly, a failure, a loser, useless, weak, I don't matter, am not important," and so on.

Notice that they are all beliefs relating to your identity, they are about 'self.' They're often not conscious thought, and you many times are not aware that you believe these things about yourself. These types of *heart beliefs* are at the root of many anxieties. Unconsciously you are worried about people discovering your shortcomings, or reinforcing them, and you don't want to accept them as being true yourself.

'Situation beliefs' and Phobias
(The following excerpt is taken from the SOHAF Comprehensive Manual) Situation Beliefs, as the name suggests, are beliefs which have come out of a situation, and may or may not relate to your identity. Phobic beliefs usually fall under this category. An example of this type of belief, might be something along the lines of having panic attacks in small spaces where you feel captive, such as an elevator. As you focus on the feeling you might, for example, identify that the anxiety about small spaces could relate to you not being able to breathe.

As your mind does a data match with other places holding those feelings you remember as a small boy playing football at school. You managed to get hold of the ball and five or six boys jumped on you and held you down. In that moment you were crushed with the ball pressed against your chest, trapped and struggling to breathe. As you focus on the situation, we ask you what will happen if you can't get away and breathe. The response is; "I can't breathe, I am going to die!" There is nothing here relating to identity, it is all to do with the situation. As we have the person embrace the fear feeling and the belief that they are trapped, can't get away, and are going to die because they cannot breathe, we ask God for His truth. Which could simply be words, or a realization that they did not die, or some other communication that sets them free?

Phobia Example Story

A phobia is an irrational fear. It is taken from the Greek word Phobos, which means fear or even horror. For example, arachnophobia is an intense fear of spiders. These phobias usually begin with an event. They can also be taken in by osmosis at an early age by, for example, observing a parent's fear of something, and now believing that the subject needs to be feared, even if you don't know why. Regardless of the source, the problem that produces the fear is a belief.

In order to help people to understand how traumatic situations can produce phobias I often use the following story when I am preparing them for ministry. (Story quoted from; Receiving Truth That Will Set You Free.) There were two little 5-year-old boys walking down a street in their town. One of them noticed a motorbike across the road and went over to look at it. As the other boy continued down the road a dog came out of the gateway of a nearby house and bit him on the leg. In that moment of trauma, it was deeply encoded in him that dogs can hurt and frighten you. His mind has made a very good memory of the event, and he is now on guard against the possibility of it happening again.

In order to counteract and compensate for this ever-present fear, he reads numerous books about how dogs are man's best friend, and that most of them will never hurt you. He is trying to counteract his experientially imbibed involuntary *heart belief* with voluntarily learnt information from his mind. This is often what we do in church and wonder why people never change or have limited growth. We give them lots of information to learn for their problems and tell them how they should think. They are willing, but cannot do it.

Perhaps this is sometimes not unlike the Pharisees, who simply told the people how they should behave, but offered no help so that they could do it. The Jesus model was to heal their *broken hearts* and set the captives free. I will explain what I mean by this statement a little further on, but back to our story for the moment. As the little boy grows up and becomes a teenager he is often invited to his friends' houses and really wants to go, but underneath there is a nagging hesitation and anxiety. He is not consciously thinking it, but underneath the thought that there may be a dog at their house is producing the anxiety. So, his inner beliefs are beginning to affect his life choices.

Many years later the 5-year-old boys are again together walking, and they are now 40 years old. As they go along a small dog comes out of a laneway near them wagging his tail. The man who was bitten has an immediate physical fear response, even though with his mind he is trying frantically to apply the knowledge that he now has about dogs, and is telling himself how it looks so friendly. His *heart belief* encoded in the traumatic event that dogs at times bite you, is greater than his logical conscious knowledge that the dog looks really friendly.

The outworking is the release of electrical signals and fear hormones resulting in a very uncomfortable fear feeling in his physical body. His friend on the other hand has an entirely different response. He feels happy, warm and 'fuzzy.' What is the difference; it's the same dog? As the friend grew up as a small boy, his family had a friendly dog that played with him, climbed all over him and licked his face. The emotions that he was feeling were coming from different experientially learnt beliefs, proceeding from a different experience of dogs.

So, the same circumstance was producing opposing responses based on what they already perceived and believed. And what they each believed was learnt in historical situations in their past. Let's move on and look at the different parts that we play in a typical ministry session.

Role of the minister
- To teach, instruct or make sure that the person understands the ministry.
- Lead them to access and clarify the problem beliefs in their *hearts*.
- Help them identify the perceived identity state or situation belief that they've accepted as truth in their *hearts*.

The minister should help the person find their beliefs by asking questions, and then allowing time for the person to explore memories.

You will need somewhere quiet, and have time to be able to concentrate. Next, let yourself feel what you believe is true in your <u>heart</u> about yourself, as opposed to trying to convince yourself that you believe what you have learnt that you should think in your <u>head</u>.

As a person looks at a memory event **you can ask questions such as**:

1. What does that make you IF? (For example; little children should be seen & not heard? Often this will be something like; 'a nothing' or 'a nobody' or 'I'm invisible.')
2. What does that mean about you IF? (For example, you can't keep up with others- it could be; 'I'm dumb, not as good as others, not enough' etc. etc.)
3. What do you believe or think about your SELF because of this or that?
4. How does it make you feel….to think this or that?

Types of questions to ask relating to the specific problem presenting:
1. Rejection/ lack of acceptance: "If I'm not acceptable, why not? What is wrong with me? What does that mean about me?
2. Fear/ anxiety/insecurity: "What will happen if……? ("What if?")
3. Anger: "what is not how you think it should be?"
4. Bitterness: "Why do you feel that you cannot forgive?" ("I can't forgive you because you've treated me like - E.G. I'm a nothing"/ Because they don't care about you, have neglected or abused you…. that means what about you that they would treat you that way?)

On the 'Elevator'

Sometimes it's helpful to do what we call the 'Elevator.' To explain this, imagine the present time as the top floor. This is the place where things that are happening in life now make you feel what you feel. As you begin to search for the source of beliefs, sometimes you will stop off at earlier strong memories. These hold the same feelings and responses, and we use these places to qualify and 'refine' the belief, or to connect with the emotions and beliefs more clearly. These are like different floors, or periods in your life.

Ultimately, we want to be at the original or initial memory, which we will call the basement. This is where you interpreted life and came to the *'heart belief,'* or conclusion about SELF/IDENTITY, or certain SITUATIONS that you now hold. This will inevitably be before you were 10 years old. As you may recall, biblically and scientifically this is when the brain is plastic, and you are forming who you believe you are.

Predicting or projecting possible beliefs

An experienced minister may be looking for what a person may think or conclude about themselves in different types of situations. They can then ask questions based on these 'possibilities.' Perhaps a person accidently was involved in the death of a pet, or something that happened to a sibling as a result of something that they did. Knowing what a person may believe in such an event an experienced minister may ask; 'do you believe that you're a *bad person <u>because</u>* everyone yelled at you because of what you did, and it was your fault?'

The minister knows that the key is finding what has been imprinted in regards to the perceived identity of the person. The person will either acknowledge that it's true, or reply, no its more like this or that. The minister has simply located them near what they believe, and the person can then refine it from there. This can be helpful, because people often don't understand what it is that you're looking for. I've never yet seen anyone agree with a belief that they don't have as the result of my proposing possibilities.

If you are receiving ministry your part is:
- To be willing to seek out and note your issues.
- To be prepared to embrace, accept and allow yourself to connect with beliefs, emotions and memories.

The work of Holy Spirit
Before I attempt to guide you through the process, it's vital to explain the role of the Holy Spirit. It is, after all His ministry that we co-labour in. Once we have identified the belief, 'He' is the only one who can bring freedom and healing. Counselling you about your belief will not bring change, even though we now know what it is and why it is present. This can be a shift that is difficult for ministers who are used to imparting their knowledge, counsel, and advice in an attempt to resolve the persons problem. It will also be challenging for those who feel the need to cast out a spirit, because that is their model, or declare or break something over a person.

The Ministry of the Spirit of Truth
- To guide and inspire the minister and the person in the session.
- To reveal God's truth and bring freedom.

The following description on how the Holy Spirit communicates truth to us is an excerpt from my book; Receiving Truth That Will Set You Free.

1. **In words**: I tend to think in words, so mostly when God uses my mind to communicate truth to me it comes in words. Interestingly I have noticed that as I have become more and more free that I also receive pictures and impressions at times, either for myself or others. Some people get stuck here because they are waiting for flashes of light, a booming voice, or an audible word from outside their body. I explain it this way. My computer

is set up with the fonts, letter styles, writing size and so on that I like. If I were to give it to you and ask you to write me a note, when you returned it to me, I might exclaim; *that is just my writing!* That's true; but you just used my faculties or equipment to communicate your message to me.

In the ministry room, having identified the 'heart belief,' I simply encourage people to let their minds go. When they hear something, occasionally people might explain that it just seemed like their own thoughts, but they heard this or that. We test and see whether or not it is God by looking at the old belief. Perhaps a person may have always thought that they were dumb. It felt true to them. Now they look for the belief and cannot find it, or it is no longer true; it has always been true to them, but now it is gone.

2. **Pictures or impressions**:
Many people think in pictures. I remember a man who was suffering from a rejection belief of some kind. When this man spent time with his own children, he would put his face up against their face as a sign of love and affection, indicating acceptance and connection. As the man was focusing on his belief and feeling his own rejection, God gave him a picture, an impression of the Heavenly Father putting His face against the mans. Needless to say, he was deeply touched, moved, and convinced of his own acceptance. In whatever way God chooses to communicate to us, it is in a sense like a *prophetic now word* from Him applied to our historical event. The main key is to discover what you 'really' believe.

I was ministering to a young man one day and as he embraced the *heart belief* that he held, the Holy Spirit took some words from a prophetic word that he had received a number of years earlier, and applied it to his belief, bringing healing to that area. Why did it not bring healing before? The young man did not know what he believed in his *heart* up until this time when we exposed it. Then the Holy Spirit applied the words to the belief.

3. **Scriptures**:
Very often the Holy Spirit will use a scripture that people know well in their minds and apply it to issues in their *hearts*. By way of example, I was ministering to a lady recently and she was in a memory where she was struggling to keep up with the other children in being able to do her school work. As a result, she had come to a conclusion and belief that she still suffered with daily, along the lines of; *I am dumb because I cannot do the schoolwork like the other kids.* As she concentrated on the school memory and felt the belief, the Lord put into her mind the book of Ecclesiastes: *Everything is meaningless!*

For her, this meant that the activity that she was basing her identity on really did not matter. This brought her freedom. If the reference that she was measuring herself against was meaningless, then the conclusion that she arrived at had no basis and could not be true either. This was not a conscious act on her part to think differently, it was the result of the truth which the Holy Spirit communicated to her. Education is good, but it is a 'man' activity, and may not relate very much to what a person will be doing in life, or the type of intelligence or skills that they possess.

4. **Realizations**:

Several years ago, I ministered to a young man who came with the presenting problem of feeling as though he was responsible for everything that went wrong in his family life, his workplace, and even to some extent the world. As he connected with the feeling, we arrived at the place where he learnt a belief something like; *It's my fault if bad things happen.* As a small boy he was traveling in the back seat of the family car. They had an accident with another car as they entered an intersection. It was an emotionally traumatic event for the little boy. As soon as it happened, his father whipped around in his seat, and said sharply, *have you got your seatbelt on?*

Now it may seem ridiculous, but in that emotionally charged moment the boy thought; *This bad thing is my fault <u>because</u> I haven't gotten my seat belt on!* These thoughts are burned deeply into our brains and hearts in moments of crisis or trauma through an electro-chemical process known as protein synthesis.

Oddly enough, as we explored the memory, he discovered that afterward it turned out that he did in fact have his belt on. He now *realized*, through the Holy Spirit, that the truth was that it was not his fault at all. He had believed that he was to blame in the moment of shock. Later, when the emotional intensity subsided it was too late to reinterpret the belief that he had already taken in, because the belief that it was his fault was already in his *heart*. But now many years later, when we visited the event, the Holy Spirit reminded him of the complete picture and set him free.

Personally, I believe that one of the reasons that this ministry is so effective is that God dwells in eternity and not in 'time' as we do. (Isaiah 57:15). He is everywhere all of the time. He is already there ten years from now, and He is there in your memory, whether you knew of Him or not, even as a child. So, we can identify your belief up here in the present time, and counsel you about it with minimal change. But when the Spirit of truth speaks into, and helps you reinterpret your memory event with His truth, He *is* actually there!

Another example of a realization could be a child coming into a room where mother and father are having a heated argument. In that moment the child believes that it is somehow their fault. Looking back and exploring the memory through the eyes of God they now realize, as they see more of the picture that was not as emotionally intense, that the parents were already fighting before they entered the room. So, how could it be their fault? God will at times bring freedom through a realization such as this. I have also seen in other instances people being set free at the moment where they realize why they believe what they believe, and where it came from, and for them that is the healing.

5. *Sensations, feelings, knowing*:
God is indeed very creative in how He communicates with us. Normally as ministers or receivers we do not know what He is going to do, or how He will do it. Sometimes He will give us insight into what He is about to say or do. I think in part this is on the job training for words of knowledge and learning to hear his voice for ourselves.

I recall one lady diagnosed with schizophrenia who had suffered severe physical and sexual abuse. As she was accessing memories and beliefs, there was a light coming into the memory picture. When the light came in, she felt peaceful and calm, safe. I was frantically going through my theology to make sure that this was something Biblical. Remembering, Jesus as the light of the world reassured me that this was something that God might do. The bottom line was that her fears were resolved.

Other people report simply feeling love. Still more, report that they just know that the beliefs they held are not true. I remember asking one lady after a session what she now thought of God. She thought about it for a moment, and then replied; *He's clever, He's very clever!* Amen. Our God is indeed very clever.

6. **Through our senses**
One lady that we ministered to had come with the presenting problem of struggling to believe God for provision. She was actually a woman of great faith in most areas of her life. However, as a child she was never sure that they were going to have food to eat. The belief that she took to *heart* as a result of that anxiety was at the root of the problem.

Immediately after we asked God to communicate His truth to her, she asked a question; *who has the bread? I can smell bread!* After assuring her that no one had bread, I asked her what the smell of bread meant to her. She reported that it meant that; *there will always be enough.* For her this resolved the issue, and as a result of her new expectations of God providing, over the next few months her family situation changed dramatically. Through our senses seems to be a much less common way that God uses, but it happens from time to time.

By whatever means He frees us we can be sure that God is always about helping people. Whether we are receiving or ministering, He uses our time doing so to learn about Him, and about His goodness. This occurs as we see His love, grace and willing ability to help His children.

Accessing the Heart via the mind and emotions
How does it work? As we have already stated, our sanctification is a process whereby we are separated from our areas of deception by the Holy Spirit bringing us God's truth. The simplicity of the ministry is that we become like little children, and listen for the Spirit of truth to reframe our wrong believing. As we enter the process, we find that as one of His sheep we do indeed hear His voice. John 10:27

Because we have a society consumed with learning and knowledge, we often find a conflict between head knowledge and *heart* knowledge. People will ask us to tell them how to think, believing that they can fix the problem without God by using their own minds and knowledge. To date I have never seen anybody successfully do that, although many try for a time.

We access the *heart beliefs* by following emotion, or by following known *self-beliefs* back to the source in the memories.

Steps to a ministry session
Let me present three common access points, or pathways to initial memories that a person may come in for ministry presenting with:
1. 1They may already have a memory.
2. They may have something in their current situation that is a stressor, or trigger mechanism, that produces negative reactions, feelings, or responses.
3. They may have something negative that they have always believed about themselves or a situation.

1. Beginning from an existing memory
If you are beginning with a memory that the person already has that has been impacting, we would most likely follow these steps:

Step 1. Go to the memory that you have. (Any memory that has been retained has been stored because it is significant.) Explore the contents of the memory.

Step 2. If you have a memory, what happened in the event? Accept and embrace any negative feelings that are present. *Pause and reflect*

Step 3. If you began with a memory that has negative feelings that you are now allowing yourself to feel – look at the negative feeling, what is it that you ended up believing about yourself that produces that feeling? [What we're specifically looking for – is a belief about your identity – that is, how you identify your 'SELF,' how you perceive your characteristics.]

We allow time for the person to examine and explore the feelings in the memory, possibly asking the occasional additional question to help them to refine the belief. We'll try not to interrupt this reflection process as much as possible. *{As suggested, identity beliefs could be: I'm dumb, useless, not good enough, unlovable…unimportant etc.}*

[NOTE: After years of ministry, we've found that people, regardless of race or personality, hold similar simple child learnt beliefs in their hearts. These relate to how they believe themselves to be.]

Step 4. This is the same for all of the pathways. Once you've identified the belief that you have about your 'SELF,' if possible, look at the event, and add in why you came to that conclusion in the memory. Why did you interpret it that way? (Qualifying statements – the; "I believed this about myself '*because*…!')

For example:
"I'm not acceptable, or lovable **because**.....?
"I'm not important, or am 'dumb' **because**....?
"I'm not worth anything, or am 'hopeless' **because**......?

Step 5. If you are prepared to accept what you believe about your SELF (identity,) in your *HEART* – and not **deny** it because of information that you now have in your mind which you learnt voluntarily later in life…. then:

Now we invite the Holy Spirit to bring His truth and perspective: As you recall this could come as ways such as; Words, thoughts, pictures, impressions, scriptures, just know, feel something, understanding why you took in the belief, seeing or realizing the truth.

2. Beginning from a current situation

If a person is beginning from something in their present life circumstances that has produced a negative emotion, response, or reaction, we would most likely go through the following steps: (Triggers in current life events are probably the most common beginnings to a ministry session.)

Step 1. What has happened that was a recent 'stressor' or 'trigger event,' that produced the negative feeling, reaction or response?

Step 2. If you are using a recent 'trigger event' that produced a negative feeling, connect with the feeling......*Pause and reflect on what it made you feel.*

Step 3. Having connected with the feeling in the current event that you are using, follow the feeling and search for the historical place or event in a memory that matches the feeling that was triggered recently...or if you know what you think and feel about yourself in the recent event, follow the feeling and belief to the earliest place that you know of where you learnt it......*Pause, go through and examine your memories.*

Step 4. Once have the matching memory, identify and accept the belief that you have about your 'SELF.' If possible, look at the event, and add in why you came to that conclusion in the memory. Why did you interpret it that way? (Qualifying statements - the; "I believed this about myself 'because...!')

For example:
"I'm not important, or worthy of being noticed **because**.....?
"I'm useless, or a waste of space **because**....?
"I'm not enough, and unwanted **because**.....?

Step 5. As with the other pathways, if you are prepared to accept what you believe about your SELF (identity,) in your *HEART* - and not **deny** it because of information that you now have in your mind which you learnt voluntarily later in life.... then:

Now we invite the Holy Spirit to bring His truth and perspective: As you recall this could come as - Words, thoughts, pictures, impressions, scriptures, just know, feel something, understanding why you believe what you do, seeing or realizing the truth.

3. Beginning with something negative that you've always believed about yourself

Step 1. What is the negative belief that you've always had about yourself?

Step 2. Embrace this negative thought, there should be a matching negative feeling.... accept, connect and focus on it.

Step 3. Now concentrate on the emotion and belief, and search for the historical place or event in a memory that matches the feeling and thinking about your 'SELF'- you need to go to the original event where you decided this about your 'SELF.'

Step 4. When you have the earliest matching memory, identified and accepted the belief that you have about your 'SELF,' then, look at the event, and add in why you came to that conclusion in the memory. Why did you interpret it that way? (Qualifying statements – the; "I believed this about myself 'because...!')

For example:
"I'm bad, and it can't be changed '**because**,' I did this or that...."
"I'm ruined, or damaged goods '**because**,' this or that happened to me...?"
"I'm unprotected, or am unsafe **because**.....?" (Possibly; 'there's no one there who cares...or...no one is in control!') This would be a 'situation' belief.

Step 5. Again, as with the other pathways, if you are prepared to accept what you believe about your SELF (identity,) in your *HEART* – and not **deny** it because of information that you now have in your mind which you learnt voluntarily later in life.... then:

Now we invite the Holy Spirit to bring His truth and perspective: As you recall this could come as – Words, thoughts, pictures, impressions, scriptures, just know, feel something, or understanding why you believed what you believe, seeing or realizing the truth.

Summary of Keys

Key 1: Accept that whatever is believed in the '*heart*' was embedded in a previous critical moment, which could be anywhere from conception on. Virtually all of these moments are going to occur in places where the identity is formative, namely prior to 10 years old.

Key 2. The earliest place where this belief was taken in is the important one.

We could term it, the original, or initial memory. Once that belief has been established and taken to 'heart,' it is used to interpret future life events.

Key 3. Having accessed the place where a 'heart belief' has been imbibed, we're wanting to frame it and give it context with a 'qualifying statement.' This will shape why we believe what we believe. You could, for example believe that you're not good enough for many reasons. When you access the original memory where you learnt that you're not good enough, this 'because' statement qualifies why you came to that conclusion. It explains why you believed what you now think about your identity, or possibly, how and why you perceive or interpret certain situations as you do.

Key 4. The ministry involves deliberately accessing the memories holding the beginnings of these unconscious beliefs. This is done by bringing the memories onto the 'screen' of your conscious mind.

Key 5. The person receiving the ministry has to be prepared to accept what is discovered that they believe, or hold as true in their 'hearts.' If they have allowed themselves to do this there will be 3 elements present. The memory, which holds the context for what they believe. The belief, and the matching emotion or feeling that is the result of the inner thinking. These normally all need to be present for wholeness to be restored.

Key 6. This could have been listed as Key 1, but I want to summarize the ministry following this Key. The most important Key is to know what you are looking for. That is, 'heart beliefs' that are contrary to what you would like to think or believe based on what you know in your mind.

It is vital to understand and accept that many of the feelings and responses that you are experiencing are coming from inner thoughts that you are not necessarily consciously aware of, and would prefer not to have.

To keep it simple we could say that the role of the person receiving ministry, is to connect with their feelings and inner thoughts. Profoundly simple, but simply profound. Once you identify and accept what you hold as truth, God can come in and reinterpret it through His greater truth and knowledge and set you free.*

*Other books with more detail on the subject in regards to negotiating blockages, other possible elements, or more complex situations are available. We recommend: SOHAF (School of Healing and Freedom Comprehensive manual) or Healing and Freedom through Truth Encounters. Both of these publications have similar material regarding this ministry.

One Line summary of the ministry
'The WHOLE ministry is pivotal on the principal that we are trying to discover what you believe in your '*heart*' that you no longer necessarily remember in words. And then invite the Spirit of Truth to set you free.'

We could say that many of our feelings, reactions, behaviours and responses are automatized. By that I mean that they are not deliberate, but stem from conclusions and programming that has already happened. They are not a meditated and thought through response to the moment.

Applying this process to disorders
When we're talking about mental disorders, we're looking at the compound effect of multiple negative identity beliefs. In our experience, in order to dismantle mental disorder, you will have to work through a number of beliefs. Remember, you can only deal with one belief at a time. This is because you have to identify the source and bring it onto the screen of your conscious mind. To put this another way, we could say, you need to become conscious of it.

So, then it is a process, working with one belief after another until the person is completely free. Resolving each individual belief is a healing in itself, resulting in a greater measure of freedom. Some people have a few deep beliefs, others have many smaller beliefs. Most people are somewhere in between, having a mixture of very impacting beliefs, and many lesser issues that still need to be dealt with. This requires commitment from both the person receiving, and the minister, who is laying down their life and time for the person in need.

Demonic Involvement
It is quite common for there to be some level of direct spiritual involvement in mental disorders. The real issue is still the beliefs that are held that give place to a spirit in some way or another. The ministry process that I have described will most times remove the place, or ground, that a spirit, or spirits work from. Here I will just note some common evidence of demonic interaction if it is present. You can access more detailed information on the connection and interplay with evil spirits as it relates to people receiving ministry in the following of my other publications. *

Signs of demonic activity:
1. The person loops or <u>replays</u> life events over and over repetitively. These can be original events, but very often will be more recent things such as betrayal, times where they've felt let down or

had injustice, rejection, or perhaps self-admonishment for perceived failures. These more recent times are as a result of pre-existing negative self-image beliefs being touched into.

2. <u>Strongholds</u> - this is where the person is held into cycles of behaviour.

3. The presence of a demon will <u>amplify</u> the problem. For example, anger, unforgiveness, ungodly control, rejection, pride, or rebellion, will be oversized in expression. These types of emotional responses are common, and very often present without any demonic interference as well.

4. <u>Resistance</u> to the ministry process of some kind, for example; inordinate control of emotions, or excessive talking leading to controlling the ministry session. Fears, or even doubt and unbelief may be present.

5. Evils spirits are often <u>attached</u> to sinful responses that result from 'heart beliefs' such as: bitterness, ungodly control, rebellion, violence, unrighteous anger, rejection, immorality, addictions, pride, deception etc.

*Healing and Freedom Through Truth Encounters, School Of Healing And Freedom Comprehensive Manual (SOHAF)

CHAPTER ELEVEN
Considering other important factors

The story of 'Bobs' ministry
Earlier in Part 1 we made reference to a 9-year boy that we were asked to help. There are a few reasons that I have put how we ministered to him here at the end of Part 1. The first of these is that the purpose of this book is to present the ministry model that we've just gone through. As I've detailed, we did not understand how God used this ministry of the Holy Spirit to free people until 6 or 7 years after we first encountered him. Additionally, the process that we're recommending as having great effect on most mental disorders would not have been applicable to his case. The reason for this is there needs to be a certain amount of use of mental faculties from the person receiving ministry.

Although we've ministered to and resolved issues such as dissociation with people who are able to cooperate and feedback, I don't think this would have been possible with Bob because of the status of his IQ, and consequently him not being able understand and interact in the process. Also, he is non-verbal, which makes his situation much more difficult to deal with. He fits into what I would estimate is less than 5% or 10% of mental disorders that the 'Truth Encounters' ministry may not apply to.

Amazing transformation
There were so many criteria on the spectrum that he met, and that he could have been diagnosed with, that nobody was prepared to label all

of his problems. In order to clarify his condition, his file described him as 'feral' as a result of his wild out of control demonically driven behaviour. His mind and actions were so hyperactive at the beginning of the ministry that he had to be asked questions 5 or 6 times before he pieced together enough of the question to respond. We came to understand that this was because his mind was going so quickly that he only heard a word here and there.

This was consistent with extreme ADHD. You would have described his whole demeanour as 'quickened' to an alarming rate, with eyes darting around everywhere. The result after ministry? Resolved. Peaceful. Calm. Able to listen and immediately comprehend anything on his level that was said to him.

Other disorders that he had that were resolved include; Sleep disorder, ODD, (Oppositional Defiant Disorder), violent and destructive behaviour, self-harming, insanity, allergies, fits, and a number of other issues which completely disappeared. He is now calm and compliant, able to hear and understand just as any other person would.

We would not describe the autism to be 100% resolved, but probably 95% dealt with. Most times today you would not necessarily identify him as autistic if you first met him, as the autistic behaviour normally is virtually non-existent. Miraculously, he at times he initiates approaching people and shakes their hands. In insecure environments there are still some signs of withdrawal if you know him.

He suffered from dissociation, and was almost continuously changing personalities. It was like watching Tarzan swinging from tree to tree. These dissociation events are currently about 90% resolved. For around 11 months of the year, he is normal and enjoys watching TV or playing video games, going travelling, walking, visiting friends, and so on, as do most people.

Notably, as we broke down the dissociation the autism resolved as well. I came to the conclusion that autism is often a form of dissociation. I recently did some research on how the scientific community see this, and many are saying the same thing. The Schizophrenia is also around 90% resolved, as this disorder operated on a dissociated part of the personality. This part only presents perhaps one month of a year with greatly reduced intensity. What I mean by this is that when this dissociative part does appear, the host person, the true identity has a considerable level of influence, whereas before he had none.

Practical lessons from Bobs story
The reason that I'm including this case study is to illustrate the difference between applying the Word of God in a practical way, and the ministry of the Holy Spirit. Dealing with people according to the ways prescribed by the Word of God has a profound affect in terms of the actions and reactions that are evoked in the person. The bible applied will build a person up giving them acceptance, value, worth, security, encouragement, grace and love. This is powerful spiritual ministry from one person to another.

Applying these spiritual attitudes removes the triggers and stressors that touch a persons' broken identity. And in the context of that relationship, covers over the issues. Although applying these principles helps, it does not produce the healing and wholeness to inner beliefs that can only be restored through the ministry of the Holy Spirit. In the case of Bobs amazing improvements, dealing with him according to God's instructions has produced profound results. However, if he was to be placed into another environment where he was ministered to in another way, according to the principles of another Kingdom as before, he would most likely revert to some of his old behaviour mechanisms.

What I'm saying is that his broken identity is not healed. This then highlights the important component of a Biblically based environment when dealing with mental disorders. Ideally, the church would teach their people how to establish the Kingdom of God in their households, and concurrently offer healing and freedom through the Holy Spirit in their ministry settings.

How then were his mental disorders resolved?
So, here is the point that I'm trying to make. Bobs story illustrates the distinction between the outworking of the word of God when it's applied through us, and the supernatural and complete work of the Holy Spirit facilitating the word of God to bring healing. We need both. But very often in the church we think that we can fix everything without the Holy Spirit by just ministering the word. Significantly, Bobs disorders were not reduced to nearly nothing by deliverance from demons, or inner healing of some kind, and certainly not by counselling, or him learning the Bible.

Deliverance
Although he was heavily, almost totally demonized, casting out demons in a direct confrontation was not how they were dealt with in this case. In 1992 we didn't know much about mental disorders, but we did know a bit about demons. We were about to learn a lot more. We've already cited Proverbs 25:28, but for the sake of the exercise we'll use it again here.

Proverbs 25:28 Like a city whose walls are broken down is a man who lacks self-control. NIV

This proverb is explaining that the human personality is like a city. In the event that its walls are broken down it has no defences to keep the enemy out, or protect what is within. In the case of a broken person, they have little defence against spiritual enemies, and are easily overrun. This was very much the case with Bob. As we've said he was wild and insane, with no self-control or self-discipline whatsoever. In other words, he had no authority over his own person. In a; 'children have rights, and shouldn't be told what to do' society, there was no other authority being exercised over him either. As a result, he just ran wild.

With no walls, defences or resistance in his personality, there was not much point casting out demons, as they would just come straight back in again. So, the first thing that had to be done was to establish authority over him for his own sake. As with any child you have to exercise authority in love, and then teach them self-discipline and authority over their own being before it's too late. If you don't, they will be easy prey to drugs, illicit sex, porn, violence and general mental confusion.

The first thing that had to be done was establish authority, knowing that the spiritual has its expression by working out through the natural. The real issue was not the demons, it was *the ground* that they had to stand on. The problem was the power that they had through unresisted cooperation from the person. We have authority over spirits, but not normally over human freewill and choice. So, someone such as Bob who is heavily broken, is also heavily deceived about their identities and their situation, and this gives *place* to the demons.

The person is deceived into believing that a demon serves some purpose, and so joins and entwines with the spirit. Now they think that what the evil spirit wants is what they want. This is done unwittingly as they may not even understand that evil spirits exist. For example, if they suffer from extreme insecurity, they may become obsessively controlling of their surroundings. If this becomes demonized and amplified, the control spirit then serves the purpose of making them feel secure. All they know is that because of what they believe they don't feel safe. So, they don't want the control to go, otherwise they will feel insecure once again.

Discipline as Love

Seemingly, often modern secular thinking is that if you love your child, you'll let them do anything that they want. This is contrary to biblical teaching, which says that if you don't love your child, you will not discipline them.

> Proverbs 13:24 *If you refuse to discipline your children, it proves you don't love them; if you love your children, you will be prompt to discipline them.* NLT (emphasis mine)

The New King James version is more emphatic, stating that you actually hate your child if you don't discipline them. At times we see parents who hate what their children do, and how they behave, as a result of their own failure to correct the child in love.

> Proverbs 13:24 *He who spares his rod hates his son, But he who loves him disciplines him promptly.* NKJV (emphasis mine)

So, initially the free run of spirits manipulating Bobs personality and faculties was taken away by disciplining him. That is, if he was manifesting, he would be punished. He quickly learnt that playing host to demons was an unpleasant experience. Now his will and decisions were positioned against continuing that behaviour. Over time it became less and less and finally stopped altogether. Although in modern humanistic thinking this may seem terrible, it was in fact the first step towards building a new self-controlled personality, leading to his freedom from demonic bondage.

In mental parlance, we were establishing a new 'host person,' thereby allowing the real person to come forward uninfluenced by these demonic entities. This simple biblical activity gave boundaries and security, and began to break down the dissociation and autistic behaviour. Bob was about as an extreme case of demonization as is imaginable. If discipline and biblical order was the beginning of breaking down this demonic power over him, it makes you wonder about the plethora of out-of-control children with mental and behavioural problems that we see in the world today. The way of the western world is not working, having seemingly abandoned our biblical roots in favour of humanistic approaches.

Inner healing

As we already stated, we didn't understand inner healing at that time. However, working from biblical instruction, we ministered to the areas that were wounded and broken. We tried to build up the walls of the personality and bring some measure of wholeness to the now emerging real person. We did this by establishing Godly order around his life, and by instigating the precepts of the Kingdom of God. His environment began to be grace, love, acceptance, security through firm boundaries, building up, and discipline in love. Over time the new host person who is Bob today was established. The real Bob is sane, calm, and enjoys life and relating to those who love him.

I include his story to highlight that along with ministry there may be environmental issues that need to be addressed. They won't bring complete healing, but they are a significant part of the development and safety of a person suffering from mental disorders. They are a factor that has to be considered in the establishment and progress of the person. Working towards the fruit of the Spirit as our basic environment in the home and church are very important indeed.

Very noteworthy, as we brought elements in his life into God's <u>order</u>, including how he was dealt with, his mental dis<u>orders</u> were resolved, either completely, or mostly. As we removed the influences created and seeded by the father who birthed the fall, the author of disorder, the 'city' was built up.

To put Bobs ministry into perspective, these 'illnesses' were either resolved or greatly reduced over many years of working with him. In stark contrast is the instant and complete healing that occurs through the 'Truth Encounters' ministry process that we've been describing. (Even though if people have a lot of beliefs that need to be dealt with, it will involve multiple sessions, and a commitment of time.)

We're now going to move into Part 2 where we want to begin to examine specific disorders and where they usually come from. We want this section to be diagnostic, and a useful reference for those seeking to carry and deliver the good news.

PART 2

SPECIFIC MENTAL DISORDERS

CHAPTER TWELVE
Healthy Perspective on dealing with Disorders

As we begin this second, diagnostic section of the book, it's important to remind ourselves that knowledge puffs up, but love builds up. People with low self-image like to feel superior to other people. These people can feel better than others by knowing about what the cause of a person's conditions may be. As the old saying goes, if you blow out someone else's candle your own will burn brighter. Consequently, people love to find fault or supposed weakness in others so that in turn they feel better about their own shortcomings and failings.

Judging where someone is up to, in terms of their issues, in order to be able to help them is whole lot different to judging who they are because of their problems. So, we understand that the information in this publication could be misused if it is in the wrong hands. It has been said that knowledge is power. We don't want people attempting to have power and superiority over others who are in need of help because they now have understanding of a disorder.

Points to make note of, and consider
1. Let me make it clear here that we rarely ask people the secular name of the issues that they're presenting with. At times we know because they have up until the time of ministry been receiving treatment from a Psychologist, Psychiatrist or counsellor of some kind. We simply begin working with the problems that they want help for.

2. The medical profession is largely specialised in this day and age, which means it is also to some degree fragmented. This in turn also means that you will often hear; "That's not my area, I need to refer you to someone else." This implies that no one person has all of the pieces of the picture. So, when you're talking about mental illness, articles present with a lot of 'possible' causes coming from different departments or specialised areas of expertise. As a result, no one really knows where these disorders began, they only have theories.

Even those who believe that these problems began in early life and formative childhood, they cannot prove it because they haven't had the help of the Holy Spirit to heal those wounds. So, even though they are right, they haven't been able to produce the results to be able to confirm that they are correct. Without the ministry of the Holy Spirit, they are left with what they can do themselves. This usually means that at best they are often only able to help people to manage their problems, and not to see them set free and healed.

Additionally, they may be trying to fix you by working on your mind, when in fact your problem is in your *heart*. *Heart* problems cannot be fixed with changing the thinking in your mind. Rather, when the *heart* is healed its negative influences on the mind are resolved, and as a result your thinking changes effortlessly. How do we know this? We've been watching God heal hearts broken in childhood for decades. We've been witnessing many of these issues and 'disorders' resolved as God brings '<u>order</u>' and wholeness at *heart* level.

3. If you begin to study specific mental disorders you will find that typically the researchers will indicate degrees of depression, anxiety, bipolar, and so on. In our experience this is dependent on factors such as: how traumatic were the circumstances or situations where the beliefs were taken in, the age and vulnerability of the child at the time. Also at times, how repetitive were the themes if the beliefs came from themes rather than specific episodes?

Another important component is how many beliefs exist that produce the condition. For example, a person suffering from depression may have a number of self-beliefs that produce the hopelessness that underlies their depression, or just one or two.

Additionally, personality may play a role in how a person might process events, and then arrive at conclusions about themselves that will become identity or situation beliefs in the '*heart*.' Some people might be very emotionally open by nature, and so resultantly are very prone to taking on a lot of negative inner thinking. The good news is that those who are very emotionally open and available, very often receive healing and restoration more easily than those more stoic, or strongly controlled in their emotional make-up.

4. Articles will often explain that a person might have multiple disorders, or overlapping problems. This is because most of the disorders begin with common or similar '*heart beliefs*.' As the Apostle Paul put it, the things that we suffer from are 'common to man.' (1 Corinthians 10:13) Or in other words we all struggle with similar things that move us out of Gods order. In this case, the beliefs that we find that people struggle with in ministry appear over and over again, regardless of gender, race or other factors.

A worldwide problem

It could appear on face value that mental disorders are primarily an issue for developed nations. We certainly have far more people in wealthy nations who are qualified to categorize and name mental issues. I was ministering in Kenya a few years ago, and happened to pick up a DAILY NATION newspaper dated 23 of October 2018. The headline was titled with the statement: 'Little effort seen globally as mental health illness cases rise.' The article stated that a study revealed that in Kenya one in four people are likely to suffer a mental health disorder. This is consistent with statistics that we've already cited that have been done by the World Health Organization. These studies indicate that for the general populace across the Earth, this will be around 2 billion people. As we've pointed out mental health could be turned around and renamed or relabelled, 'very unhealthy thinking,' particularly in regards to how you see yourself, and how you perceive that others view you. These perceptions would include anxieties about how people may deal with you as a result of how you think that they might regard you.

The article went on to point out that 2 out of 3 mental conditions are chronic conditions beginning in childhood. It stated that 4 out of 5 Kenyans who commit suicide are depressed at the time of their death. It went on to say that 5 out of 6 Kenyans with mental illness do not receive treatment. The paper projected that the cost to the global economy will be 16 trillion dollars by 2030.

It really is of prime importance that the church, the largest global people care organization on the planet, is fully equipped to deal with the issue as God intended. With that in mind we're going to investigate the most common of these mental disorders, and propose where to begin to look in terms of the root beliefs that are behind these problems.

Our goals and intentions as we examine specific mental disorders

In this section, at the beginning of each disorder we're going to try to explain the typical kinds of root *'heart beliefs'* that you're likely to find behind the problem. Then from that basis we can hopefully discern and have an explanation as to why the thinking, feelings, responses, behaviours and reactions exist and are present. And why the mental state of being of the person is distorted and corrupted.

I'm hoping that you'll see the connections, and understand the *cause* and *effect* behind unresolved thinking problems. We'll be attempting to take a diagnostic approach to the *fruit*, exposing the causes and typical beliefs, along with revealing the most common roots that you can expect to find with these specific mental disorders.

So, as we begin to explore these mental problems, I want to say up front that just as physical diseases generally come from the same few basic *'heart belief'* roots, so do mental disorders. As I've said, over the years we have found that people from across the world suffer from the same basic underlying beliefs that produce these problems, and we have found ourselves ministering to the same things over and over again. For example; Rejection beliefs, anxiety beliefs, inferiority beliefs, worthlessness beliefs, inadequacy beliefs, injustice beliefs, insecurity beliefs, are all common to man.

We've pointed out previously that if, perhaps, you feel worthless, it's because you believe that you're worthless for some reason. This is the cause or root. The fruit, or result, might be that you now feel frustrated or hopeless that you will never be able to do, or be, what is required for you to be of value. This may be behind an issue such as depression. But you require the root *heart belief* along with the qualifying statement, the *because* statement for freedom. So, we'll endeavour to unpack some of these underlying 'lynch pin' beliefs.

Specific Mental disorders causes and beliefs

As we go along, I'll endeavour to explain how these thoughts, emotions and responses to life, almost exclusively come from *heart beliefs*. That is to say beliefs about your SELF, your identity, who you perceive yourself to be. These then leave you trying to resolve these issues by working out how to be acceptable to others, and how to fit into the world.

We need to note here, that in practice it requires an investment of time to hear a person's story. It can also be time consuming to work through the beliefs that trouble them one at a time. (Skill levels in achieving this, and the amount of time required changes with experience.) Once you realize how important that the person is to God, and how much Jesus went through to pay for their freedom, it's relatively natural to be committed to the process.

Following is a list of common 'mental disorders' that plague mankind. We can gather information from what man has observed over time, but have the wisdom and understanding to discern what is behind these problems. For us this comes from decades of ministering to these disorders. Depression and anxiety are the most common so we will place them at the top of our list. What I'm going to be detailing here is a summary of what is generally accepted about these disorders.

I have collated this information from research in recent years as more and more people who come for help have labels attached to their problems. I've then added conclusions and suggestions in regards to what you may be working with, basing these on what we have learnt from years of experience in applying Biblical precepts to these maladies.

Diagram 6

TYPICAL ROOTS AND FRUITS OF MENTAL DISORDERS

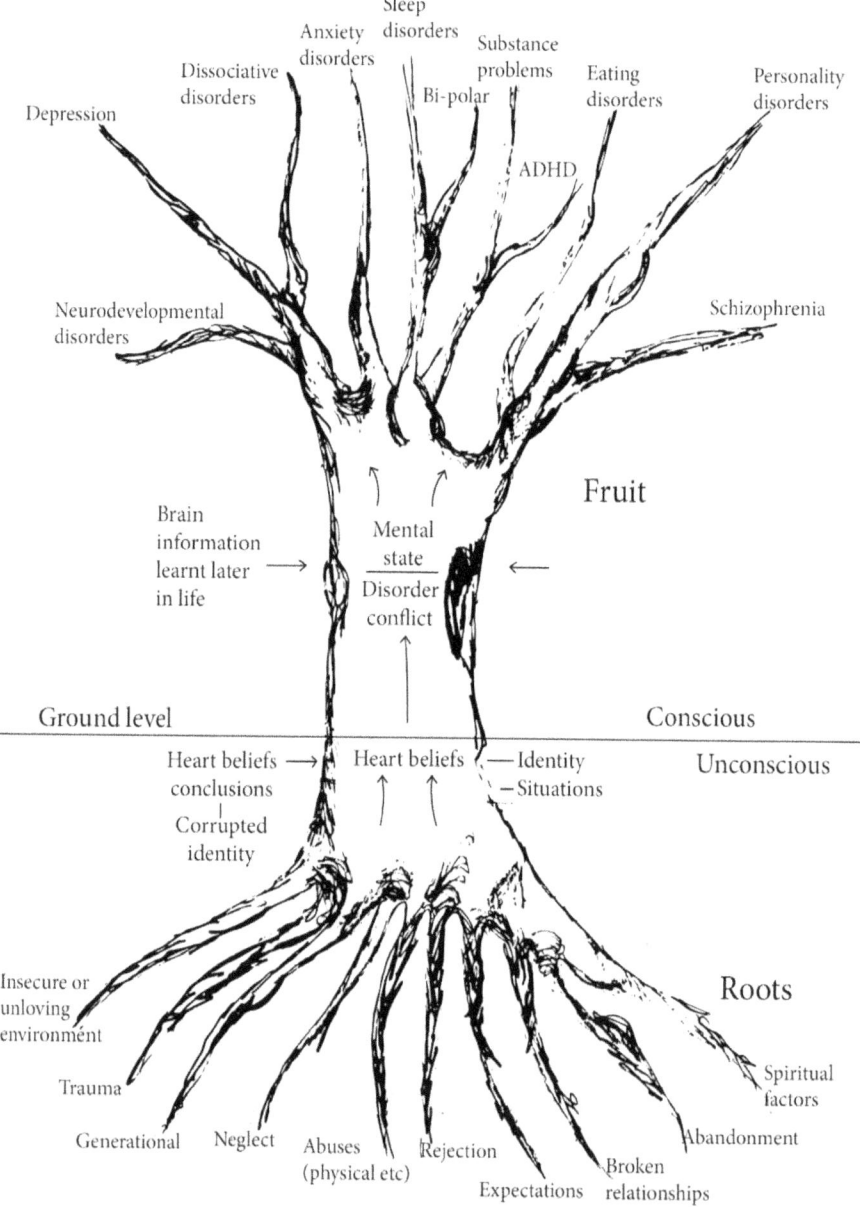

CHAPTER THIRTEEN

Depression

Depression is reportedly the most common mental disorder. There are 2 main types which have been titled exogenous or reactive depression, and endogenous depression. Exogenous means from outside causes or stressors, and endogenous means emanating from internal causes or origins. The resulting feelings are the same; a sense of being overwhelmed, it's too much to bear, feeling pressed down (hence **de**pressed), hopelessness, and despair.

Exogenous or externally rooted circumstantial depression
Reactive or exogenous depression is the result of external circumstances. For example, a number of years ago my wife and I owned a vineyard. At the same time I was working 2 other jobs. So, even though I was young through that period I had limited time and energies. From the house we could see the whole acreage across the hill and into the valley. We could not afford to pay someone else to prune in the winter time, so having to do it myself was a stress and a burden that I could do without. As I would go outside early on a cold and frosty mornings, I could see all of the several months of work in front of me. It seemed an overwhelming task with all of the other things that I had to do.

It would feel as if I would *never* get there, it was too much to cope with. I was probably not clinically depressed, but it felt depressing. I hope that gives you the general idea of depression that is a reaction to your outside circumstances.

It could be that your months behind in your housework, or your credit card never seems to come down, you can't get the weight off, it seems impossible to give up that addiction, get through that mountain of study, or resolve that problem relationship. Any or all of these compounded can be implicated in mediating exogenous depression. Up front let me say that whether you are talking about depression from internal or external sources, the root problem of hopelessness is the same.

In the case of reactive depression, the hopelessness that you are feeling most probably will be from thinking such as: "I'll *never* get there, I'll *never* be able to get it done, or perhaps there is no-one to help me." Maybe, "I can't cope, it's too much, overwhelming!" Generally, these circumstances are eventually dealt with in some way, and this type of depression, which proceeds from external factors is resolved.

Endogenous or internally sourced depression

This form of depression is the one that is the most damaging. The reason for this is that it cannot normally be resolved through a change of circumstances. The problem is that the root of this type of depression relates to what you believe in your *heart* about your identity. That is who you are, how you are, how you perceive the characteristics that you hold that make up *self*. This is problematic because you don't normally know what these beliefs are, or where they came from. It seems hopeless and overwhelming, because you don't think that whatever you perceive your identity to be can ever be changed. These *heart* beliefs leave you forever anxious and worried about what to do to repair the issue.

> Proverbs 12:25 Anxiety in **the heart** of man causes depression…….. NKJV (emphasis mine)

So, these beliefs produce anxiety, (which is commonly found along with depression,) because to you it's completely *hopeless* that you <u>will ever</u> be able to change your state of being, which emanates from whatever you perceive and believe about your identity. This is the key to depression. For example, you may be locked in to believing something along the lines of, "*it's hopeless*, I will *never* be able to be what I'm meant to be, or should be." Or, "I will *never* be able to be what they want me to be, or expect me to be." At times: "I'm meant to be perfect, but *never* can be!" Or, "There's something wrong with me that I can *never* fix!" Maybe even: "I can *never* be like others…. it's impossible, hopeless!"

These beliefs are the *hopeless* component coming from an identity or self-belief that is held. Healing the self-belief is the key to setting the person free from the depressive *hopeless* belief. For example, let me suggest some possibilities of what you may believe which could be something along the lines of; "I will *never* be able to be what I'm expected to be **because**; I am too dumb, too ugly, sickly, unable to meet the standards, not like other people, useless, not perfect, too small, too young, too big, the wrong gender," and so on. It stems from whatever it is that you believe that you should be, that you believe inside that you can *never* change.

That's why it's *hopeless*, overwhelming, and produces such despair. It weighs on you, pushing you down, or depressing you as we know it. It is not normally necessarily conscious thought.... and most times it's in the *heart*. You may just know it as feelings, or a general response and reaction to how you perceive life. People who have, for example, suffered sexual abuse may believe seemingly unchangeable things such as: 'I'm damaged goods, I am no longer like other people, I'm dirty, guilty...." etc. etc. If you believe that this can *never* be changed then that is *hopeless*, depressive.

High expectations and lack of encouragement, a harsh, or an abusive or critical environment can produce anxiety about your performance. From these environments proceed conclusions about your SELF and identity. These ever-present internal beliefs remain unresolved, and often lead to depression. So, it's not the rejection in itself, it's the beliefs that result from not being accepted that are the root of the problem. Remember, there was an event or a place in your early memories and history where you learnt these beliefs, and accepted that they were true about you.

How do I know that this is true? Because I have seen depression consistently resolved if people are prepared to commit to the ministry.

Some depressed people believe that they *can't ever* be what they need to be, but at the same time don't want to let go of their own solutions to the problem. This could include blaming everyone else for how they feel. It could also be holding on to medications as their answer, rather than opening up for ministry and embracing and accepting their internal beliefs. (If a person is on medications, we're not advocating going off these without medical advice or supervision.) Some secular and Pastoral models promote denial of what you believe and feel about yourself. Just tell yourself that it's not true. Sadly, this rarely, if ever resolves the hidden belief.

Depression producing environments
This disorder is often produced by the expectations of primary figures in our formative years of life, such as parents. If these authority figures are influenced by performance-based environments such as generational expectations, or cultural standards, they project this conditional

achievement-based acceptance onto their child. (This would normally occur with the best of intentions, wanting your child to be more successful and acceptable than perhaps you were yourself. However well meaning, it still imprints negative inner thinking onto the subject.)

For example, today we see societies with high education standards who have high rates of depression and suicide. We were in South Korea a few years ago and were shocked to hear that the typical high school student has class from 8am until 9.30pm or 10pm. This was Monday until Saturday, up to 16hrs a day! The suicide rate in that nation was formerly the 2nd highest in the world and is now in 4th place. It remains the highest for developed nations. From Korea we travelled to Vietnam. I enquired about education in their nation, and the person that I asked reported that they began at 7am, and were trying to emulate the success of South Korea as a role model.

When everyone in a society is trying so hard to achieve, it is inevitable that those not suited to academic endeavours may end up believing that they are inferior to others. And, more importantly, that there is nothing that they can do to change the elements that they believe make up this diminished identity. Putting acceptance based on success in these areas, particularly early in life, is a breeding ground for depression. I see this 'identity shaping' pressure being exerted on children in many developing nations as they try to emulate, so called, successful societies.

A few years ago, in Africa I was asked to speak to a group of High School students immediately prior to their exams. I knew that the parents were wanting me to pressure them to achieve. I understood that perhaps somewhere between 10% and 20% of them are actually gifted for scholastic achievement. So, much to the horror of the attending parents, I spoke on the top 50 most successful people in the world who never finished school. Generally, those who thrive in academic settings are those who think in the same way as those who put together the curriculum.

The entrepreneurs' can be found staring out the window working out how to change the world, along with the musicians, artists, adventurers, chefs, and others with creative God given gifts. It's of prime importance, to avoid shaping identity by trying to conform our children to societal standards and requirements for acceptance.

Between 6% and 10% of people in the U.S. and Australia reportedly suffer from depression and anxiety. This is a very significant statistic, and indicates that perhaps we're internationally not the great role models that we're supposed to be?

Let's look at conclusions from my research in regards to what you can typically expect to be present with depression.

Causes and roots of depression

It's generally accepted that historical abuse of some kind is usually present in people who may suffer from depression in later life. They may be triggered by dealings with other people that may bring up, or tap into the negative self-beliefs that are programmed into the person. This could be physical, sexual, emotional or verbal abuse. These are the grounds for the *heart beliefs* that are operating underneath the consciousness, and are the real root of the problem.

Depression may be the result of the collective power of multiple beliefs, or just one or two. I recall ministering to a man in his 50's who had suffered with depression all of his life. In the session we identified a memory where, because of the high expectations of the parents, he believed that he could *never* be enough, that is, be what he was expected to be. So, he had a belief something like; 'I'm a failure, *because* I will *never* be able to be what I should be able to be.'

The Holy Spirit brought God's truth and perspective to the man in this initial memory. With his head in his hands, still staring at the floor, the man reported out aloud; "I'M OKAY!" For him that meant that he was alright as he was, God didn't expect him to do or be more than he already was. Identity restored, the man who many years later I still see from time to time, has never suffered from depression again. In fact, his life circumstances would probably depress me! But the root of his depression was in his self-beliefs, coming from his history.

It's not always that simple, but many times it is.

'Triggers' that may precipitate depression

Sadness, or grief resulting from loss can be another stressor that can precipitate depression. This could include the death of someone who was important in your life such as a mother or father. We've found that the hopelessness and depressive component of this is not only the loss of the person, but many times relates to the loss of opportunity to ever receive affirmation from this person, because this may be the one that they believed that they couldn't ever be enough to please.

Additionally, a person could for example be overwhelmed with sadness and loneliness. (This often stems from a *'heart' belief* learnt in early life such as; that there is no one there for them that loves them, or cares about them.)

Cleary anyone can experience grief and loss. This does not mean that everyone will necessarily go into a depressive episode. Depression will involve a number of other factors such as feelings of low self-worth, negative thinking and negative expectations for the future. These could lead to feelings of despair and thinking about suicide as a supposed solution. Grief in isolation will probably more likely involve the sense of loss, and possibly the feeling of being empty. Other feelings such as joy or pleasure may still be inaccessible until any related beliefs are dealt with.

Other feelings of loss could come from:
- loss of purpose if you lose your job, and that which you felt gave you value
- divorce or retirement. These events can make you feel that you are no longer enough, which runs close to the fundamental problem that you hold about yourself at 'heart level,' that you're not enough, and can *never* be enough, no matter how hard you try. So, once these items that you seemed to be succeeding at, or achieving value in are removed, you go into depression.
- long term chronic illness or pain which appears to have *no hope* of cure. Interestingly as depression is resolved it often proves that the illness improves or is gone as well. The same 'heart belief' is the root cause of both, affecting mind, but finishing in the body with hormonal imbalances and eventual illness.
- some medications can trigger depression
- social isolation (This could come as the result of other mental disorders such as anxiety issues)

The Generational Component
It has been stated that if you have a family history of depression then you may indeed more likely be at risk. Clearly if your parents grew up learning that they had to achieve this or that goal, or meet this or that expectation or they would not be worthy of acceptance, then it follows that they will very likely follow their own parenting model and transpose that onto you.

At the time of writing there is no science to support that there is a gene that causes or contributes to depression. That means that if it travels in the family, that their environmental issues such as I've just described are most likely implicated. It is spiritually transmitted in the sense that parental behaviours such as; mental, emotional, verbal, physical or sexual abuse is not inspired by the Spirit of God. It is the fruit of the programming of another spirit. (Obviously these abuses can proceed from other sources as well.)

Complications of masking behaviour

Many people turn to substance abuse of some kind to comfort themselves, or to alter their state of consciousness and mask, or temporarily alter the negative feelings. Invariably even if drugs or alcohol make you feel better momentarily, in the end they will promote depression. What goes up must come down. People using these drugs think that it's the drug that makes them feel better, when in fact it is usually the large releases of your body's own feel-good hormones that produces the improved feelings. Often the pharmacological action of the drug that makes you feel 'up,' or better, by releasing large quantities of these hormones and neurotransmitters, will also inevitably deplete them, and you'll be more depressed than before.

Reportedly one in three people who have substance abuse issues will also suffer from depression. Even overeating as self-comfort can contribute to, and exacerbate depression by eventually further destroying self-image and self-worth. With the sexual revolution beginning in the 1960's mental problems particularly in women increased at an alarming rate. Once again, devaluing yourself with illicit sex to feel wanted actually contributes to your lowered sense of identity. Research into what was initially know as 'free love' statistically showed that it was anything but free, and actually cost a great deal in terms of self-value and broken relationships.

A significant number of people are on various prescription medications to help with their depression issues. The myriad of side effects that comes with these drugs is truly remarkable. Many of these medications are designed to target the low self-image coming from the corrupted identity emanating from distorted *heart beliefs*.

The effect of these negative *self-beliefs* on your chemical body is diminished levels of hormones and neurotransmitters such as serotonin and dopamine. So, if you don't feel good about yourself, your body doesn't produce the chemicals to elaborate your thinking into your body to make your thoughts a physical reality and feeling. Over time they become deficient and depleted. The process then is to try to treat the end of the line, the fruit, by trying to enhance or make these neurotransmitters stay in your body longer. We need to go to the root of the problem, and the fruit will take care of itself without drugs.

Many of these drugs are used to treat other disorders such as anxiety, bi-polar and so on. Some of the improvements that these medications that are used to treat depression have, has been reported to be more than 90% a placebo response. In other words, you think you feel better, because you expect them to make you feel better. You have to ask yourself if all of the side effects are worth it? Other reports suggest that people using these drugs show improvements for a time, but then return to their original condition. The problem here is that those using the drugs are then afraid that if they go off them that they will be even worse.

I'm sure there are those people who have genuine benefits from these interventions, but wouldn't it be better to resolve the need for them altogether? If you begin to like and accept yourself then you will feel better about yourself and life, and your body will respond by producing more feel-good hormones such as dopamine and serotonin.

Others try to resolve the inner feelings by some kind of lifestyle change. For example, reportedly young homosexual and transgender people have a higher rate of depression and suicide than the general population.

These transgender, or homosexual people might consider that societies lack of acceptance of them is at the root of these statistics. But what if some of these attitudes are simply triggering what they often already believe? As you may recall, the basis of depression is inner beliefs such as; it doesn't matter what you do you can *never be* what you believe that you should be, or *never* be able to do what you need to do for acceptance. In the case of gender issues, the root can often be a *heart belief* that you're not acceptable or loveable for some reason if you are not a gender other than what you are. That's a hopeless situation!

And whether you have acceptance from society or not will not fix programmed inner beliefs such as this. This is evidenced by the fact that much of western society both accepts and supports those who choose this path, and yet there is still much anger and resentment from those with these issues. In summary, many of these choices are the result of attempting to come up with your own solution to fix the problem, and be what you think that you need to be. In the end, as you think in your *heart*, so are you. You state of being will be the outworking of what you perceive and believe about your identity.

> Proverbs 23:7 For as he <u>thinks</u> in his <u>heart</u>, so is he. "*Eat and drink!*" he says to you, But his heart is not with you. NKJV (emphasis mine)

Permit me to share a story that is typical of the types of belief-based issues that we encounter. A friend sent an article written by an American

Paediatrician. In the course of her practice a young boy who wanted to be a girl, and insisted on it being so was brought to her by the parents. After asking questions the Doctor found that what had happened was that a little sister was born into the household, and that the little girl received a great deal of love and affection. Reportedly, the little boy came to the conclusion that you are only loved if you are a girl. A predictable course of action would be to decide that you are in fact a girl, and this seemingly resolves the problem. You can imagine the self-conflict and identity issues that are likely to unfold through life when what you feel that you *need to be*, is not in harmony with your physical being. And that this will *never, ever*, be completely resolved.

This is a fairly controversial area that needs to be addressed, but addressed sensitively, not least because of potential legal ramifications in today's world. Consequently, I will put these gender issues aside for the moment, and perhaps cover it in isolation in another publication in order to not produce any detrimental effect on the acceptance of the other materials presented here.

Symptoms of Depression
In order to help identify depression in someone that you may be ministering to, I have collated the symptoms that most articles would expect to be present in the condition. I've then added in a few that I have found to be common to the disorder myself. Most people have experienced some kind of depression at some point in life, and certainly many of us have had these feelings that I'm about to propose, either in isolation or together. If you don't have them all, it does not mean that you're not depressed. And if you exhibit some of them it does not mean that you are.

Typical feelings associated with depression:
Hopelessness, low self-worth, overwhelmed, can't cope, worthlessness, guilt, sadness, misery, frustrated, angry, disappointed, alone, isolated, unhappy, no self-confidence, anxious, irritable, crying for no obvious reason.

Let me elaborate on why guilt is included in the list of feelings. As you recall, the root of depression is often coming from not being able to be what you believe that you should be for some reason, or not being able to do what you should be able to do, which makes you feel unworthy, unacceptable and unable to change yourself. Guilt comes when you have either done something that you shouldn't have, or not done something that you should have. If these are locked into your history, they produce depression.

For instance, if you've done something bad or unacceptable early in life you may have imbibed the belief that you're bad or unacceptable for some reason. Guilt about your perceived identity now follows you everywhere. The reverse of this is if you were always expected to achieve, perform, and please those around you in your formative years, then you may have encoded a belief that you're a failure, or a letdown, or not enough. Now you feel guilty for not being more, or for not being able to do more.

Typical thinking for those suffering with depression:
'I'm worthless, a failure, I'm no good, not what I should be, it's my fault, (guilt).' This leads to negativity about self, others and life. They might always feel like they're letting down, or not enough for those around them. These people may end up hating themselves and rejecting themselves for their perceived weaknesses and faults. They are unable to forgive themselves for their mistakes and shortcomings. They may judge themselves harshly and reject themselves. Not liking or accepting self can be a part of the downward process leading to suicide. As a generalization, the self-rejection is a continuation of the parental rejection received early in life.

As a consequence of the above self-beliefs, common are depression thoughts such as: 'There's nothing good for me, I'll *never* get there, *never* be able to do what is required to be enough.' 'People would be better off without me, life isn't worth living, it's too hard.' 'Everything is going to go wrong, it's hopeless, my issues are too difficult to solve.'

As a result, the depressed person thinks that it's hopeless, and ends up being negative about self and others. Along with the feeling of hopelessness the person can feel helpless. Nothing will *ever* get better, and nothing can be done to improve the situation.

Outworking's of depression beliefs in your body:
Physically a person may present as; tired and fatigued, run down leading to illness, sleep problems, overweight or underweight, perhaps a loss of appetite, headaches, pain, dread and anxiety in the stomach, digestive problems.

Effects of depression on activities and social life:
You may lose interest in things that you formerly enjoyed doing.
You may want to withdraw from others and stay home.
You may lose productivity and not be motivated to complete tasks.
You may rely on alcohol, drugs or other substances to meet your needs.
You may have difficulty thinking things through and making decisions.

(This could be because you have anxiety about getting things wrong, which in turn will prove that the beliefs that you hold about your shortcomings and weaknesses are true.)

Additionally:
Because you have become so hard on yourself you may also be hard on others. Because you don't feel that you are enough or acceptable, then you project that outwardly onto others. Your tolerance of others can become low. You are angry and irritable, everything and everyone gets on your nerves. You have no peace inside, and may be restless, agitated, and if this boils over you could be violent.

Perhaps we can finish here on depression by reviewing and reinforcing the types of situations that you would be looking for, and some sample *heart beliefs*. We can look at our summary statement boxes, which include the underlying causes of depression.

Summary of the types of beliefs that we have consistently found that produce depression;

> 'This will never get better or be resolved. It's hopeless! My situation will never change.' The overarching implications of these beliefs; 'HOPELESSNESS.' These beliefs are usually characterised by a 'never, ever,' component. With exogenous depression it could be something such as; 'I'll never ever get all of my debts paid,' or 'I'll never, ever get all of this work done,' or even 'I'll never, ever be able to fix my relational situation.

> In the case of endogenous depression which emanates from distorted identity, you can include other beliefs that produce thinking that is usually unconscious, such as; 'No matter what I do I'll never, ever, be able to be what I need to be.'(E.G. For acceptance, approval, to be enough.) Or 'I can't be what I should be.' Other beliefs; 'I'll never, ever, be able to not be what I am.' (E.G. Bad, useless, damaged goods, a hopeless case, a loser, a nothing, weak, not as good as others.) So, inner thoughts with a sense of 'never be,' 'can't be,' 'won't be able to ever,' are the types of things that are behind depression. Remember, these will have their root in a belief about SELF, and will be found in an initial memory event, or events.

Next, we're going to move on to study anxiety problems. These are common in people with depression, with both conditions often occurring together. This is further evidence and confirmation of what we have found over and over again. That is, many 'disorders' share the same root *heart beliefs*.

CHAPTER FOURTEEN
Anxiety and stress related disorders

Truth and love are the key to freedom
At times when I have been teaching on fear and anxiety, I have asked if there is anyone in the congregation who has no fears or anxieties at all. To date I have never seen a hand go up. We could say then that virtually everyone is impacted by anxiety in some way. Let me repeat that a lack of truth about God, and/or about your own acceptability to Him and others is usually at the root of anxiety. It goes back to the fall of mankind. Beginning with Adam and Eve, people no longer believed that they were worthy of protection and acceptance because of their sin. They now perceived through the resultant distortion of identity that they were in fact beings that should be receiving judgement and punishment. If we remain anxious and fearful, it is because we have not yet received truth of God's grace for our sin in our minds, and more importantly in our inner parts, or *hearts*.

> *John 1: 17 For the law was given through Moses, but grace and truth came through Jesus Christ. NKJV*

Generationally we have received this imprint of the unacceptability of our old nature. Until the inner beliefs behind this old nature are dealt with, and the deception that we're not loved by God is resolved, our expectations tend to be for negative outcomes around our lives. We gravitate towards expecting judgment and no good thing for us. Fear and anxiety if we are without healing through truth is the most likely outworking of this state of being.

> 1 John 4:18 There is no fear in love. But perfect <u>love drives out fear</u>, because fear has to do with punishment. The one who fears is not made perfect in love. NIV (emphasis mine)

Fear and anxiety can be relentless, tormenting, because we cannot get free and come to peace. So, we end up in a constant state of restlessness, and unsettledness, robbing us of peace. Torment is the word used in the New King James version, which displaces, and is seemingly the antithesis of a sense of wellbeing….or a sense of everything being well in our being. It's to do with a feeling of things not being right in some way.

> 1 John 4:18 There is no fear in love; but perfect love casts out fear, because <u>fear involves torment</u>. But he who fears has not been made perfect in love. NKJV (emphasis mine)

The extent of the anxiety epidemic

Anxiety affects 40 million adults in the U.S. each year, or 18.1% of the population. Anxiety disorders are reportedly the most prevalent mental health issues in the U.S. They are said to affect around 30% of adults at some time. These disorders most often begin in childhood. (I would suggest almost always before 10 years of age.) They may not become fully evident until adolescence or later as life circumstances and stressors fully expose their presence.

The estimated cost to the U.S. economy from anxiety disorders is between $42 and $47 Billion each year, (more than 4 times the GDP of Rwanda), with mental disorders in general topping the list of the costliest conditions in the U.S. at $201 Billion per annum. At the time of writing, it is recorded that one in six Australians are experiencing depression or anxiety, or both.

Anxiety can produce physical problems such as thyroid, adrenal or heart arrhythmias, which in turn can produce further anxiety. If we accept that the normal reason for these bodily imbalances is as the result of anxiety to begin with…. we can see that the chicken certainly comes before the egg in this case. Additionally, there are many prescription medications, along with recreational drugs, that can produce anxiety as a side effect. This includes some 'anti-anxiety' drugs which can produce anxiety as a chemical action or reaction in the body. So, whilst the genesis or Etiology is in childhood, there may be other complications and factors that may need to be considered and investigated in a ministry setting.

Some reports indicate that women are statistically more prone to anxiety than men. This could relate in part to their hormonal make up, with men on average often having 20 to 25 times as much testosterone as women. Also possibly implicated is the fact that the female gender in general is more wired for relationships and nurture than men, who tend to be more task oriented. This means that women generally are more vulnerable to being hurt by the breakdown of these relationships.

Men commonly operate along cognitive lines, trying to problem solve with logic, and so when an event happens, they tend to close up shop emotionally, and attempt to rationalize a solution. However, men are still hurt and anxious underneath. Girls are more emotionally based and readily feel whatever is presenting in their situation.

Defining anxiety

Anxiety is an emotion. As you may recall that before an emotion is a feeling, it is a thought or belief. As we go along it's profitable to remember that the emotion is a matching chemical elaboration that makes what we think and believe a reality in our bodies. Again, don't forget that the beliefs and thoughts that produce anxiety are most often not a conscious activity, it's coming from underneath in the *heart*. It will certainly be felt in the emotions via the release of various hormones and neurotransmitters, which along with inducing these emotional feelings finishes in your body producing phenomena such as; fast heart rates, high blood pressure, rapid breathing, sweating, and fatigue.

The tiredness is often the result of depleting stocks of stress hormones such as cortisol. Along with being implicated in the anxiety emotion it has other functions such as helping balance and store blood sugar that produces energy. Fear which would not be termed as anxiety is considered to be a response to a specific observable danger. Perhaps a storm, violent situation, or being confronted with a potentially dangerous animal, such as: a lion, a bull, a big angry dog or a snake. These will raise your cortisol and adrenaline levels as well, but after the moment has passed, they will return to normal. Anxiety is like continuous, pervasive, often low-grade fear.

A definition of anxiety is: 'a persistent or intense and excessive state of fear and worry about everyday situations.' Anxiety is seen as a type, or subtype of fear that is more general, less focused. It is many times considered a future oriented fear, which can occur without an observable or obvious stressor. It can be triggered by stressful situations such as having to do some public speaking, or exams, or a work interview. When these stressors produce anxiety, they indicate underlying problem beliefs that need to be dealt with. Anxiety does not go away and can get worse over time. As we age what is known as the amnesic barrier, which is the wall that we put up to protect us from our perceived identity, breaks down. That is, we lose the emotional strength and ability to hold down negative feelings about *self*, or sometimes specific types of situations.

Types and categories of fear/anxiety

Having ascertained that anxiety is a type of fear, let's look at the two broad categories that I've concluded that fear comes under. The first is 'fear of harm,' and the second is 'fear of rejection.' As near as I've been able to work out all fears come under one of those two broad categories.

Fear of harm
Under our first category, 'fear of harm,' you could list anxieties such as; fear of pain, fear of death, fear of lack of protection or provision, fear of loss, (which means that you will be harmed emotionally, or for example, financially.) We could go on with fear of illness or poverty and so on, but I think that we have the general idea. Additionally, I have identified two types of fear which I call 'circumstantial,' or 'historical.' Circumstantial would be a present tense event that you have never experienced before, such as being confronted with a natural disaster like a bushfire or an earthquake. So, your fear is to do with your current situation. When this is resolved, your fear, stress and anxiety are also resolved.

With most anxiety disorders, the source of the anxiety is rooted in *heart beliefs* that you've imbibed and concluded in fearful situations in your historical past. You may recall in part one of this book that we described two main kinds of beliefs. *Situation or situational beliefs, and identity beliefs. With anxiety under the 'fear of harm' category you will almost exclusively find these beliefs proceeding from emotionally charged situations in the past.

Researchers suggest that the part of your brain that is considered to be the fear centre is called the amygdala. When you encounter a fearful and emotionally charged situation, it's as if the amygdala decides something such as; 'wow that was scary, I better make a good strong memory of that, and then be predictively on watch that it never happens again.' Once these type of *heart beliefs* are in place they remain until you're set free by the Spirit of truth. Phobias nearly always fit into this type of 'fear of harm' situation belief.

Fear of Rejection
With the second category, 'fear of rejection,' we would include anxieties such as; fear of failure, fear of embarrassment, fear of not performing

to expectations, (we call this performance anxiety,) fear of not being enough, and so on. These anxieties are about people not accepting who you are, that is, your identity. As such, they are identity beliefs.* As we've said, our identities in regards to who we are, and how we are, are formed in our *hearts* in childhood, almost exclusively before we are ten years old.

Once we've been rejected, we fear it happening again. It's not the rejection in itself, it's what we believed in our *hearts* about our identity because of the rejection that matters. So, now we fear a rejective or non-accepting event that makes us feel, or seems to prove, that what we already believe about ourselves is true. Often then, it's an anxiety about a perceived weakness or shortcoming being exposed. It often causes us to withdraw from potentially rejective situations, or others, isolating ourselves as a self-protective behaviour.

Situation beliefs, and identity beliefs can be reviewed in Chapter 10.

So, when a person comes for ministry how do we know what the persons fear or anxiety is? Put simply, it will be whatever they're afraid of. If they examine and focus on the emotion, they will usually readily categorize the anxiety belief. It will be rooted in the expectation of a bad or negative outcome of some kind. It will be either in regards to rejection or harm of some sort. It will be projecting off something learnt in our history that something bad will happen. Even when people come with a current or present situation that is producing anxiety, you will almost always find that they're interpreting that event through things learnt in the past.

In other of my books, I have described how a few years ago we were scheduled to minister in Kenya. As it happened their national elections ended up being scheduled for the same time. Our friends in Kenya became very anxious about these elections because they often result in violence. There are around 42 tribes in Kenya with the biggest 6 of these representing around half of the population. Clearly, all of these tribes want their candidate elected to lead the nation, and if their person doesn't get elected, they can become very unhappy.

We felt quite peaceful about the trip and went anyway. We had not grown up with violent elections, so we had no historical situational precedent or programming to make us anxious. In comparison the locals had grown up with election time as a very unstable and insecure time. These experiential beliefs now were producing anxiety when this political cycle came around.

Let's now begin to break down the most common of these disorders.

Anxiety disorders

Anxiety issues are generally sectioned into different types by the secular mental health professionals, so let's begin to examine them here. People who experience anxiety as a profile may exhibit symptoms that are identified as being in more than one anxiety condition. This is because the 'root' beliefs can occur producing different 'fruit' in multiple numbers of conditions under differing titles. Anxiety will also present in various other mental disorders such as depression, bipolar and so on.

Common 'types' of anxiety
GAD-Generalized anxiety disorder

GAD is when people present with generalized and excessive anxiety and fear over a protracted period of time. We personally describe this as a 'fear profile.' In our experience these people often grew up in anxiety filled environments, and commonly had parents who were fearful about everything as well. This exposed them to soaking up the seeming need to fear, and taking in these beliefs of the parents by osmosis.* (The process of gradual or unconscious assimilation of ideas, knowledge, etc.) These people constantly worry about everything and anything. Health, work, relationships, school, will your children be ok, are you saved?

They appear to move from being apprehensive about one thing, and then to move to the next. There is not necessarily any specific trigger, as they worry about everything around their lives. After all, if when growing up the ones who should have been able to provide safety and security are in fear themselves, then it stands to reason that you need to be worried too! Even if you don't know what exactly it is that you are worrying about.

<u>Symptoms</u>
It's generally accepted that these people will consistently or constantly feel: Restless or on edge, experience tension in the muscles, struggle to concentrate, or with attention, feel fatigued, (fatigue is often the outworking of stress related glands being overworked and now undersupplying hormones), have problems sleeping, and possibly as a result feel irritable.

SAD – Social Anxiety Disorder

This disorder is characterized by people presenting with excessive fear, or anxiety that relates to one or more social situations where the subject will be observed by other people. For example, public speaking has been considered to be the number one anxiety producing stressor in the U.S. This could include performing in front of others, meeting new people, or general public settings. One study even suggested being watched while they are eating, eating in public or even being in public. Individuals with SAD fear being humiliated or rejected in these settings, and will typically try to avoid or withdraw from these situations. If they do have to be present in these circumstances, they will most likely be very stressed and anxious.

The amount of anxiety experienced may well be much more than is appropriate realistically. This is particularly in regards to the actual likeliness of them being dealt with negatively. Most people will experience some level of stress if they are put into the position of public speaking, but for people with SAD this is a situation producing extreme fear or anxiety. The fear of rejection that they suffer from, will usually produce other dysfunctional coping behaviours or efforts to avoid these situations. This may lead to them being excessively in control of their environment, or possibly withdrawing emotionally even if they are present, or hiding.

People with this condition usually have an intense fear of being put down, criticized, disapproved of, humiliated or embarrassed. This is because these are the kind of abuses that are in their history which have produced the '*heart beliefs*' that are behind the condition.

A possible sample of beliefs that produce this type of anxiety could include; 'I shouldn't be here, I should not be seen or heard,' (which means that you believe that you're some kind of low life, or lesser humanity...... people may describe this *heart belief* as, 'I'm a nothing, or I'm invisible).' They could believe things such as; 'people won't like me if I speak up,' 'I'm a nuisance,' 'I'm not approved of,' 'I'm in the way,' etc. Or all of the above, possibly learnt in the same or different events in childhood. Additionally, they might believe things such as; 'They'll think I'm dumb if I say the wrong thing.'

Panic disorder
This is when a person has intense panic attacks. They will feel overwhelmed by these often-uncontrollable bouts of anxiety. There will be an outworking in the physical body which may produce excessive sweating, shortness of breath, or dizziness and chest pain. This condition is diagnosed when these attacks are recurrent over a period of time. Panic attacks appear suddenly, whilst anxiety attacks come on more gradually and may vary considerably in intensity.

Panic or anxiety attacks can come from situation beliefs such as; 'I'm going to die...there's no one there to protect me.... I'm all alone, I don't know what to do.... everything is out of control,' and so on.

Phobias

Phobias are when a person experiences intense fear regarding particular situations, certain objects or items; such as snakes, spiders, blood, heights, flying, enclosed spaces, storms, bullying, violence or germs. Phobias are normally specific intense fears. Even the thought of these or a potential fear situation will usually provoke a rapid and immediate fear/anxiety response and reaction. This could for example include a fear of travel by air or having an injection.

Some time ago we ministered to a young lady with a thyroid problem. Understanding that the disorder was almost certainly related to anxiety we ministered to every fear that we could find. An unexpected by-product of her being freed from her anxieties, was that along with the resolution of her thyroid problem, (Which supposedly could only be supported with hormone treatment!) was her delight that she did not have a panic attack when they re-did the blood tests.

The word Phobia comes from the Greek word Phobos, which means fear. There can be many types of these fears or phobias. They don't generally relate to your identity. They normally relate to fearful *situations* that you have been exposed to. The problem is that the level of fear is often not proportionate to the threat. For example, people could be afraid of a snake that might be in the bushes, even if there isn't one. As a result of these anxieties people may go to a lot of trouble to avoid these situations or objects that they fear.

We've ministered to many people who have presented with a fear of flying. We saw one lady who my wife had ministered to a few years ago. We asked how she was about flying now, and she responded that she has since been around the world several times.

A lady bank manager that I was discussing church finances with a number of years ago, looking at my bank account, noted that I travelled overseas a lot. She said that she wished she could do that but had a phobia about flying. In passing I related to her that often when people have a fear of flying that we find the source in an event such as someone as a small child getting out too deep in a swimming pool or creek. They can't touch the sides, and can't touch the bottom. As a result of that *situation*, they believe that they're out of control and will die. She looked at me in amazement, and told me that she remembered just such an event from her own childhood. When you hop on a plane, you can't get out when you want, can't touch the bottom, and are certainly not in control! They won't let you drive that's for sure. Your programmed heart belief interpretation of the situation says something like; "That's close enough to what I'm afraid of!" And now you have anxiety, but most times you don't know why.

Agoraphobia
Agoraphobia is now considered to be a condition within itself. Formerly it was considered to be a part of the panic disorder profile. It involves the presence of fear and extreme anxiety about being in situations where a person believes that they cannot escape. For example: On public transport, in an aeroplane, being in a crowd, enclosed spaces, which could include stores, airports or church. It includes being away from places where the person feels in control, such as outside your home.

The symptoms are similar to having a panic attack in that they present whether you are in the situation, or even thinking about it. You may experience intense anxiety about being trapped, unable to get away, being powerless, overwhelmed, or fear that there is nobody there to help or protect you. In severe cases, a person with agoraphobia may stay at home continually. They are frightened of the fear feelings from the exposure to these circumstances, and even at times fear their fear, in the sense of having a panic attack that they cannot control in public.

At one time we ministered to a lady who had such a fear. As we heard her story, she revealed an occasion when she was working outside of opening hours in a large multi-storey city bank. While she was there an intruder broke in, and even though she did not come in contact with him, it was still a very frightening event. We felt that surely her Agoraphobia had begun in this anxious moment, even though she was in her 30's at the time that the break-in occurred. When we couldn't resolve the beliefs, I felt prompted to look back further into her history.

As she focused on and embraced the beliefs and matching fear feelings, she recalled a memory as a small girl living on a farm. Her mother and father were going to a neighbouring property for dinner for the evening, and her older brothers were charged with looking after her. When the parents left, the brothers also left soon after to go and connect with friends. The result was that the little girl was left alone, terrified in a creaky old farm house believing that she was alone and unprotected, and that someone was in the house who was going to get her.

Other events such as times of sexual abuse often contain circumstances that can produce these '*heart beliefs*' and consequent feelings.

Separation anxiety disorder

Separation anxiety disorder is as its name says, when a person displays disproportionate anxiety or fear relating to being separated from a person. That is, they display fear that is excessive considering their age, and where their emotional and mental development has come to. They become stressed when they are separated from the person, or even think that they will be separated from them. This could extend to environments that they associate with the person such as their home.

They may also be anxious and worry about becoming unattached to these primary figures in their lives. As a consequence, they may experience episodes of <u>fear about being left alone</u>. They may also suffer regularly from dreams or nightmares where separation occurs. Events such as being separated from family at a critical early age can be behind this disorder. It now is of prime importance to them that everybody that they believe should be there for them, are there.

Obsessive Compulsive Disorder

This is where a person has irrational thoughts and feelings that are unwanted and cause anxiety. The person may acknowledge that these thoughts and fears don't make sense, and yet they are compelled to try to alleviate them by carrying out particular behaviours or going through rituals. As the name for the disorder suggests, they are under compulsion to fulfill these behaviours, obsessed with the necessity for them to be performed. In ministry, in order to identify the *'heart belief,'* or programming that they hold we ask questions such as; 'what will happen if you don't do this?' For example, a person might feel the need to be constantly washing their hands, clothes, or household items, because of a fear of being made sick by germs. What will happen if you don't wash, or how will this affect you if it isn't done?

I once heard a story of a lady who was a compulsive hand washer. When she was a small girl a visitor to their household had ejaculated in her hands. In the confusing traumatic moment, she couldn't understand what this was and why it happened. Decades later she still believed that her hands were unclean, and she was still trying to wash it off.

Some people will check the door is locked over and over. Possibly they grew up in an unsafe neighbourhood where mother was always making sure that the door was locked for safety. The child unconsciously continues this behaviour as they grow up, not necessarily knowing why, but feeling that you have to make sure it's done to feel secure. Other times you may just believe that you have to make sure that you've done everything properly, otherwise you will receive disapproval or get into trouble. It is still belief based, and still has a source and origin, even though there may not be a specific event. It may just have been a constant theme through the formative part of life.

Stress problems
PTSD (Post traumatic stress disorder)
PTSD is diagnosed when people have ongoing symptoms of stress after a traumatic event. For example, they've been involved in a violent situation, an accident, a major trauma event, such as a disaster or even a war.

The symptoms following these events could be that you are on alert all of the time and cannot relax. You may experience dreams or upsetting flashbacks containing fearful or impacting elements of the episodes. Typically people experiencing PTSD will avoid anything relating to those types of events.

Some consider that PTSD can follow relationship break ups such as divorce. In practice, what we have found over and over, is that such an event tends to trigger a large amount of the negative *identity beliefs* that you hold, all at the same time. The intensity of the pain relating to the divorce may be greater than any one of these beliefs in isolation. So, it's easy for the sufferer to conclude that it is not connected to past memories or pre-existing beliefs. But as we process them one at a time the PTSD from the current event lessens, and then resolves completely.

Usually people involved in divorce, or other relational breakdowns, will consider that the pain that they are feeling is all because of the treatment that they're receiving from the other person. In fact, what is happening is that the pain that is felt through the rejection, is coming from pre-existing pain connected to previously imbibed identity beliefs.

RAD Reactive attachment disorder
RAD is a condition where an infant or small child has failed to form an emotional connection with their parents or primary caregivers. These children may reject, or not desire to receive encouragement or comfort. They may even be fearful of these current parents or caregivers. This is the case even if these key people are caring and loving. They will usually have trouble forming significant relational bonds with others as well.

These children often don't feel secure and safe, and could report feelings of loneliness. They many times have difficulty containing their feelings and emotions and could be sad, or be easily irritated.

Who is most likely to experience RAD?

As you might expect RAD is reported as mainly presenting in children between 9 months and 5 years old who have been subjected to abuse of some kind. This could come through being neglected emotionally, not having their physical needs met, or from some other form of abuse. Evidently RAD can be misdiagnosed as some other behavioural problem that is behind their distorted emotional state.

Common predisposing factors for RAD

- Children removed from primary caregivers after they have already bonded
- Children who have been in foster care with a number of different families
- Children who may have been in a childcare institution such as an orphanage
- Deeply emotional losses of critical relationships in early childhood

Research points to a lack of secure caregiving, love, emotional nurture, and bonding leading to RAD developing. As a result, these deficits leave a child feeling not cared about, alone and abandoned. The '*heart beliefs*' that result from this treatment, prevent a child from making a healthy, secure emotional bond with caregivers. This can be compensating behaviour, in that they're unconsciously self-protecting from further rejection. These beliefs create a 'force field' where attempts to nurture are reframed as more potential places for hurt and neglect. Lack of trust, and insecurity many times lead to controlling behaviour later in life.

In normal healthy relationships with primary caregivers, children build trust and security. They encode *identity beliefs* that they are worthy of being looked after when their needs are consistently met. They learn that they are cared about, and can trust the parent to provide for their needs, and be there for them when required.

Some of the suggested types of situations that place a child at a higher risk for developing RAD are as follows:
- Not feeding a child who is hungry for an extended period
- Not attending to, or comforting a child who is distressed, and crying (A distinction needs to be made here. Small children, even babies know when they are loved and cared about by all other treatment and attitudes towards them. So, if a child needs to sleep, and is put to bed for their own good...but doesn't want to rest, they may cry in disagreement with your decision. With babies that we have dealt with

over the years, the question always was; 'are there tears?' Tears meant genuine distress and the need for comfort. No tears, could simply mean bad temper, or an attempt to take control of the parenting!)
- Not taking the time to interact with a child through; touching, holding, affirming looks or verbal communication.
- Providing these needs, but not consistently, or only when it suits the caregiver
- Not bathing, or changing nappies when necessary
- Too many people looking after a child, without having the opportunity to become familiar, bond to, and feel secure with them.

To here we have discussed the omission of items that a child needs to *believe* that they're valued and secure. In other words, things that aren't done that should be done. These children often act up in an attempt to gain the nurture and attention that they require to meet their needs. If they believe that no one cares about them, or is there to provide for them, then they really are taking steps and making an effort to make sure that it happens. As I've said, as adults, these people often continue this behaviour by being controlling, and making sure that people do things for them.

Additionally, there are things that are done to a child that will lead them to conclude that they are not; safe, secure, valued, loved, significant, important, cared about and so on. This would include any kind of abuse from a parent, caregiver, adult, or even an older child. This could be physical, emotional, verbal or sexual abuse.

Observable symptoms of RAD
Typical symptoms in infants and young children may be different from child to child, but common signs include:
- Lack of eye contact, and a reaction or avoidance of physical touch, particularly with parents or caregivers
- Tantrums; anger, easily irritated, sad or unhappy
- Defiance, disobedience, or even arguing
- Absence of normal emotions when dealing with others
- Not showing guilt or regret over actions
- Exhibiting affection towards strangers, whilst projecting fear or lack affection towards parents or caregivers. (Most likely this is still an attempt to fill the nurture void that the child is needing through a person who is not close. So, rejection from them doesn't have the same anxiety or implications to reinforce *identity beliefs* that they may have, as those people don't represent a relationship that is necessary for security.)

Later in life these children will possibly gravitate towards being withdrawn and emotionally unavailable. They may not show affection to, or seek affection from caregivers or others, and keep to themselves out of fear of further rejection. Independence then, is their solution to possible hurt.

OR

As stated, they may look for affection from strangers by being excessively friendly. Mostly these children are emotionally immature for their actual age.

CHAPTER FIFTEEN
Common Personality Disorders

Personality disorders and stigma
When psychologists talk about 'personality,' they're referring to the patterns of thinking, feeling, and behaving that make each of us unique. No one acts exactly the same all the time, but we do tend to interact and engage with the world in fairly consistent ways. This is why people are often described as 'shy,' 'outgoing,' 'meticulous,' 'fun-loving,' and so on. These are elements of personality.

Because personality is so intrinsically connected to identity, the term 'personality disorder,' might leave you feeling like there's something fundamentally wrong with who you are. But a personality disorder is not a character judgment. In clinical terms, 'personality disorder' means that your pattern of relating to the world is significantly different from the norm. (In other words, you don't act in the ways that most people expect.) This causes consistent problems for you in many areas of your life; such as your relationships, career, and your feelings about yourself and others. But most importantly, we need to know that these patterns can be changed!

As we discuss the topic of 'personality,' we're examining the combination of qualities or characteristics of behaviour that make you uniquely you. So, we could define a personality disorder as when these patterns of thinking, feeling or behaving, are out of order in a negative way. This means behaviour that we would not describe as normal, balanced, or centred. This relates to how you would respond to, relate with, or engage with other people. Your personality is largely a reflection of your perception of *identity*, that is, who you perceive yourself and your characteristics to be. Whether you are shy, outgoing or fun loving, are all strongly connected to how you see your-SELF, and how you believe others see you.

Therefore, if you have a 'personality disorder' it does not indicate that there is something fundamentally wrong with who you are, but rather it is the outworking of the *beliefs* that you hold that <u>there</u> is something that is fundamentally wrong with you. The behaviour is your response, reaction or effort to live out, or compensate for these *beliefs*. As the SELF-*beliefs* about *identity* change, the patterns of interaction with others change as well. I believe that everyone on Earth needs to possess God's truth and a healthy answer for; 'who am I,' 'where do I fit,' 'what am I here for,' and, 'what's it all about.?'

Mental health articles typically state that personality disorders will never be resolved. As with many other mental disorders they would suggest that they can only be managed, or improved through therapy or medication of some kind. We have not found this to be the case in Christ. I recently ministered to a young lady who came in with the presenting condition of BPD. (Borderline Personality Disorder.) As with many others she'd gone through many years of secular treatments of various kinds. People were intimidated by the title of her disorder. This particular girl proved to be quite easy to minister to. She accepted, and cooperated with the ministry process in a simple way, in spite of years of contrary instruction about what to do to deal with her condition.

She did not complicate the process by trying to working it out in her mind, and she felt and accepted what she believed about her identity. We worked through 5 or 6 different *heart beliefs* in about a 45-50-minute session. (This is unusually fast, but it happens occasionally.) She went immediately from hating herself, to accepting, liking, and valuing herself. She no-longer wanted to cut herself, or to self-harm because of self-anger stemming from what she had previously believed about herself. She reported an immediate change to an eating problem that she had suffered from, and some substance issues began to resolve from that moment on.

She had further sessions relating to how others treated her, but many of the core beliefs behind her disorder were resolved in that initial short session. (Note: She had been through the work up and preparation material, so she understood the ministry model prior to that first meeting.)

BPD Borderline Personality Disorder

BPD is a problem that is diagnosed in adults after the age of 18 years old. As a disorder it is identified by fear of abandonment or being left alone, low self- image, unstable moods, being impulsive, self-harming, being depressive and even suicidal. People suffering from BPD can experience notable changes in mood and respond emotionally to day-to-day events. BPD is defined by being triggered by relational stressors, and as a consequence this can cause relationships to be unstable. This may in turn produce anxiety, depression or self-isolation. In fact, you can expect other disorders to be present along with BPD such as:

Depression, Bipolar, anxiety disorders, substance abuse, eating disorders. (Anxiety and mood disorders commonly co-exist with personality disorders.)

Common Symptoms of BPD

- A constant and strong fear of rejection or abandonment, particularly relating to people who care about them. This includes a fear of being left alone, and there being no one there for you. This can make you 'cling' on to people, making sure that they are there. This controlling behaviour can have the opposite effect, and push people away because they feel smothered. (The simpler that you keep this ministry the better it works. If people fear rejection or abandonment, then you are looking for the historical place where this has happened before. This may include pre-natal events and certainly often comes from early childhood.)
- Volatile or unstable relationships, including how you feel about people, and how you feel they relate to you can change very quickly
- Self-harming such as cutting, indicating self-rejection or self-bitterness (As with any self-harming, you are angry with your-SELF, punishing *self* for the things that you believe are negative and unacceptable about your person. This may have been concluded as a result of why you interpreted that you were abandoned or rejected to begin with.)
- Impulsive behaviour may produce activities such as; dangerous driving, binges, impulsive spending, and so on.
- Having moods constantly influenced by distorted self-image, you never really feel whole and complete. These moods can change quickly and dramatically. For example, one moment you may feel good about yourself, and the next minute be filled with self-loathing. This lack of clarity about who you are and what you want from life may result in changing employment or your location often, as well as goals, churches, values and even sexual orientation if you consider

this to be the reason for your rejection and abandonment. These mood swings are not like depression or bipolar as they typically pass quickly, in minutes or over a few hours.
- At times explosive anger responses, a 'short temper.' This could include acting out, throwing or hitting items, yelling, fits of rage. This behaviour is usually followed by remorse and guilt after the event. As with any anger, it is expressed outwardly, but it also has an inward element, where you are angry with yourself. You are angry with others for making you feel what you already believe about yourself, such as being unimportant, or not enough. But you are also angry at yourself for not being able to be what you think that you need to be for acceptance from people who you value in relationships. People with BPD can often spend a lot of time and thinking on being angry at themselves because of their inner beliefs.
- Easily feeling bored or a sense of emptiness, resulting in being restless or easily irritated – suicidal thoughts - anxiety. This pervasive, and often chronic feeling of emptiness can stem from '*heart beliefs*' where they believe that they are, for example, just; 'nothing,' 'nobody,' a non-entity. Some describe it as just being 'wrong.' They try to fill the inner empty void with drugs, alcohol, sex, food or even career. But nothing ever resolves the feeling, it is just masking behaviour.
- People with BPD often have trouble trusting the intentions and motives of other people towards them, leading to suspicion, and even paranoia.
- In certain stressful events that connect with their trauma history, a person may become overwhelmed and disconnect from the present situation. They could feel vague, cloudy or foggy. This can be the action known as dissociation.

People with BPD are uncertain about their *identity* in terms of who they are. They feel as though everything is unstable, their emotions, thinking, moods, behaviour, and as a result their relationships. Self-image, what you want in life, making decisions, even what you like or prefer can become confusing, or even overwhelming. You would be described as touchy, sensitive, easily upset even by small things.

What causes BPD?
As with many other of these conditions you will most commonly source physical, sexual, or emotional abuse during childhood. Additionally, neglect, instability, insecurity and trauma through early childhood or prenatally can precipitate the development of the disorder. Trauma could include separation from a parent, or a caregiver, even if they were physically

present, but were emotionally absent; (such as people with addictive problems, or their own mental health issues.)

Narcissistic Personality Disorder

As we begin to profile NPD let me make a general statement. People hold or believe delusions, or are deluded, because the delusion suits them, or most likely because it meets a need to believe certain things about themselves. So, it's a choice, conscious or unconscious, even though it's a distortion of the use of their imagination. It's like wearing a mask or creating a persona, in the sense that it's put in place to build the self-image to what is desired, or is felt that is needed to shore up self-worth and damaged *identity*. The problem is that it's unreality, not truth, often grandiose. The Apostle Paul talked about people being puffed up by idle notions by their unspiritual minds. Col 2:18

What is known as psychosis is the phenomenon where people lose touch with reality. In a sense NPD is like a very mild form of this, where people lose touch with the truth about their identity, and are deluded about their real state of being.

Those who suffer with NPD generally exhibit poor social skills, predominately because they are fixated on their own self-importance, and are not necessarily aware of the needs and feelings of others. (This varies from slightly to extremely) The inner thinking is that; "everybody should just do what I think, because of course I'm right – I'm superior!"

As a consequence, they are intolerant of lesser, inferior people who they don't consider are valuable or significant. Their unconscious thinking, shaped by *heart beliefs* could be along the lines of; 'their needs, feelings, or value don't fit into my thinking…. I know that I am better, more *important*, superior.'

NPD is probably more common than people realize, and is often co-occurring with possible rebellion and lack of submission issues. Because in the *heart* they believe that they're *not important*, they compensate by creating a persona and self- delusion that they are not only important, but the only one who is *important*. Now, like Satan whose corrupted *heart* caused him to lift himself up, the NPD mirrors the conclusion of that fallen being; 'if I am going to raise myself above, why should I submit to another – someone else?' In his case, for Satan this was God, and he evidently held an inner attitude something like: "I don't want it to be all about God, I want it to be all about me!"

For Satan, his pride produced rebellion, he wanted to be in control, above other lesser beings, have his will be done, and bring people under his plans. So, we could say that pride is a part of the imprint of Satan on our fallen nature. If as Christians we are healed of the causes of this, we are happy for it to be all about Christ and not us. Perhaps this is what the Apostle Paul meant and was alluding to when he stated; 'no longer I, but Christ who lives in me!' That is, it's no longer about my realization and importance, it is about Christ being lifted up!

(Because NPD most often comes from not being valued or treated as *important*, it can run with low self-image and depression, or other issues.)

NPD Narcissistic Personality Disorder Profile
NPD is a disorder where people have an inflated opinion of themselves, an unrealistic or grandiose sense of superiority and self-importance. They believe that they are 'special,' too good for anything ordinary or mundane. As such they often only want to be associated with significant people who have status. They have a strong need for the admiration of others, consider themselves very important, and expect to have the attention of others. Because they believe that they're better than others they expect to be recognized as such. This can occur even when they have actually achieved nothing, and so it is at times unrealistic.

It can make them unhappy when they are not afforded the praise or special prominence that they believe that they deserve. They present as superior or above others, often proud or conceited, which can make them unpleasant to be around. They project; 'I am and there is no other!' They appear to have high image of SELF, with high self-esteem, believing that they are superior and more important in comparison to other people. Because they believe that they're special, they expect special attention, admiration and praise.

People consider them to be self-centred, (It's all about me!) and arrogant. A narcist means 'someone in love with themselves,' or at least the idea of the self-image that they have created. It is a word that means basically 'it's all about me.' Probably beginning in childhood where nothing was about you.... even though you may have had material wealth and provisions, you could for example have been sent to boarding school. Now you are sidelined, *unimportant*. To counteract this the delusion begins. As we've said, a delusion is where your imagination creates a perception that you would want to be true.

Narcissists are often demanding, because in their minds, of course people should be serving their ideas! In general, they don't respond well to anything that they perceive to be criticism. This would be registered as an attack on this monument to self that they have constructed over the void of *unimportance* and inferiority. As is often the case, the opposite of how they present is what they really believe in their '*hearts*' about themselves.

Although narcissists seem to love themselves inordinately, usually this is brittle at best. What they love is the idea of the grandiose image of themselves that they hold. They're in love with the idealized, inflated image of self that they have created to compensate for the deep feelings of *unimportance*, inferiority and consequent insecurity about self. This is why they have such strong reactions to those who appear to be tarnishing this image of supremacy by disagreeing with them, or suggesting changes to how they do things. These are perceived as attacks on their person, or negative criticism.

In order to maintain the delusion of superiority they play down the accomplishments and abilities of others, whilst exaggerating and being boastful in regard to their own talents and achievements. They gravitate towards being high achieving, success oriented, and seeking power. They may at times be drawn towards risky behaviours to prove their superiority, or be prone to activities such as gambling in order to achieve quick success. They are generally competitive and ambitious, gravitating towards doing things to prove and justify their superiority.

Comparison will often be a part of the profile, along with making judgements on the inadequacies of others, their lacks, or weaknesses. Many times, NPD has actually begun in childhood settings where there has been some kind of comparison that has left them feeling and believing that they are inferior or *unimportant*.

In the Church setting if they are acknowledged, and they're able to work in the institutional system, they may rise to the top in leadership situations. As a Christian there may be a 'sanctified' version of this problem where some of the 'fruit' may be lessened, or harder to discern, because of a mixture of Biblical values and knowledge, along with other aspects of spiritual growth. But the problem remains. If NPDs are not acknowledged, generally, they may stay out of the immediate church environment, being unable to submit to 'lesser people' who do not admire or acknowledge their 'great gifting or spirituality.'

If this is the case, they will often interpret the perceived lack of acceptance and promotion as because the Church, that is Pastors and authority figures, are wrong about everything, and conclude that they, themselves, are right about everything. They may believe that they have a special relationship with God, have a 'hotline to heaven,' and receive special revelations. Remember a delusion is where your imagination creates a perception that you would want to be true. For Christians with this disorder, you add in a God who is limitless in power and potential, and because of your perceived superiority, you expect to be promoted and used for great and marvellous things.

This being the case they feel that it's right to bypass the acknowledgement of mature members of the body of Christ. Often, they will believe that they are called as Apostles or Prophets, who God will use for grand things, correcting and leading the leaders and telling them how things should be done.

Because they consider themselves as better than everyone else, they appear to be confident. And of course, you will appear confident if you've come to the conclusion that you're superior to everyone else. The difference between confidence and pride is that if you are confident, you are content in your God given identity as an individual. You have no need to prove anything or compare, because you accept that others are also unique individuals. They are also, one-of-a-kind creations. But with pride, you believe that you are over, or above others. God opposes the proud, because it is the nature of Satan having a manifestation through a broken person. He does not hate the person, He detests this self-centred, selfish nature because of how it diminishes others of His creation.

In reality, people who have good self-esteem and a healthy self-image are usually humble, with a true perspective of their person and gifting. That is, they have a sober picture of themselves. God wants us to be confident and accepting of who He created us to be. Whereas those suffering from NPD will be full of pride, considering themselves on a pedestal, better than others. A little discernment can be required here, because with NPD you can see pride and low self-image in the same person. This can look similar to a person with healed identity who presents as confident and humble. Pride is fallen confidence, and low self-image is fallen humility. Humility is a healthy perspective of knowing that you are an imperfect created being, but at the same time that you are God's creation, fearfully and wonderfully made. Psalm 103:14, Psalm 139:14

People with NPD may not accept or admit that they have the problem, because to do so they would have to admit that they're not superior and supremely *important*. This would diminish the self-image that they've built to convince themselves that they're not inferior and consequently *unimportant*, which is in fact the type of '*heart belief*' that they usually hold. Sadly, it's generally difficult to get people suffering from NPD to come for ministry. After all, how could there be anything wrong with them, they are superior and have everything together. Mostly they present for help with some other co-existing problems such as depression.

*There is some evidence that physical problems such as strokes are the result of specific anger related to a lack of recognition from others. In practice I know of at least two stroke cases that I have dealt with who were NPD and had anger issues of this type.

This personality disorder produces broken relationships. This is because they are not interested in what anyone else thinks or has to say. They are consumed with self, and may become angry if people don't see things their way.

Summary of Symptoms and characteristics of NPD
- Behave or present as arrogant and self-*important*
- Expect to receive special treatment because of your *importance* and superiority.... feel entitled
- Tend to exaggerate or boast about your abilities or achievements (to highlight why you're so *important*)
- Need or demand acknowledgement, praise, and admiration from others
- Prone to unreality about being lifted up in success, power, or even in regard to your appearance
- Use up other 'lesser' people in the process of building your image. They expect people around them to comply with their every wish and desire, believing that what they want, they should get.
- Because they present as so confident, narcissists can be very convincing in telling you what you should do or think. If your own self-image is not whole, you may be drawn to them, as they may make you feel that you need their approval because they are successful and have everything together. It's unlikely that they will ever recognize your needs, probably making you feel even lesser than you already do because of their dismissiveness of your person. They're not seeking partners, only people who will praise and acknowledge them. Their image is everything for them. They can present with a very magnetic

and charismatic personality. You can be drawn into the great things that they are doing, or going to be doing.
- Have difficulty considering the feelings or needs of others, having never developed the ability to identify with what others may need or want. They cannot place themselves in the other persons situation, and as a result lack empathy. They are pre occupied with SELF and simply don't consider how their behaviour might affect others. They are only concerned with their own wants and perceived needs. Your existence is only significant to them in the sense of meeting their own needs. They cannot engage in healthy reciprocal relationships because they do not really care about or respect others. They have no remorse or guilt about using others, and if it is pointed out that they are, they will not be able to understand what you mean.
- Have some kind of negative reaction to criticism
- People suffering from NPD may well feel entitled to come into your home, and for example, change the channel on your TV set without asking, put their feet on your furniture when you wouldn't on theirs, have a loan of your possessions without asking, go through your personal items, or drop in even when they know that you have other guests, or are busy with some kind of activity. They will give you advice and share their undisputable opinions without you asking for them. Someone has even proposed that they will have no hesitation in taking your ideas or work and using it for their own glory. This inordinate level of presumption stems from this inner belief that has been adopted; "I am, and there is no other. I am the only one who is *important!*"
- Narcissists will often see the shortcomings in others that they themselves have, but cannot see or admit to having faults themselves. For example, they may accuse others of having pride. They project these traits away from themselves to protect their own inner feelings of inferiority. They seek to deny their own weaknesses, failures, shortcomings or mistakes.

In Christianity people suffering from NPD may well exhibit considerable faith. They have an underlying belief because of what they consider about themselves that produces an inner rationale something along the lines of: "Of course, God will use me, and has great things for me.... I'm amazing!"

Most narcissists will need to be right and win the discussion concluding in the place of ascendency. So, don't waste your time trying to have a reasonable discussion, because ultimately whatever you say will have to be overridden or topped. They are unlikely to listen to you no matter how rational, measured or logical your presentation. Proverbs can appear to be unkind in regards to this attitude;

Proverbs 26:12 Do you see a man wise in his own eyes? There is more hope for a fool than for him. NKJV

How does it begin?
Researchers usually have concluded that the roots of the problem will be found in one of the following kinds of areas:
Childhood neglect or abuse of some kind. (This is in fact what we have often found.) A person interprets these situations as that they are *unimportant*. For example, sexual abuse means that you are just there for the other persons use.... therefore, you are *unimportant*. Verbal abuse, excessive criticism or discipline can cause you to believe that you only matter and can receive acceptance if you can meet certain standards. So, if you can't you are inferior and have no *importance* or value. Neglect means that you aren't worth taking the time with. Once again meaning that you must be *unimportant*.

What you're looking for in ministry is events or themes that caused the person to conclude that they are not *important*. The way the person has responded and coped is by deciding that they're in fact <u>the only one</u> who is *important*. So, believing that they are '*not important*,' becomes compensated for by seeing themselves as '*more important*' and valuable than others. They now consider others as idiots, low lives, or lemmings, and project onto others an attitude of; "what you think, is not valuable or important." "I am above, better, and know better."

Everyone can suffer from pride at some time, just as most people suffer from some measure of low self-image or inferiority. We're not describing this type of generic pride here; what we're suggesting is an inordinate presentation of extreme self-importance. It comes from low self-image that has led to beliefs about value and *importance*.

Neglect could include a child being left by a parent at an early age.... or a high achieving or absent parent who may be too preoccupied with their own projects to put the time and value into you. Sadly, this could even be occupations such as Pastors where they are busy doing God's work, preparing sermons, or looking after everyone else and neglecting their own children. Excessive or unrealistic expectations and standards from parents can make you feel inferior and unworthy because you cannot live up to them. And now as a result you feel that you have no value.

Additionally, being spoilt or pampered can lead you to believe that you're special, more than others, or more important. Being spoilt or pampered and given possessions or privileges doesn't necessarily mean that you haven't been emotionally neglected. Even a lack of discipline can be interpreted by a child that they are not worth the time, or important and matter enough to be straightened out. Instead, they are 'bought off' by being given things to appease the busy or preoccupied parents' conscience, or to facilitate their desire to be left alone by the child. So, there still is a possible mix of being treated as special or important, but also being emotionally neglected.

We've gone to great lengths to help with discerning the NPD profile. What you are looking for in a ministry setting will be places where a person has imbibed a *heart belief* or conclusion for some reason that they are not valued or important. This could have begun anytime from conception onwards. For example, a father leaves when the mother discovers that she is pregnant. The child can take in that belief that the mother is feeling, that we're not important enough for him to be around. Sibling comparisons, expectations from parents and so on are all possible beginnings.

Simply follow the feelings of no value back to its origins and seek truth for the person from the Holy Spirit. As with any problem there may be multiple beliefs from multiple events contributing to the disorder.

HPD Histrionic Personality Disorder
As we've said repeatedly a personality disorder comes from a distorted self-image, which means that the self-perception of a person's identity is corrupted in some way. This is again the case with HPD, where a person seeks the approval of others to build their self-esteem. People may go to considerable lengths in an attempt to be noticed. Once again, the inner belief is that they're not *important*, with the qualifying, or *because* statement being related to why they're not worth noticing. It produces a different outworking in behaviour.

I was once travelling on a bus with a lady who commented on some young people walking on the footpath who had shaved off their hair. She said, "I think that is so great that they don't care about what people think of them!" I was thinking; 'if they really don't care what people think, why do they need to try to prove that they don't care by doing something like that?' It's as if they're trying to convince themselves and others that they don't care at the same time. I recall a young man at a church camp wearing bright clothes and sporting a big pink Mohawk haircut. It was as if the inner person was screaming out; "would someone please notice me, ... please!"

Unlike NPD, people with HPD often have very good people skills. They are very aware of what people might think about them, and are influenced by what others are doing, and they are sensitive to their environments. They may use their attentiveness to others to manipulate those around them into making them the centre of attention. In fact, much of their behaviour is orientated around getting this attention that they crave. I remember another young Christian lady who would swear to shock other Christians into noticing her and giving her attention. In ministry we found a; 'would somebody please notice me' event back in her early childhood. She believed that she was unimportant, and compensated with various attention seeking behaviours, including dressing provocatively.

Typically, people suffering from HPD are quite functional socially, or in the workplace. As a result, it is not considered to be a debilitating disorder, and often it goes undiagnosed. As with NPD it would normally come under scrutiny when it is identified with commonly co-existing self-image and identity problems such as depression, or anxiety. At times these problems will come to the fore through the breakdown in a key relationship, such as marriage.

People with HPD can present with the following;
- Theatrical, or dramatic and have exaggerate emotions
- Speech or physical presentation that is intended to create an impression, and draw attention
- Assumes that relationships have a greater depth than they actually do
- Seeks to harmonize with others and so is influenced easily by people
- Will express shallow emotions which adapt quickly to whatever appears to be necessary to maintain the attention of, and inclusion by others
- Doesn't like situations where they are not the centre of attention, where they're not being noticed
- Is prone to flirtatious or provocative behaviour
- May struggle with routines (get bored easily)
- Can act without thinking, make snap decisions
- Do dramatic things such as threaten to commit suicide to get attention (I was ministering to a lady one day who was fading out in the ministry session. As I asked her a few questions she revealed that she'd overdosed, so I had to race her to the hospital. This was not the first time she had done this. There was a need for her to be

fussed over, and for people to be made to notice her and prove that they cared about her. She also suffered from cooccurring disorders.)

Causes of HPD

As with virtually every other disorder, mis programming of identity is normally the root cause of HPD. This can come through osmosis, that is learning from others in the family that exhibit this kind of behaviour as a solution to their own emotional deficits. Then when their environment creates a corrupted picture of their person, they gravitate towards the behaviour that they have seen modelled and appears to be the acceptable way to cope.

Mostly, it will present because as a child they have not received attention. They have then constructed patterns of behaving that have worked at some level in gaining that attention.

Possible reasons for believing that they are not worth noticing or giving attention to by parents or caregivers could be:
- Parents failing to take the time to discipline
- Parents who are present, but absentee because of drugs, career, escaping their own issues through media, being focussed on dealing with adult relational problems that are present
- The arrival of siblings who appear to get all of the attention
- Households where parents consider children as unimportant, 2nd class citizens that should be 'seen and not heard'

Remember, you don't need to remember all of these names of problems. To simplify the process, you may often not know how people behave outside of the ministry room. All you know is that they come with a presenting issue of not believing that they are worth noticing and being treated as important for some reason. So, your steps to ministry will be to find out what they believe in their hearts about why they are unimportant. Identify the memory where they learnt this. Find out why they came to that conclusion. And then seek the Spirit of Truth for His input and freedom.

There are other less common personality disorders that can easily be researched. Behind each of them you will find some kind of SELF belief that has affected their identity in a negative way. For example: APD, DPD, HPD, NPD, PPD, SPD.

Antisocial Personality Disorder (ASPD)

This disorder is characterized by having no regard for the feelings or rights of other people. They disregard rules, along with what is normally accepted as right and wrong. They normally manipulate or abuse others, and can present as rebellious, defiant or antagonistic. They commonly end up as law breakers and are prone to drug or alcohol abuse. Along with these traits, people with ASPD typically can't manage responsibilities, being unable or unwilling to exercise discipline over themselves, or possess the organization necessary to care of others, such as their own families.

Symptoms may include:
- A diminished sense of, or disregard for right and wrong
- Little or no respect for others, being motivated purely by self-interest. Distrustful of people's sincerity and trustworthiness in general. (This can give some insight into the genesis of the problem and type of historical memory events that you will encounter)
- Problems with being deceitful or lying (People who lie generally fear rejection, so they say what they think you want to hear. Additionally, they believe that if they tell the truth that you will see them in a negative way, expecting this because of how they perceive themselves.)
- Pride, arrogance, superior and opiniated. (Emanating from beliefs around low self-image and inferiority)
- Lack of empathy for others, even animals. (They may even like to see others suffer, because they carry hurt themselves)
- Dangerous or risky behaviour, with no regard for how this might affect others
- Abusive, violent, hostile, aggressive and inconsiderate in relationships
- No remorse about hurting others, a lack of empathy
- Living in the moment, being impulsive
- Irresponsible, impulsive, no thought of consequence of actions
- Illegal behaviour or criminal activity

Evidence of the disorder is usually apparent before mid-teenage years, manifesting with chronic behavioural issues such as; being destructive, stealing, aggressive towards others including animals, disregard for the law and rules.

Causes
Perhaps the best way to explain potential causes is to share a case history from a number of years ago. A man presenting with everything on the lists

that we've just described was brought to me for help. He believed that he was an impossible case, as many had tried to help him before. As we examined his history, I learnt that he was born out of wedlock to a mother who had substance issues. He was adopted into a loveless, demanding, legalistic, and at times violent household. One of the most crucial *heart beliefs* that we processed was that imprinted on his identity as a child was that he was <u>bad</u>. If you believe inside that you are bad, then as a man thinks in his *heart*, so is he. As a consequence, this man lived the life of a bad person. If you believe that you are bad, why even try to be good? He was angry with everyone, especially anyone or anything that represented authority, because as a child it was authority figures who had abused him. He was also particularly, and understandably, annoyed by anyone who appeared to be good.

So, why should he now submit to, or trust these people, or obey their laws and rules? His selfish parenting model had taught him that these figures were all about themselves, and that your life was just to make them happy. Again, inner reasoning from *heart beliefs* concludes; 'if no one cares about you or your needs, why should you care about those of others!' Through the freeing ministry of the Spirit of Truth he made great progress, and it was very satisfying to see the changes in his family dynamics, work habits, and cessation of some dubious activities. As with many other mental disorders the secular world considers that this problem cannot be resolved.

CHAPTER SIXTEEN

Bipolar disorder

Bipolar disorder is a common mental illness with reportedly nearly 6 million adults in the U.S. suffering with the condition. The disease is identified and characterized by dramatic and unpredictable mood swings between depression and mania.

Research reveals that people are often first diagnosed with clinical depression because they may not yet have had a manic episode. These episodes can present years after the onset and identification of depression, and the diagnosis then moves to bipolar disorder.

An important key to identifying *'heart beliefs'* here, is noting that commonly in an episode of depression, that a person suffering from this disorder may experience overwhelming feelings of *hopelessness* and worthlessness. This can lead to thoughts of suicide. This is an attempt to resolve the *hopelessness* and despair which is proceeding from the distortion of personal identity. Because the persons negative self-beliefs relate to never being what they think that they need to be for acceptance, then it follows that if they compensate by convincing themselves that they're more than enough it seems to resolve the problem.

So, they swing from believing that they not enough, and can *never* be enough, (depression phase), to believing that they are not only enough, but that they are ascendant beings, superior to others, excited and energised about their state of being. (Manic phase) It's almost like being depressed and hopeless about your low self-image, unimportance and failings, and then to compensate swinging to an elevated state of self-importance and high self-image. In my opinion, it is like adding NPD (Narcissist Personality disorder) to the depressive state. I did some research to see if that was consistent with the summation of others and found that some mental health professionals have come to the same conclusion. The person does not remain in either state permanently and swings past centre and order from one extreme to another as you will see in the diagram in this chapter.

Symptoms of Bipolar Disorder

Bipolar is identified by extreme mood swings. It was formerly known by the term Manic/Depressive because a person can range from being in an extremely low condition (depression), to an extremely heightened state, (Mania.) I use the word 'extremely' because most people go through times of feeling a bit flat, and other times where they feel good about themselves because they are achieving. For those suffering with this disorder, it is a marked change which could continue for weeks or months.

Depression Phase

Following is a composite of lists that I collated that relate to how a person might feel and behave during the depressive phase of the disorder. In brackets are my suggestions why this behaviour might be present. In the Depression phase you may experience the following symptoms:

- Feeling HOPELESS, sad, or empty most of the time (You believe that you can *never* be enough)
- Suffer feelings of WORTHLESSNESS (If you can't do or be what you are meant to be able to, then you have no worth)
- Have a sense of GUILT, despair and hopelessness (You feel guilty because you believe that you haven't done what you should be able to, or have done something that you shouldn't have, and that means that what you now believe about yourself can never be changed)
- Be overcome by SELF DOUBT (Because you believe that you are a hopeless case, a failure, consequently you have no confidence in your abilities – even if you have actually achieved in life! The inner belief remains until you are set free by the truth of God by the Spirit of truth.)
- Experience suicidal thoughts – plan or attempt suicide (A perceived way to deal with, or resolve, the persistent negative feelings)
- Feel pessimistic and negative about everything (If you cannot resolve not being what you should be, then you don't expect anything good for the future)
- Be lethargic, and lack energy, fatigued, irritable (This can be the result of poor sleep patterns, or hormone depletion from constant anxiety)
- Have difficulty sleeping, wake up early, lose your appetite (Your mind often attempts to problem solve during the night. Even dreams can

contain created situations that prove or reinforce your worst fears about your identity)
- Have a loss of interest in life or activities, not feeling pleasure (The result of the pervasive sense of no hope of anything ever getting better)
- Find it hard to remember things and concentrate, indecisiveness (You will be indecisive because if you try something and get it wrong you will prove the inadequacy that you believe that you have)
- Become delusional, have illogical thinking and even hallucinate (Perhaps an attempt to deny what you actually do believe about yourself)
- Either restless or slowed down behaviour

Manic phase

Following is a composite of lists that I have collated that relate to how a person might feel and behave during the manic phase of the disorder. In brackets are my suggestions as to why this behaviour might present.

They may:
- Feel SELF-IMPORTANT (Compensating for feeling unimportant)
- Feel very happy, even elated (remember, they are now in a mode where they not only think that they are worth something, indeed they believe they are greater than others, and this self-deception of being not only enough, but more than enough, produces happiness - remember emotions are an elaboration of thinking)
- Have an exaggerated sense of SELF-CONFIDENCE or well being
- Spend money on things that they really can't afford and would not normally want (Remember underneath this is a sense of worthlessness, so when the pendulum swings to this phase they have themselves believing that they are deserving and worth anything that they want)
- They may have big plans and ideas (Accomplishing these ambitious enterprises will make them worth something and give them value, and in this state their expectation is that their grand schemes will come to pass)
- Be very energised, feeling full of energy, racing thoughts
- Not feel like eating or sleeping
- -Be very talkative, or talking very quickly, hyped up
- Become annoyed easily (remember they are in an exalted state, like NPD others are lesser in their thinking, and should recognize their superiority)
- Experience psychosis, where you see or hear things that are not there, or become convinced of things that are not true. (This is a part of the process of choosing delusion to resolve troublesome inner beliefs)

- Have difficulty staying on task, be easily distracted
- Feel anxious or distressed
- Be delusional, exhibiting disturbed or illogical thinking, which can result in poor decision making, and these choices may bear a consequence. They possibly could even hallucinate.
- Some may cycle rapidly or swing from a depressive to a manic state without having a 'normal' period in between. Others may present with a concurrent condition with the symptoms of depression and mania together. For example, being restless and energized, but at the same time be feeling depressed.

People who suffer from bipolar disorder may have episodes of depression more often than episodes of mania, or more phases of mania than depression. There may be periods of having normal moods between phases. At times people may be shocked at the behaviour that they have exhibited. Reportedly the degree of mood swings in bipolar disorder varies widely. Some people may only have a couple of bipolar episodes in their lifetime and are stable in between, while others have many episodes.

CAUSES

The secular world acknowledges that Bipolar can have its roots in childhood. That it can develop in a child who experiences a lot of emotional distress of some kind. The outworking of this in Bipolar may be that the child doesn't develop the ability to regulate and control emotional states. This will be as the result of some emotionally traumatic events, episodes or themes in early childhood that shape beliefs regarding self-worth and identity.

These could include:
- physical, verbal, emotional or sexual abuse
- neglect or lack of nurture (a deficit of affirmation)
- losing a significant primary carer giver (This could include a parent passing away, or leaving at a critical stage of childhood. The child interprets the event by believing that they are not enough, and if they were more the parent would have remained. It could also be a parent who is physically present, but unable to offer relationship and nurture because of their own deficits)
- genetic inheritance (Science doesn't consider that there is a Bipolar gene that passes to a child. In practice we have found that it passes through families because the parent programs a child's 'heart' beliefs through how they treat the child. In other words, if the parents have perhaps grown up under criticism, perfectionism, or harsh attitudes, then they will most likely act this out on their children. In doing this

they are propagating the disorder through the generation line. (In Exodus 34:6-7, and Deuteronomy 5:9-10, we see this principle of the sins of the fathers visiting or passing to the next generation.)

Triggers or stressors that may instigate the disorder
Symptoms may worsen through stressful events such as a relationship breakdown of some kind, physical, emotional or sexual abuse. These events can bring the responses to beliefs to the surface. Even overwhelming problems in life such as workplace, loss of job, or an activity where the person felt that they were achieving acceptance. Or relational breakdowns where previously the person may have felt that they were being enough may bring on or worsen symptoms.

Possible Related conditions
People who suffer with Bipolar symptoms will often have other conditions such as for example:
- Anxiety problems
- Conditions like ADHD which shares many of the symptoms and roots
- Alcohol, drug or eating disorders. (These come as the person attempts to comfort themselves or mask the negative feelings and emotions that are present.)
- Physical problems such as; heart disease, (often as the result of anxiety, or even anger issues), thyroid, and or adrenal imbalances and insufficiencies, (again rooted in anxiety issues), headaches, weight problems and so on.

Summary
We've already covered the *depressive side*, where you're feeling what you truly believe about yourself, as with other depressive conditions. With the depressive side perceived or actual failure taps into the beliefs. The *manic side* is a countermeasure and solution type response to the *hopelessness*, worthlessness and low self-image coming from *heart beliefs* such as; I'm nothing, broken goods, not what I need to be for acceptance, and so on. This manic profile is generated by, and can present as;
- The need for success – the need to be someone special...above others
- Self - deception (even delusional) about abilities (hence risk taking, and even believing that they'll be right about their gamble)
- Insecurity
- Beliefs regarding worthiness
- A person could flip from believing that they are world class at something...to performance anxiety about being good enough. [This is coming from the real belief of not being up to standard and able to do or be what people want you to be]

- A feature of the problem in depressive state is guilt etc
- In a manic state 'self-importance' will be prominent (Seeing themselves as dealing better with life than others. The person will consider how good they were in dealing with situations...ascendant above others who would not have coped as they did.... superior)
- The bodily outworking is that these swinging states can cause a disruption and imbalance in hormones and neurotransmitters such as dopamine, serotonin, and noradrenalin. So, it will affect both physical and mental conditioning, because these hormones are implicated in the mediation of physical, emotional, and mental actions /states.

I include another pendulum diagram as a summary and illustration of the dynamics of bipolar disorder. Centre being normal ordered thinking, in balance with peaceful acceptance of self.

It swings from one side to the other. We all do a bit as we try to get settled about our identity and where we fit into the world. In this case it is more exaggerated and on a sliding scale depending on the severity of the disorder.

Diagram 7

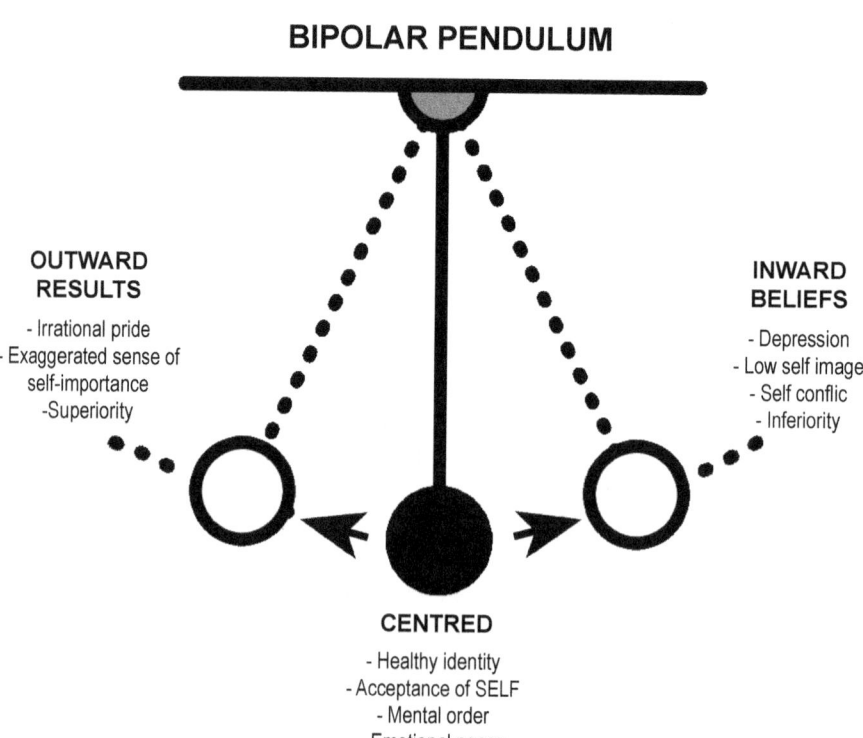

What am I looking for in Ministry?
People that I've ministered to with Bi-polar usually have similar *heart beliefs* as those suffering from depression. They've generally been programmed early in life by beliefs such as that there is something wrong with them. Some of these people have grown up in Christian settings where there is a lot of religious activity, but not much time for nurture and affirmation. Indeed, the expectations to meet spiritual expectations can become a part of the profile.

Many times, there has been a parent, almost always the father, who has been harsh and demanding with his expectations on the child. So, you're looking to work through these early childhood events that have mis-programmed the identity. Bipolar disorder is slightly more complex to work with, or at least to understand. It's resolved using the same simple technique described in Part 1, Chapter 10.

CHAPTER SEVENTEEN

Sleep Disorders

The AMA (American Sleep Association) reports that sleep problems are common throughout the World. One article that I studied cited that sleep disorders have an impact on as many as 50 to 70 million adults in the U.S., and that insomnia is the most common amongst these disorders. It is another disorder that we commonly see resolved through the type of ministry model that we are proposing here.

God can of course do anything at any time. At one time while ministering in Africa there was a man who came out in the prayer line reporting that he had not been able to sleep for a very long time. Not being in a circumstance where we could minister in the usual way, I simply prayed for him. The next day he returned with his wife and daughter reporting that he'd slept perfectly. Both his wife and daughter were healed of complaints the same day. Anything is possible. However, many times sleep issues are rooted in anxieties, and God will most times want to resolve those for your general peace and wellbeing.

We will briefly examine the 5 main sleep disorders, remembering that disorder means that something is out of order.

1. *Insomnia*
Insomnia is diagnosed when you either don't sleep well or deeply, or you cannot get to sleep at night, or stay asleep. It could be the result of other sleep disorders, or mental or mood disorders, particularly anxiety or depression.

I ministered to a lady a number of years ago who was almost frightened to go to bed, and when she did, she would lie awake for hours. When she did fall sleep, she would often wake up with panic attacks. We back tracked her problem to a childhood event where she had been pushed off a slide at school and lost consciousness. When she woke up in hospital her parents were not present, and being small she was afraid of what might happen. She had beliefs that she was alone, not protected, and that she was going to die. After those beliefs were resolved she began to fall asleep almost immediately upon going to bed. I still know the lady, and once those anxieties were resolved, perhaps 10 or 12 years on she has never had another panic attack.

We have a promise from God that He will bring us to the place of being free from these troublesome inner thoughts, and give us restful sleep.

> Psalm 91:5-6 *You will not fear the terror of night, nor the arrow that flies by day, [6] nor the pestilence that stalks in the darkness, nor the plague that destroys at midday.* NIV

Short term insomnia
Short term insomnia can be related to circumstantial stresses which are normally resolved over time, and then regular sleep patterns are restored. This could include sleep disruptive events such as Jet lag where you rapidly change time zones and you now find it is daytime when you would normally be going to bed. Unresolved issues, for example in relationships, can cause sleeplessness as your mind overworks trying to find a solution. Medical conditions that cause pain or discomfort may be another reason for transient or short-term sleeplessness. It may also be the result of medications or over consumption of substances such as coffee or highly caffeinated drinks.

Many years ago, I ministered to a lady who was set free of a number of problems. She decided that it would be good if her husband came and saw me as well. I asked him what he needed help with, and he said that he had trouble sleeping. The thought popped into my mind to ask him if he drank much coffee…his reply was; "no, not much, only about 12 cups a day." I recommended that he reduced that to 3 cups first and then see what happened. He never came back, so I'm assuming that he either didn't want to cut down on his caffeine intake, or he did, and it resolved the problem. Drugs and alcohol can also have an impact on sleep habits. In any case, with transient insomnia, organizing your schedule or life in a way that you can be more relaxed, and have less on your mind where possible, can help a lot with resolving your sleep issues. Personally, I write lists of things that I need to do to get them off my mind. I know that it's all on the list for tomorrow, rather than trying to remember everything, and then go over and over it in my mind throughout the night. Your mood before bed and whether you are feeling anxious, stressed, sad, or happy and contented with life, will all have an impact on the quality and depth of your sleep.

Probably around 25 years ago I found myself in a situation where I had 3 jobs, a church, my own family dynamics, and fostered sometimes multiple children at a time, who usually came packaged with a variety of problems. The result was I could not get into a deep sleep and was tired all of the time. I was not feeling good about trying to get some sleep with pills, but in the end was forced to try them. They didn't work anyway.
While I was away on a ministry trip, I friended a youth Pastor from Switzerland. We started telling each other jokes, and eventually got the 'giggles,' laughing uncontrollably. This proved to be a huge emotional release for me. After these pent-up stresses were released, I went and slept perfectly, after possibly six months or more of insomnia. I remained sleeping well. The point is that stress and anxiety can make a big difference to our sleep quality.

Persistent Insomnia
This is where your sleep problems are ongoing, unresolved or chronic. You may find it hard to fall asleep, or stay asleep, resulting in daytime drowsiness or tiredness. It's not uncommon to have poor sleep one night, and then a better rest the following night as a result of being exhausted. Or it can be a longer cycle of many days of insomnia, followed by a few restful nights. Typically, people who suffer from this disorder cannot sleep even if they are tired, and this can create a pattern.

Because anxiety is the most common reason behind this, we hear expressions such as; 'wired and tired.' In other words, they are unrefreshed by their sleep time, and may present as stressed and/or irritable as a result. Your quality of life is diminished in general, and you may have trouble thinking clearly or concentrating. You may also feel tense and unempowered to go into social settings, and as a consequence withdraw from interacting with others. Physically people report associated digestive troubles or headaches. Some common medications used for sleep disorders have been found to cause some measure of brain damage, and others are highly addictive.

A typical example would be a lady that I ministered to at one time, who had anxiety beliefs about her safety and security. These came from troubling fearful events in her early childhood. For some time, she'd been on medication to help her sleep, and as a result she suffered from all kinds of side effects, and also was now addicted to the drug. We worked through the beliefs behind the issue and she began to sleep perfectly, eventually being able to detox and withdraw from the medication.

Very often people have beliefs sourced in historical events that cause them to 'worry about tomorrow.' This is a common cause of poor sleep, and so this inner thinking needs to be resolved for a person to come to a place of peace and restfulness. They are anxious about tomorrow, but it's projecting from beliefs learnt in things that have happened in their past.

> *Mathew 6:34 Therefore do not worry about tomorrow, for tomorrow will worry about itself. Each day has enough trouble of its own. NIV*

In our experience people need freedom from God, which comes through His truth and perspective to the heart many times before we can trust Him with everything. In that place of inner assurance, we can expect to sleep peacefully.

> *Psalm 4:8 I will lie down in peace and sleep, for you alone, O LORD, will keep me safe. NLT*

2. Sleep Apnoea

Sleep Apnoea is a common disorder where your airway becomes repeatedly blocked and you stop breathing. This is a serious condition where you may snore loudly. When you become deprived of oxygen you wake up gasping or choking, with a sore or dry throat. This can occur once a night or hundreds of times depending on the severity of the problem. As a result of your lack of sleep, through the day you can feel drowsy, tired, irritable, and suffer from headaches.

Treatment
Being overweight is a common cause, so weight loss by some means can eradicate or at least improve the condition. Some people only suffer when they sleep on their back, so changing positions can help. Others use dental devises, or wear a CPAP mask using the low air pressure machine to keep the airways open. Others opt for surgery to resolve the problem. Some Christian commentators suggest that this disorder is also connected to anxieties of some kind. The only person that I recall ministering to who had this condition was set free from *heart belief* issues, but also lost considerable weight in the process of dealing with the sleep apnoea that he was suffering from.

3. Narcolepsy

Narcolepsy is a relatively rare disease affecting around 0.05% of the population. People suffering from Narcolepsy may suddenly fall asleep without warning. Some studies have shown that at times Hypoglycaemia (low blood sugar) may be implicated in Narcolepsy, or at least overlap with the condition. This certainly makes sense if you suddenly fall asleep during or shortly after a meal, which is a time where your blood sugar levels can be dramatically affected.

Many cases are considered to occur as a result of low levels of a brain hormone known as orexin or hypocretin which regulates sleep. This deficit is thought to occur as the result of an autoimmune response attacking the part of the brain that produces the hormone. This may point to *heart beliefs* where a person does not like themselves for some reason, much the same as beliefs that are at the root of other autoimmune actions on the body. Personally, I don't recall having dealt with a case up until this point, so I can only surmise what the actual cause may be.

In general, people diagnosed are unable to regulate their sleeping cycles, and as a consequence report insomnia, daytime tiredness, drowsiness and other symptoms common to sleep disorders. This pattern of disturbed sleep may indicate underlying anxiety issues as with other sleep problems, along with possible negative self-image beliefs that produce the autoimmune component.

We used to have a man in our church who had served as air force ground crew in World War 2. When there was an air raid on the airstrip where they were working, they would all run and get into trenches that were built. Others were jealous of this man, because once in the trench, and as the raid began, he would instantly fall asleep. So, this Narcoleptic type event was triggered by extreme fear. After the raid he would wake up and go back to work. This is certainly an indicator that at least in some circumstances, fear could be a trigger for a person to hit the overload 'circuit breaker,' in order to disconnect temporarily from a real or perceived stressor.

4. Restless Legs Syndrome (RLS)

RLS is described as an uncontrollable urge to move your legs while resting. Your symptoms are usually worse when you are inactive, possibly getting worse at night. Your legs may ache or feel as though something is crawling in your muscles. This may be partially alleviated by moving around or stretching. Researchers suggest that this may be the result of an imbalance in the hormone dopamine which is implicated in sending messages to muscles to control movement. Iron deficiency may also be involved, along with nerve damage from conditions such as diabetes, varicose veins or Parkinson's disease.

Once again, some researchers believe that anxiety may trigger or worsen RLS. In fact, it is reported that RLS is usually present along with significant psychosocial issues. A part of the accepted treatment regimens used for dealing with RLS includes behavioural therapy. This means that dealing with the psychological disorders implicated through ministering to *heart beliefs* may also resolve the bodily outworking of the inner thinking which presents as RLS.

5. REM Sleep Behaviour Disorder

REM means rapid eye movement, and it relates to the deepest part of your sleep cycle, which would ideally go for 90 minutes per night. It reportedly is a stage of sleep that produces important hormones that will positively affect mood and health.

This REM Sleep Behaviour disorder is characterized by physically acting out realistic, violent or other unpleasant dreams while asleep. It affects 0.5% to 1% of adults, and may occur along with degenerative neurological conditions. Most people experience a type of muscle paralysis during REM sleep, but when you have REM Sleep Behaviour Disorder this does not occur. As a result, you can seriously frighten or hurt yourself or someone who is near you by shouting, screaming, talking, laughing, hitting out, punching, or moving your limbs around whilst asleep.

Those suffering from this problem will exhibit all of the usually daytime symptoms associated with sleep disorders such as; irritability and tiredness. Additionally, you might feel alone because others may not understand what you are going through. Research indicates that anxiety, PTSD (post-traumatic stress disorder), and depression are risk factors for this disorder.

We can conclude that it is Gods desire that we have 'truth in the inner parts.' And once we have received this truth that sets us free through the ministry of the Holy Spirit, our expectation can be that this will result in restful sleep.

> *Proverbs 3:24 When you lie down, you will not be afraid; Yes, you will lie down and your sleep will be sweet. NKJV*

CHAPTER EIGHTEEN

Dissociative Disorders

What defines a dissociative disorder?

These disorders relate to issues with memory, self-perception and identity. They result in corresponding problems of mental function, negative emotions, and the associated reactions and behaviour. When 'triggered' by a stressor a person detaches from these problems, and in order to cope they go into a dissociative state. This can involve loss of memory or amnesia, and they may additionally have the feeling of being outside their body. These dissociative events relate to escaping from, or coping with, beliefs that have begun in previous traumas. The result of this detachment or disconnection from the feelings can include separation from one's own identity, current circumstances or activities, and may involve a lack of continuity in thoughts.

I recall the first person that I ever dealt with who suffered from dissociative states. They were unable to remember or retain information. It was like chopping your garden hose into lengths. There was not a continuity of flow for what you were trying to explain to go right through the system. It was like putting water into a hose, but finding that it leaked out before it found its way to the other end.

It's considered that these disorders are largely an 'involuntary' process where people escape from reality. This occurs as a response to a perceived need to distance from traumatic memories. Disconnection is made from negative beliefs about identity, situations, and the resultant thoughts and feelings coming from past events. Dissociation occurs on a sliding scale beginning with simple phenomenon that we all experience, such as day dreaming when we're bored. Many years ago, when I used to drive my children to school, they would often comment that 'dad's dissociated.' What they meant was that I had lost connection with the conversation or what was going on. Usually, I was wrestling with resolving someone's situation, or deliberating about the meaning of a portion of scripture.

We all remember times where we are, for example driving our car, and realize that we don't consciously remember where we have just driven, or if the traffic light that we just went through was green or red. We have disconnected from the conscious reality of the moment that we're in.

Dissociation as a coping phenomenon
The more extreme end of the scale is where a person dissociates to escape from an overwhelming situation or event. This could be; violence, abuse, war, trauma, an accident, horror. It is where we hit emotional overload. A place where we perceive that we cannot cope with our circumstances. Most modern houses are equipped with what is known as a circuit breaker on the electrical system. If there is some kind of fault in the wiring, or an appliance, or it is overloaded, then in order to protect the whole system from potential damage or burn out, it trips out and stops the flow of power through the system.

When you are very young you are very sensitive to mental and emotional overload. For example, if you are small and being sexually abused you don't understand anything about what is going on. It is a 'shock,' overwhelming, and your mind can't cope. If the same event happens when you are, say, 20 years old, although traumatic, you have some understanding of what is going on, and why.

In these intense situations where your mind 'trips out' to protect your whole system, it begins with amnesia. This is where there is seemingly no access to memory of events, and can extend to the creation of other identities that seemingly are able to cope with the situation. *(See Dissociative Identity disorder)*

Because of the insecurity we have about our identity or safety from these events, stress can be a trigger to move us into a dissociative state. So, we could summarize by saying that it is the minds way of coping with the overload of some kind of trauma or abuse. It is not considered to be a personality disorder, but can certainly coexist with many disorders.

The result of dissociating may be that you feel that the world around you is not real, or at least you are not connected to it. Additionally, along with detaching from the world and trigger situations, you may disconnect from yourself and reality about yourself. This is because of your self-perception. It is essentially a coping mechanism which can be a partial and short-term disconnection from immediate stressors, or involve a much longer episode extending for several weeks or longer.

If you experience dissociation that involves time loss you may be diagnosed as having Dissociative Identity Disorder. It can become an automatic response to certain kinds of stresses. People who experience this disconnection can at times report that it is as if they are observing their lives from outside their body.

Examples of more partial type dissociative manifestations, could be having memories, but being disconnected and not feeling any emotion. (This could also be suppression, where you've pushed the unwanted feelings away over time.) It could present as an inappropriate emotion for the content of the memory. Or you may have feelings and emotions, but have disconnected and have no memory picture. (This could also be suppression.)

Because dissociation often begins from some kind of abuse or trauma, it may at times be considered to be a symptom of some other primary mental disorder such as; depression, anxiety, bipolar, BPD, post-traumatic stress disorder or schizophrenia. These other disorders can share similar identity beliefs and the same type of events that produce dissociative states. Clearly drugs, medication, or alcohol may also be used to deliberately go into an altered state, dissociate, and move into unreality. Even media, to some extent, may be chosen and used to disconnect from reality. Some ritualistic practices such as certain forms of meditation or trances are other 'voluntary' means of achieving controlled and deliberate dissociation.

Causes
As is the case with many mental illnesses, these disorders most commonly occur beginning from childhood sexual, physical or emotional abuse. As we've stated, often the reason for this is in early childhood, when the child is most vulnerable, forming their identity or self-image, and in a state of brain plasticity. Another reason that they are more vulnerable to establishing dissociation in these formative years is their lack of knowledge.

So, a sexual event is more confusing and overwhelming for a child than an adult as they have no knowledge or understanding of what is happening. Coupled with this, as a small child who is overpowered, they don't know what to do. The result is that there is no physical escape, so they freeze, may feel numb, lose feeling and connection with the event, and escape with their minds. The likelihood of a dissociative pattern being established is exacerbated if there is no protection or help to interpret the event from an adult, or if indeed the caregiver is the perpetrator.

This means that they are more likely to cope through detaching than someone who is older. Once this is established as a method of coping, it may become a pattern of stress response that is used later in life. This can happen even if there is only the perception of the possibility of further abuse, rejection or a trauma situation.

Less commonly dissociative problems are found in children who have suffered major neglect, grown up in unpredictable household environments, or in nations where danger and terror may be present in the culture, or even natural disasters or accident situations. Other cases have been reported from medical procedures or invasive operations that are traumatic early in life. Once the dissociative process is in place, it will remain until it is resolved through processing the beliefs encoded experientially in previous memories. As a result, disassociating might become the coping method of choice, and you may not develop other normal means of dealing with situations.

A dissociative person could also break the event into separate parts so that the memory doesn't have to be dealt with in full. People report being in the room as the abuse is happening, but virtually watching it happen to themselves, but not feeling as though they were a part of the event. They can feel like this in the ministry process where they feel like they are outside of the event in the memory, looking in.

You often first have to resolve the belief that they hold as to why they can't be a part of the memory. This could be something such as; 'if I'm there I could die,' or 'I will be out of control,' or 'I'll be powerless,' 'it will be too confusing,' 'I won't know what to do,' and so on. These beliefs, are common thinking coming from the memory event, and are often the reason that the dissociation is in place to begin with.

Symptoms
Common symptoms found in the various categories of this disorder include: memory loss, feeling disconnected and withdrawn from yourself, not experiencing emotions, time loss, amnesia around events and people, a perception of unreality, no defined sense of identity, an inability to cope with stress, depression and anxiety including suicidal thinking or activity, relational adjustment issues, and other mental issues.

Types of dissociation

Characteristics of dissociative categories:
1. Depersonalization/Derealization Disorder
Depersonalization is the sense of detachment from your own self in mind or body. It is a disconnection with reality, as if you're observing events from outside your body. Some have described it as watching a film clip of themselves and observing their thoughts, feelings and activities, but from a removed place.

Derealization is when a person experiences a blurred perception of reality, and feels detached from their circumstances or surroundings. They may know that something is not right, but still feel as though people and the world around them are not real. Typically, these symptoms begin in early childhood.

Dissociative Amnesia
The primary symptom is extreme memory loss. This means more than normal forgetfulness and relates to: forgetting information about yourself and everything about who you are and your identity, (this could extend to your entire life history although that is considered rare) other people in your life, not being able to recall events, (this could include traumatic accident situations) parts of events or periods of time. This can occur for minutes, hours or on occasions weeks, months or more.

As is the case with other types of dissociation it is considered to be sourced in childhood abuse related mostly with emotional abuse or neglect. These people may not consider that it's important or relevant to access memory.

This is the most common type of dissociation that we deal with in the ministry room. Most often it has begun in a sexual abuse event in early childhood where the person has been overwhelmed by the circumstances that are occurring. To be able to cope they put themselves outside of the event in their minds. Future events are generally interpreted through the beliefs and conclusions about identity and the situation learnt in that initial event. (Although at times other beliefs may be added to those existing beliefs in later events if there were other dynamics involved.) The memory is now put aside and is not accessible or remembered. I have ministered to people who have suffered multiple sexual abuse events, with no memory whatsoever of any of them.

These people generally come for help because of anxiety or dysfunction around sexual activities, without knowing or having any reason why this is the case for them. For example, one young lady was unable to have sexual relations with her husband. She didn't know why as she had no previous memories. When we uncovered why, we found that she had been abused by a close member of the family. When this happened to her at a very young age it was such a traumatic and unacceptable moment that her mind 'tripped out' and put the memory aside. She was set free, and as is usually the case, much to the delight of her husband, was able to have a normal sexual relationship.

We would perhaps describe this as 'partial dissociation,' because a normal state of being can generally be maintained, and a general or main sense of identity exists, although damaged.

Dissociative Identity Disorder
This used to be referred to as multiple personality disorder because people changed from one personality to another. Sufferers feel as though there are two or more people inside their heads, each with their own ways of thinking and perceiving life. Hence multiple personality disorder, because more than one personality that they feel they need to cope has been established. One person that I dealt with even created a personality of insanity. This meant that they didn't have to deal with anyone, or work with reality at all.

*To help understand and simplify the reasons behind constructing these personalities, let me offer a few thoughts. Remember, we have one soul, one mind, one heart, so we're never multiple people. Creating these personalities serves some kind of purpose. Many people who aren't dissociative create different personalities to cope with certain situations or stressors as well. People often present with *masks* or *personas* if they feel unsafe in being who they really are. E.G., a person who becomes the 'life of the party,' because they don't believe that they're acceptable or worth noticing if they aren't funny or extroverted.

History teaches us that famous comedians are often depressive in their private life. So, creating another personality is a common way of compensating for perceived negative identity beliefs and feeling worthy. Others might dress a particular way, or change their hair colour to be who they think that they need to be to be able to cope with their environment. In church this might be people who appear as hyper spiritual, or the opposite, legalistic. Or even in the most minimal way the miracle in the carpark occurs before the church service, and everyone turns into a perfect Christian with no problems before they enter the service, in order to harmonize and be acceptable in that environment. This may be an entirely different appearance to how that person presented when they were out on Saturday night!

When I was a very young Christian, I was still trying to work out how I should present in that new Church situation. So, I was very conservative. I was talking in a reserved way with my Pastor one day when someone I knew from more worldly environments walked by. I had a completely different, colourful, full personality response to this person in the street. I looked back at my Pastor, who was clearly in shock, and wondering about me, who is this? Later I was set free from the identity beliefs that created the insecurity about my acceptability that produced the harmonizing behaviour.

Any of these ways of presenting yourself, are most times not based on the truth of who you really are, they're founded on who you think that you need to be in specific situation. Very often, they are in essence a deception, but they serve a purpose in you being able to feel safe in your environment. In much the same way, in many cases, although much more extreme and isolated, these dissociative identities are created to deal with different stressors.

Common symptoms of DID
In the case of DID, (dissociative identity disorder) because you have constructed these altered identity states within you in order to cope, you are often likely to have trouble defining a single identity that you identify with.

At times in these cases, all of these identities have their own characteristics which may include; Different names, different voices, mannerisms, genders, food preferences, and even at times physical needs such as glasses. They may differ in how they relate with others, and commonly also present with dissociative amnesia. These different states of your identity may be in control of your personality, thoughts, responses and behaviour at different times depending on the circumstances and your 'triggers.' Having only one mind, you can only be operating in one of these identities at a time.

Remember these presentations are to cope with particular perceived threats or situations. Although these various personality presentations appear to be different, they are still all manifestations of one single soul, mind and *heart*. All of these parts, or presentations, still add up to being one person. Clearly, the division is more marked than when what is considered a normal person changes how they respond in different situations. The trauma/s have made more distinct and strong parts that they have constructed to deal with these more dramatic situations. So, in these cases they present as completely different personalities that take over the operation of consciousness.

Each one of these personality presentations will probably have a different way of thinking and relating to circumstances and the world. Some people are aware of, or experience one main identity that they consider the most to be themselves, and this is termed the 'host identity.' In the process of resolving DID with one person that we worked with, we had to establish, build up, and draw out the true identity as 'host.' We called this identity; 'the executive member of the board.' In other words, it was the presiding personality who made the decisions and chose the behaviour that was going to present. And then we went about dismantling the reasons why the other parts had to be created. Much of this was dealing with fear and insecurity issues.

(Because these other identities are based on deception and trauma, there is often a demonic element that needs to be dealt with. At times this can be because these identities may have taken up sin responses that give place to an evil spirit, such as; violence, self-hatred, hatred, bitterness, rebellion, ungodly anger and so on.)

Some people experience memory loss when another personality presentation takes over unbidden, and they don't have memory of what happened while that other person part was in control. They may not be able to stop these personality projections from taking control when exposed to certain stresses. Once again, the degree of presentation of these projections can be occasional through to extreme. These people can at times be dissociated for weeks or months, with no memory of what happened whilst they were in that condition. Some of the terms for these personality presentations include: alternate states, states of consciousness, alters, alternate personalities or identities.

Explaining Flashbacks and 'Triggers'
A flashback is where people may become aware of a piece of memory of some kind. This can happen when you deliberately try to remember, or unbidden, when you have a specific stressor that relates to the piece of memory experienced. This experience from the past could be in pictures, sensations, smells, body memory, (such as a feeling of dread or panic in the pit of the stomach). People with suppressed or repressed memories can also experience this, but in the case of someone dissociative it may trigger an episode or feel as though you are reliving an overwhelming trauma event.

I recall ministering to a young lady who had been sexually abused all of her life. She was in her 20's and believed that she had never had sex prior to her marriage. As we ministered to the problem of depression and sexual dysfunction that she came with, she began to have flashbacks. Snippets of the many abuses that had happened throughout her life. As she was able to accept one piece of information, others pictures and memories began to appear piece by piece. Eventually we were able to work through, and resolve all of these memories and see her set free. These fragments of memory came back over a period of weeks, not all at once in the ministry session. It involved her husband's love and support, giving her the security and safety to accept what had happened.

Pulling the trigger on a gun is the mechanism that sets a response in motion. When we talk about disorders and refer to 'triggers,' we are describing something that relates to something that we already believe, that is triggered or stressed and produces a mental, or emotional, response or reaction. This could be something perceived in the situation that you find yourself in; a sound, smell, sight, sensation, taste, or even an event in a movie that relates to your inner trauma producing belief. A lot of things can be 'triggers,' very commonly how people deal with and relate to us will produce a response of some kind.

Issues that predispose dissociative processes
Sexual, emotional, or physical abuse, along with extreme neglect place a child at increased risk of developing dissociative disorders. Almost all sufferers have experiences of overwhelming abuses in childhood, often of a repetitive nature. Statistics indicate that around 90% of cases in Western society present from some kind of childhood abuse or neglect. Indications are that around 70% of these cases attempt suicide at some point.

Associated issues and coexisting disorders
People suffering from dissociative disorders are prone to other issues such as: sexual problems, suicidal tendencies, drug and alcohol misuse, self-harming, depression, anxiety, personality disorders, eating disorders, sleep disorders, and various physical symptoms. Remember the *heart beliefs* in regards to identity or situations are often the same, which is why the disorders commonly are present and overlap or co-occur.

Treatment /Ministry to Dissociation
Ministry involves dealing with the reasons or beliefs that caused the dissociation to begin with. This can be beliefs taken in or concluded when interpreting terrifying or overwhelmed events. There will often be 'objection beliefs' to connecting with and accepting initial memories of the events. This can include; fear of death, being out of control, being trapped, an inability to accept the situation because it is too terrible or unacceptable, or the choice to deny what is now believed about self. 'It cannot be,' 'I won't be able to cope,' are possible reasons why the dissociation occurs in an event.

These beliefs are resolved as with any other beliefs using the "Truth Encounters' process described in Part 1, Chapter 10.

CHAPTER NINETEEN
ADHD

About ADHD
In 1775 German physician Melchior Adam Weikard first described attention deficit in six pages of his publication. He noted how sensory stimuli would capture a patient's attention and divert him from his thoughts. He wrote that 'it is easier to perceive impressions through the sense organs than to form or retain ideas, to recover past memories or do other reflective operations.' He noted that 'each sense can disturb us in our thoughts or thinking, distract us from our object, and draw our attention to something else. Of all the senses, this most often occurs with hearing and sight. The result is distraction, lack of attention, inattention.'

As the name Attention-deficit/hyperactive disorder suggests, the condition is characterised by a diminished ability to stay focussed due to their heightened, restless, hyperactive state. They could be described as; 'fast,' or 'quickened.'

Symptoms in children and teenagers
This list of symptoms is normally observed before the age of 6 years old. They will be seen in multiple environments that the child may be in. As the name suggests a sufferer will be easily distracted, inattentive, have a reduced attention span, lose things, be unable to stay on tasks, move from one activity to another without completing things. They present as forgetful, have difficulty with organization, and be careless with what they do.

They will tend to be impulsive, (act without thinking,) impatient, (unable to wait for their turn,) interrupt others speaking because they can't wait for them to finish, be restless, unable to sit still, excessively talkative, hyperactive, and be fidgeting all the time, (A lot of physical movements,) not seem to have an awareness of danger.

Additionally, they may have issues interacting socially, seeming to be intolerant, inconsiderate or impatient with others. Because they struggle to focus and complete tasks it can reduce their ability to do well in activities such as education.

Possible co-occurring conditions in children and teenagers with ADHD
These other problems are not always present along with ADHD, but you may observe disorders such as; anxiety disorders, ODD - oppositional defiant disorder, where a child presents as rebellious and unable or unwilling to submit to others, especially authority figures. Conduct disorder – a tendency for extremely anti-social behaviour. Other problems such as depression, irregular sleep patterns or difficulty getting to sleep, ASD – Autistic Spectrum Disorder, learning issues such as dyslexia, or epilepsy.

Causes of ADHD
Researchers report that the cause of ADHD is not clear, and that study continues in an attempt to identify whether it has come from a child's environment, key moments in development, problems with the central nervous system, or genetic factors. In some circles it is even considered to possibly be a neurodevelopmental disorder.

Most commentators say that there is no difference between ADHD and ADD which is now considered to be an obsolete term.

It's worth making note that low self-esteem is considered to be a common personality feature with ADHD. As we've been saying there are often a number of identity beliefs that contribute to low self-image. This makes sense when we note that these identity beliefs will also be found at the foundations of the other possible co-occurring conditions that we've listed. Although low self-esteem can come from abuses, it can also come from neglect in some areas of life, which in my opinion and experience is very often at the root of this disorder. In the process of developing an attention deficit, it may well be that they have had a deficit of attention from parents in specific areas.

Let me offer my observations and experience of people with ADHD. Again, the name itself points to the root cause of the problem. These people often have lacked attention in some areas of life at critical stages of childhood while their brain is in a state of plasticity and while their *'heart beliefs'* are being programmed. It appears that those with ADHD most often have grown up with a *lack of supervision*, which often includes a lack of discipline. They may have had general rules such as; don't leave the house, or don't cross the road. But beyond this parents may have been preoccupied for some reason.

This could be because of career, isolating themselves because of their own issues, parents who were absentee, or those who were present in the house, but absent to give attention and supervision to the child because of drug or alcohol abuse. It could be parents dealing with an illness. Perhaps the adults were just plain selfish and couldn't be bothered investing the time into *supervising* the activities of the child, with a; do what you want but don't bother us attitude. They may themselves be ADHD and self-focussed. In that case they are probably propagating the parenting model that they grew up with, and so the issue becomes generational.

In any case, the inevitable result is that the child grows up being programmed to believe that there are; no boundaries, no restrictions, no limits, and no rules. So, you just do what you want to do, when you want to do it. This is certainly consistent with the symptoms, where a person suffering with the condition can be rebellious or defiant when someone attempts to set rules, limits, restrictions and boundaries around them. Or tries to *supervise* them, when this is not how they perceive that they should be treated.

To some extent I believe that it is a societal condition. In the 1960's we saw a rebellion against limits and rules, and indeed against maintaining the Bible as our standard. Throwing off the rules began in the garden of Eden, and is an ever-present spiritual dynamic trying to ensnare anyone exposed to the right conditions. Western or so called, 'developed' societies now have an aversion to excessive restrictions, and have become a 'my rights' culture. Many who grew up prior to that era, who grew up with excessive discipline without love, then had a 'knee jerk reaction,' deciding to not do that to their own children, and so brought them up without boundaries, absolute freedom, and rights to <u>self</u> without discipline.

The problem, at least in part, seems to be that this excessive freedom, or lack of supervision, begins early in the child's life, where they haven't been required to learn self-control. Later, they are out of control, because for them there are no limits or restrictions. We have to learn to be under control as a part of the process of learning self-control.

Experiences with cases of ADHD
We found in small children that the dis-order disappears when order and *supervision* come. Many years ago, we were in a foster care program and had numerous children through our household, many of whom were labelled ADHD or ADD. Later when we left the program the senior case worker informed us that they used to send the difficult children to us. In those days we came to term ADD as; 'Appropriate Disciple Disorder!' At that time this was partly tongue in cheek, but it does in fact pretty much often hold true. Clearly, the older the children were, the more entrenched behaviours had become, and the more difficult they were to reverse.

I recall one little girl who was ADHD who stayed with us weekends for quite a long time. She was around 4 or 5 years old, and I recall well the first Friday night when they dropped her off. Her condition was obvious, she was totally out of control. As usual I decided to invest some time into her and sort it out immediately so that we didn't have to deal with it all weekend. I began to supervise her and give her some limits, restrictions and boundaries. As was normally the case she was quite resistant and defiant to having rules. I sat her on a chair in the corner instructing her that if she behaved, sat still for 10 minutes, and did what she was told she would be able to play with the other children.

I was very gentle about it, but unyieldingly firm. After a few minutes she got off the chair. So, I put her back on explaining that this was sad for her, because now she had to begin her time again. This time she lasted about 5 minutes. Back she went, commencing her 10 minutes from the beginning again. This time she went the distance. While she was sitting there, I could see her observing that the other children all did as they were told. It was almost like; 'I don't know why they're doing that, doing what they're told, but that must be how it works around here!' It was over. She came under the authority of the house and calmed down. Does that sound too simple. *Supervision*, guidelines.

Clearly this was a new environment for her that she was trying to adjust to. If an ADHD child is your own, and in your care, they will respond much more slowly to you, because they have experiential knowledge of you giving them a lot of freedom. It will take time for you to change, but the child will change too. This little girl was just as well behaved as any others, went to church and was calm all weekend. On Monday morning her case worker came to pick her up. This worker was amazed as she looked at the little girl who was sitting quietly watching an old Shirley Temple movie on the TV.

The worker came to the conclusion that the child must be tired. I informed her that this was unlikely as she'd just had 11 hours sleep! What was remarkable, was that the moment the little girl changed environments and hopped into the case workers car she became agitated. The wipers were on and off, the windows were going up and down and she was climbing all over the seats. That set the scene. From then on, she would come into our household and settle for the weekend, and then go back to the old ADHD pattern when she went into the other environments. As I understand it the parents had substance issues and so were unable to *supervise* their children adequately.

The Importance of cultural environments
We often minister in places such as African nations. Many of these countries have continued with the standards of discipline modelled to them by European nations such as England and France that formerly governed them until the 1960's. These former governing nations have supposedly advanced, but in my opinion, in reality have gone backwards by taking Biblical discipline out of the family unit. This is to the detriment of their children and a general consequent deterioration of society. I include my own nation in this group. In these African nations the only place I have seen a child out of control, disrespectful, or throw a tantrum is in airports. I imagine that this is because these wealthier parents and children have been adapting to the ways of the supposedly successful societies that they can afford to have exposure to.

The world is changing everywhere with people learning from what other nations are doing, and what attitudes and accepted values are through access to smart phones and social media. This has been happening in many of these nations before our eyes over the last 10-15 years. Humanism is insidiously working its way across the globe. I'm off subject!

The scriptures clearly instruct us about the importance of supervision in the form of discipline. The theme of these verses is that with discipline; you'll have a good life. When we try to modernize the counsel of scripture it is at our own peril. Or in this case the peril of our children, who are the future of our world. It's a grave mistake to modify the Word of God through the eyes of our own understanding, or qualify it to suit our own opinions.

> *Proverbs 13:24 If you refuse to discipline your children, it proves you don't love them; if you love your children, you will be prompt to discipline them. NLT*

Ministry to ADHD

I recall a lady that we ministered to who had all of the symptoms of ADHD. We knew her for a number of years before she began to receive ministry and freedom for various problems. We always knew her as a person who, legs crossed, would restlessly have her leg rapidly jigging up and down. She did not come for ministry for ADHD, so we just ministered to various anxiety beliefs related to identity and self-image, and some anxieties proceeding from situations. As we went through the process over a number of brief ministry sessions, her leg slowed down as her anxious thoughts were resolved. And when all that we could find had been worked through her 'jigging' eventually stopped altogether.

We still know her well, and she is still quite calm, symptoms resolved, along with having her associated problems that she originally came for dealt with.

Christianity and ADHD

In a Christian setting someone may grow up with love and affirmation but still have no boundaries, limits, or adequate *supervision*. For those in the World system it could be because the parents are drug addicts or alcoholics, or because the parents are absorbed in their career, opportunities and ambitions, so they aren't focussed on the child, and give them no boundaries. In the church, perhaps parents are so concentrating on the work of God, or Church activities trying to please God, or attempting to fit into a religious setting, and in so being preoccupied they unwittingly neglect their child.

If a child never had *supervision*, boundaries, limits or restrictions themselves they do not understand to instil them into the child. There can be a plus here in a sense in the shaping of a Christian. Even though they will need to learn that there are limits and must be accountability to others, the upside is that is that if you've grown up with love and value, and learnt that God is good because dad and mother were good, then you don't expect or believe that God will stop you or limit you in His work. This may produce bold faith. And to you there are no boundaries or limits to what can be done or achieved, because it is true that God is for you, and limitless.

This can make you unstoppable, have limitless faith and expectation, believe there are endless possibilities, be confident, (self-confident), because nobody ever stopped you before! So, you KNOW that you're significant. The downside is that you will still struggle with the areas of ADD/ADHD that are negative, and these will cause you problems working with and relating to others, which can in turn make you ineffective in your ministry. These probable issues are listed below. So, even if seemingly you have some benefits, you will still need to work through the negative aspects of your profile.

*Although the condition is termed a mental disorder, I believe personally that it is usually more a case of behavioural conditioning, with a belief component regarding acceptability of certain attitudes and activities.

Adult symptoms and the reasons and inner rationale behind them
ADHD as an adult will still often have its source in if you've grown up with no controls or limits on your behaviour. This produces behaviour that you're not completely in control of. These are driven by the inner belief that you should be able to do whatever you want, no boundaries. Then, for example, if people begin suggesting things to you that you could do, you interpret it as they're against you. It seems to you that they're telling you what you should do, which goes against your programming and beliefs. It feels like *supervision*. You feel as though they telling you what to do, when, in fact, they may be just trying to help you do what you're doing better. This can produce an inordinate reaction. Let's now collate the normal symptoms associated with the condition:

- Impulsive, spontaneous or impetuous. – (You just want to do what you want, when you want, no limits.)
- Lacking organization and problems prioritizing. (Organization is a problem because you never had to discipline yourself to achieve a goal or task, because you just did whatever you wanted to in the moment.)
- Difficulty staying focused on a task. (You grew up flipping from one thing to another without having to complete anything.)
- Struggle with time management. (Again, time is a boundary or a limit, a restriction that you have to fit into; this is not in your programming.)
- Easily frustrated. (I can't do what I want when I want to.)
- High activity or even **restlessness**.

- Not good at planning. (Untrained to stay on a task.)
- Mood changes easily and often. (This can at times be reactions to others, including sulking or being angry if you don't get what you want.)
- Problems completing tasks and following through. (Staying on mission is difficult, because you may just suddenly want to do something else...and why not!)
- Volatile temper. (If you're used to just doing what you want, then you expect others to do what you want as well, and often they won't.)
- Poor coping with stress. (There is no stress in working without limits and restrictions, you just do what you want. So, having deadlines or guidelines is a stressor.)
- Because of poor organization you may exhibit problems dealing with more than one task at a time.

Reports suggest that people suffering from ADHD may have reduced symptoms as they get older, but others may have continued problems. As with any disorder the symptoms are on a sliding scale from mild to severe. One article that I read suggested that many adults are not aware that they fit into this diagnosis. They just know that they might find it difficult to prioritize, organize and focus. (This could of course be for other reasons.) For them this could mean missing appointments, meetings or social events.

They may become impatient when they cannot do what they want when they want. This could mean that could get very irritated, or have outbursts of anger waiting in queues, for example, or being held up in traffic. That doesn't necessarily mean that you are ADHD, as most people experience most of these symptoms at some time in their lives. We are talking about severe and recurrent symptoms. And in particular when these ongoing, persistent, and disruptive symptoms can be sourced back to early childhood.

It's also worth noting that a lot of adult sufferers of ADHD present with other mental disorders, for example; anxiety, depression, bipolar or other mood, personality or substance disorders. Let me say again, and reinforce that the root *'heart beliefs'* behind these problems are common to many of these dis-orders, and so are the situations that they stem from.

Studies have observed that ADHD can run in families. We have already pointed out that if your own parenting model was not having had the *supervision* type attention given to you in applying boundaries, limits and restrictions, then you will probably consider it appropriate and even desirable to allow your child to live without boundaries as well. From the same root beliefs, a child can sense or perceive that supposedly they are not worth investing the time into that is required for disciplining and *supervising*. The resulting *heart beliefs* about worth and importance could be implicated in other disorders such as depression or anxiety. Many agree that key moments in development may play a role in the onset of the ADHD problem. This is consistent with the model that we've presented.

Reports indicate that there could be environmental factors implicated as well such as exposure to chemicals, your mother doing drugs or alcohol during pregnancy, (she is ignoring restrictions and limits,) or premature birth, but they are not sure, and indicate that these might be a part of the cause at times. These are areas that I could not comment on.

Further evidence of the possibility of ADHD
People suffering from ADHD, along with co-occurring conditions might; Struggle at school, find relationships hard, suffer from low self-image/inferiority, have a pattern of failures. They may also have difficulty securing or keeping employment, have issues with drugs or alcohol, make poor financial decisions, be prone to illegal activities. All of these issues can worsen anxiety, worry and depression, leaving them 'wired' and nervous. They could also struggle with understanding concepts, and they may have a diminished ability to communicate with others.

CHAPTER TWENTY

Eating Disorders

Eating disorders are considered to be serious mental health conditions. They're characterized by an unhealthy, or out of balance relationship with eating. They involve a preoccupation with body shape and exercise. These disorders are considered to be complex mental conditions that go much deeper than just being about food. Around 4 out of every 100 people or 1 million people in Australia are cited as being affected, and as many as 1 in 7 people will struggle with an eating disorder in their lifetime. In the U.S. that figure is around 30 million people across their population.

Current data points towards eating disorders appearing along with anxiety, low self-image, emotional problems, depression, and the abuse of substances. The evidence is that these issues generally develop in teenagers and younger adults, and more commonly in girls than boys. In my opinion and experience this gives us insight into the self-esteem issues that are most often at the root of the problem. Today we're in a society where physical image is largely held as a measure of worth and acceptability.

People who suffer with eating disorders may present with being intensely concerned or dissatisfied about their body and appearance. They can have an inordinate fear of weight gain, and subsequently feel anxious or guilty about eating. Some people fear being out of control around food, even stressed that they cannot achieve or maintain the supposedly necessary image.

Eating disorders potentially have a long-term consequence on health if they are not resolved. People with these disorders mostly tend to cover up their problem, so it is not always immediately obvious that they have an issue at all. Again, if we look at our pendulum as it relates to what is normal or centred, we see that these eating patterns can be either eating too much or too little.

An obsession with food can be to mask or comfort people who have unresolved emotional issues. It can also be an attempt to control some aspect of life. As we've pointed out, for example, meeting the image that is perceived as acceptable and desirable. Let's examine the most common eating disorders.

Anorexia Nervosa
This is probably the most well-known eating disorder, and is where a person has an intense fear of putting on weight, and a preoccupation with body shape. They will starve themselves or be obsessed with exercise to facilitate conforming to the image that they believe that they need to present with. Reportedly a significant number of people suffering from anorexia will use vomiting, diet pills, or laxatives as a means of preventing unwanted weight gain.

A key feature of this disorder is the distorted self-perception of their physical condition. They often see themselves as being overweight when in reality they are in fact extremely underweight. Reportedly, anorexia affects under 1% or less than 1 in 100 people in Australia.

Studies suggest that the obsession may begin gradually, perhaps trying to bolster their self-image for some kind of event. Driven by the need for acceptance and conformity to what society is promoting as desirable, it soon moves to a preoccupation with weight. This can be promoted by cultural ideals to be thin, and exposure to media that exacerbates this thinking. Notably some eating disorders are virtually completely absent from cultures that have not been exposed to the Western promotion of the 'ideal person' being thin. This may be some kind of indicator as to why twice as many women as men suffer from these types of eating disorders.

Anorexia has reportedly increased 36% every 5 years since the 1950's. Given the proliferation and increase of media, and its programming of social acceptability through that same period, it's no surprise. If you already hold a belief that you are not acceptable, then it is just another reason why. Now your body cannot conform to what is supposedly needed to be good enough, desirable, or possibly even loveable. You're once again not up to expectations.

What we are witnessing is culturally driven acceptability. Interestingly society is changing with a return to curvaceous celebrities becoming the trend. The result is that now we see girls having breast enlargements and buttocks implants in order to conform to these new norms. Men increasingly are hitting the gym to grow big muscles. All of these are about *identity* and driven by the need for acceptability. Notably 2 out of 3 eating disorders affect women. This is perhaps not surprising, being fuelled by something innate in the natural order of things, and that is that women are as a generalization more wanting to be attractive and desirable.

For many, no matter how much weight they lose it is never enough. Anorexics may constantly think about food and often exhibit symptoms consistent with Obsessive-compulsive problems.

Some people suffering with anorexia may wear loose clothing to hide the extreme loss of weight that is occurring. They will often be obsessed with what and how much they eat, and have rigorous routines around diet and exercise. From the overflow of their '*distorted identity, self-image, which is their heart belief*' you may hear them express that they're fat, when it is abundantly evident that they are not. The medical profession considers anorexia to be a <u>dis</u>ease. Their inner thinking about their perception of self and identity is not at peace, so they are not at <u>ease</u> about their image.

One young lady that we ministered to was regularly hospitalized because of this disorder. Sparing all of the details of her ministry session, we found that she believed that she needed to look like a very skinny model who was popular at the time. This became yet another reason why she was unworthy, sparked off by earlier pre-existing beliefs that she held about her identity. Once she was set free the parents reported that, to their delight, she returned to normal weight.

Bulimia Nervosa
Around 10% or 1 in 10 people who suffer with eating disorders have bulimia nervosa. People with bulimia go through cycles of eating a lot of food, or having food binges, and then go to extreme lengths to remove the food they have taken in. Many of these dramatic measures known as 'purging,' are the same as anorexia, compensating for overeating by excessive

exercise, laxative misuses, diet pills, or forced vomiting. They may be angry or disgusted with themselves for having over eaten. Many times, they report feeling out of control.

This sense of being out of control will generally relate to their sense of not being able to meet expectations, or not be what they think that they need to be by resisting the natural desire for nourishment. Eating is a natural urge for survival. This could include, 'cave ins' in terms of self-control that result in binge eating, and guilt. This is not too surprising as a backlash when you try to deny the natural need and desire for food.

Sufferers of bulimia also have a distorted perception of what is required for an acceptable body image. As a result, they also see themselves as fat, and have an extreme fear of gaining weight. A point of differentiation with anorexia is that they don't appear to have the delusion of being fat when they are actually unnaturally thin. As a result, in spite of their obsessive behaviour they often maintain normal weight. Attempts to hide their weight loss and eating behaviours share similarities with anorexics. In both cases those suffering may avoid social events that involve eating and may choose to eat alone.

Amongst accepted treatments for bulimia, we find the use of anti-depressants and cognitive behaviour therapy. This gives us an indication in regards to what we have been proposing as the root to this issue. This is still a self-image-based problem that is based on *heart beliefs* about their acceptability. This now extends to appearance because of its proposed premium as a characteristic that makes you acceptable. We've ministered to many girls who believe they're ugly from some growing up event, such as being mocked by nasty school kids for being slightly overweight or having a pimple. This contributes to the distorted picture and belief about *self*, and becomes a seemingly vitally important part of their identity that demands to be resolved.

Binge Eating Disorder (BED)
This is where people often binge eat very large amounts of food, as opposed to overeating all of the time. They may do this even when they are not hungry, which indicates some kind of emotional triggering of the pattern. In much the same way as bulimia they may feel angry with themselves, guilty or disgusted about their eating episodes, and feel distressed at their inability to control the cycle. Feeling bad about what they have done then precipitates the next binge, which clearly is often about comforting yourself about feeling bad about your identity to begin with.

This shows us that bad feelings about their performance, perceived failure and acceptability, is actually the main root behind the disorder. So, the worse they feel about themselves because of their bingeing the more likely they are to do it again. They then go and eat very large amounts of food, often in short periods of time continuing the cycle. Once the binge has begun, they have a sense of being out of control. In order to compensate for this feeling, many times, they will be on diets or fasts in attempt to cope with the negative feelings that have been elicited by the binge.

Nearly 50% of eating disorders in Australia fall under the category of binge eating, and it is considered to be one of the most common eating disorders in the U.S. This disorder is distinguished from anorexia and bulimia by the fact that they don't try to purge the food through vomiting, laxatives, fasting, or intensive exercise. As a consequence, they will usually present as overweight or obese.

As with other eating disorders it usually begins to appear in teenage years or early adulthood. Perhaps in part this could be attributed to the removal of parental controls and influences. Mental health experts indicate that the average age for this disorder to appear is around 25 years old, and is common in both men and women. Over time it can lead to a variety of health problems because it precipitates obesity.

A further indicator of *'distorted identity,'* or *'heart beliefs'* as we describe them, is that the problem is many times cooccurring with depression, and is commonly treated with antidepressants.

OSFED (Other specified feeding or eating disorder)
OSFED shares symptoms with other eating disorders without completely fitting with any other diagnoses. Around 1 out of every 3 people suffering from an eating disorder fit into this category. Again, a distorted perception of body image is commonly observed.

Summary
With any eating disorder it is necessary to realize the serious implications for health, relationships, and self-acceptance. Not surprisingly, given that eating disorders are mostly directly related to not accepting or liking yourself, (because of what you believe about yourself,) that there is a strong connection to autoimmune disease. As we have pointed out earlier, everything begins with a thought. Your immune system is designed to attack threats or enemies of your wellbeing. If the *'heart belief'* that you hold about your *'identity'* is that you are letting yourself

down, and consequently are the enemy of your own acceptance, then your immune system plays out you not liking yourself and attacks your body in some area.

It's almost like an internalized version of self-harming, cutting or headbanging, which is an obvious physical outworking of this lack of acceptance or dislike of '*self*,' and may present as an urge to harm yourself in some way. So, we can identify this tie in to propensities towards autoimmune disease in people with eating disorders, as a spiritual and emotional playout of a person's state of being in regards to self-perception.

People suffering from eating disorders will also often present with other methods of dealing with emotional pain from their distorted identity, such as the use of alcohol or drugs. Emotional signs of eating disorders are consistent with other kinds of coping behaviours or addictive profiles, for example; low self-worth, low self-image, low self-esteem, negativity about self, and with eating disorders this has often become specific to appearance or body image.

Consequently, the outworking of these negative inner thoughts and emotions will be anxiety, and feeling depressed and out of control. Remember, depression comes from overwhelming *hopelessness* that you can *never ever* be good enough. That is, you can *never be* what you are expected to be. So, the anxiety around food is that if you are not in control of it, then the image that you perceive that you need to attain to be good enough and acceptable is hopelessly unattainable.

Hence the guilt and disappointment with *self* that you feel if you fail and eat uncontrollably. This fits with three observed personality traits that place you at risk for developing an eating disorder such as perfectionism, (from- the need to get everything exactly right to be good enough and acceptable) neuroticism, (means- insecure about life and sees the world as distressing, unsafe, or threatening), and impulsivity. (Means- having a problem with emotional or behavioural self-control)

Where do eating disorders begin?
As with most mental problems, eating disorders begin with events that program a person's perception and beliefs about their identity, significance, and worth. These are greatly impacted by many life events, and can include episodes of emotional, verbal, physical or sexual abuse. Additionally, they can be programmed into *the heart* in early school years through lack of acceptance of some kind, including children bullying or mocking a person.

Additional thoughts on general eating problems

As a generalization, out of order eating habits that would not fit on the mental disorder spectrum, often involve some measure of self-comforting, even though it may be lesser in expression. For the same reason you may have a propensity or weakness towards other excessive or addictive behaviours such as too much alcohol. This may be on a sliding scale influenced by factors such as your mental and emotional condition, programming through how your family chose to deal with these types of pressures, and/or generational or cultural issues. For many Christians a social drink is unacceptable, and so they gravitate towards food for self-comfort.

Of course some people become addicted to excessive food, alcohol, or drugs in their pursuit of pleasure. In many nations today media promotes a plethora of food shows and movies, or where people drink or smoke, making these things appear desirable. If you are in a culture where this is affordable, you will possibly follow this programming. The old saying is that the devil will give you either too much or too little. The result of this imbalance is illustrated by, for example, the statistic that two thirds of Americans are considered overweight. More than one third of adults in the United States fall into the category of being obese.

Obesity is now considered to be an epidemic right across the globe with one in 8 people being described in this way. Contrasted with this is the statistic that around one in six people worldwide are undernourished. If we live in societies that can over indulge there is an ever-present temptation to do so, and it is fairly easy to simply develop bad habits.

Ministry to eating disorders

Ministry involves identifying the beliefs and feelings that the person holds in regards to their image and identity. Once they are free of these, most commonly people are no longer driven or triggered by these factors, and are free to adopt normal patterns and disciplines over time. Sometimes these changes occur immediately following a ministry session.

CHAPTER TWENTY ONE
Substance Misuse Related Disorders

What is substance misuse or abuse?
Substance abuse is considered to be a dependence or addictive disorder which involves excessive use of alcohol, drugs or even tobacco. Estimates indicate that around 1 in 20 Australians misuse substances in this way, with between 20 and 24 million Americans being cited as having at least one addiction. Around 1 in 5 Americans who have an anxiety disorder or suffer from depression also have a substance abuse disorder.

Evidently, as with other mental disorders, it generally co exists with additional problems and is separated for the purposes of specific study. More than 5% of deaths worldwide each year are considered to be caused by the use of alcohol, which is the most commonly abused substance. Reportedly 1 in 6 Australians consume dangerous levels of alcohol. We can see that it is a global problem. Substance abuse can in itself damage the brain and body, and as a consequence it is considered to be a major cause of mental illness.

We understand that there is a root as to why people misuse it, but, further mental disorder is an added component, or complication that is a serious result implicated in the use of these substances. Drugs such as LSD damage your chemical brain, and this opens doors to psychotic, delusional behaviour, along with a general licensing of unreality and a loss of perspective and truth. You really are opening yourself to untruth, distorted thinking, and deception about life and your own identity.

People using drugs such as marijuana, methamphetamines, cocaine, speed, ice, heroine, ecstasy or LSD statistically exhibit a considerably higher rate of mental illness than the general population. When we are discussing drugs, along with illegal drugs, we can include misusing prescription medications. Dr. Henry Wright in his popular book, 'A More Excellent Way,' cited an article from USA Today, April 24th, 1998. It listed adverse reactions to prescription drugs as the 4th most common killer in America, behind heart disease at number one, cancer at number two, and strokes at number three.

The following year, November 30th 1999, the newspaper updated to number three cause of death, properly prescribed and administered FDA-approved drugs with side effects. So, we can see that drugs, whether recreational or prescribed, have a significant impact on all areas of function in your person.

Habitual or addictive use of substances can affect every area of life. Your mental and emotional wellbeing, physical health and relationships, will all be impacted by your problem. Indicators of there being a problem with substance abuse may include trying unsuccessfully to cut down or give up, even though you are aware that you are being harmed. Another problem is needing an increasing amount of the substance to achieve the same results because of developing a tolerance. An additional indication appears if you're experiencing withdrawal symptoms if you try to stop using the substance.

Addiction is considered to be the physical or psychological need for a substance. Often a habit is formed when a person regularly uses these substances. This can begin simply from enjoying the feeling that the drug produces.

The choice of substance can be influenced by observing parents or others using drugs while growing up, and this is considered to create a high risk of developing the problem later in life. The addictive element of these substances varies considerably with some being mildly addictive, and others being extremely addictive.

One problem with drugs such as alcohol is that in some people it increases the incidence of other disorders such as anxiety, depression, or other mental illnesses. It is also documented that substances and medications can be causative of mental disorders in people who didn't formerly have them prior to the use of drugs. This can include amongst other problems:

bipolar, depression, anxiety, OCD, sleep disorders, psychotic problems, neurocognitive disorders and sexual dysfunction. For example, side effects such as anxiety can be observed in some anti-anxiety medications. Some anti-depressants can induce suicidal thoughts.

The flip side is that people with mental and emotional disorders are more inclined to misuse substances to ease their symptoms far more than other members of the community. This in part could be because drugs release 'feel good' hormones, such as dopamine. For example, the pharmacological action of cocaine on your body is a massive release of dopamine, resulting in suddenly using up all of the feel-good hormones that would normally keep you happy. What goes up must come down.

Now your body has to replenish your store of dopamine, which is slowly replaced. Perhaps this is why you need more and more of the drug for the same affect, trying to wring out whatever your tired-out glands can produce. Psychostimulants such as methamphetamine have a stimulating effect on your adrenal glands. Once these glands wear out you can be subject to issues such as adrenal insufficiency, which is where your glands cannot produce enough of the many health-giving hormones that they would normally supply.

Why are people predisposed to drug addictions?
As we have already stated, many of the people who develop substance misuse have anxiety, depression, poor self-image, and other mental problems or circumstantial stresses. The action of the substance triggered by the activation of the brains reward system is considered by some as central to issues stemming from drug use. Equally, actually being productive or successful may be associated with feeling like you should be rewarded, and that this feeling of achievement should be enhanced. Even mild addicts may feel that they should have something following 'a good day's work.' These could be times where you believe that you're doing, or did good work for example.

In fact, the feeling of reward as a response to the use of drugs can be so strong that they favour taking the substance over the undertaking of necessary, or other regular activities. Whilst most drugs work differently in the body according to the category of the substance, the feelings of pleasure that are associated with the reward system are similar.

Dealing with substance misuse disorders
Because of the tendency for co-existing mental and emotional problems

with substance misuse, it is sensible to deal with both of them at the same time. People often begin to misuse substances in an effort to self-treat mental and emotional disorders. It becomes their solution to how they feel.

Given the fact that a '*distorted identity, or heart belief*' as we term it, is usually behind both problems, then the answer to take the power out of the issue is usually the same. First, we deal with these *self-beliefs* in regards to *identity*. Next, we need to be realistic about the time needed to slowly resolve the chemical and habitual elements of the addiction.

As with other disorders severity varies greatly from person to person. Some people have low levels of self-control and resistance, which means that they are more vulnerable to developing addictions if they have exposure to drugs. For some people who don't have as deep a problem, it may be relatively easily resolved. For others with a stronger addiction, or something of longer duration, it can be a lengthier process with a number of factors that need to be worked through over time. This can be because of personality, or the determination and commitment of the person to break the cycle. In severe cases hospitalization or rehabilitation whilst detoxing from the substance/s may be required.

People often are unaware of the severity of their problem, or deny that they are addicted at all. Clearly, they are more likely to accept the input of others if they are dealt with respectfully. Nobody wants to be told that they have a problem and that they 'just need to get it sorted out.' In effect this would be like telling them that there is something wrong with them, and this implies that they are not good enough or acceptable. In most cases those are the types of underlying beliefs, with consequent negative feelings, that led them to the substances to begin with. So, to treat them this way is more likely to drive them towards their addiction than away from it.

The underlying causes of the substance misuse will need to be addressed. Childhood rejection through verbal, emotional, physical or sexual abuse will need to be worked through and dealt with by resolving the corresponding *heart beliefs*. Once these emotional triggers are dealt with, the will of the sufferer to be free can be engaged, and use of the substance can be slowly reduced or immediately stopped. In a sense, coming to truth about your identity, and feeling happy about, and accepting yourself, displaces the counterfeit version of feeling good induced by the substances.

The connection between association and addiction

Our brain to a large extent operates by memory and association through 'cues' or 'triggers.' These remind us of certain things that we do that are connected to an event or activity. For example, at the moment I'm attempting to lose some weight. I'm achieving this by fasting in the morning and only having a small serving of vegetables for lunch. These aren't very filling, so I began to have a small handful of nuts afterwards to make me feel a bit more as though I have eaten. By doing this regularly I have created an association between the meal and the nuts.

The meal is the 'cue' or 'trigger event,' and my brain then reminds me that there is something that follows my lunch. So, I have created a habit, and I feel that if I don't get up after my meal and get the nuts, I'm missing out on something that I now perceive that I need to have.... or can't do without. It's a simple example of an association that needs to be broken down. I don't think that nuts are a very addictive substance, but it still requires effort if I decide not to have them.

Imagine that you are going through a period of time where you are stressed and under load. As a result, you are feeling a bit tired and run down. One day you happen to have a caffeinated soda drink. The caffeine and sugar give you a bit of a boost and you feel a bit happier and a little more energized. Your brain stores this information in a file titled; 'feeling flat and what to do about it,' in the limbic system area of your chemical mind. The next time you feel flat your brain does a data search on information relating to this problem. Right on the top of the list is a record that drinking caffeinated soda gave you a boost and made you feel a little better in the past.

So, your brain has kept a record and created an association between tiredness and the boost received from the drink. Clearly if you continue to be tired you will continue to access that file titled; 'feeling flat and what to do about it.' Before long, you have developed a habit. If you serve the habit long enough, over time it becomes an addiction. It is important to create God habits and associations, and avoid developing unhealthy habits which end up with mastery over us. We are not 'religiously' suggesting for a moment that drinking caffeinated soda is sin! We are just using it as an illustration of the workings of association and addiction.

We do however recognize that it is important to not create habits that potentially can get out of control. It is best we model ourselves on the advice and wisdom of the Apostle Paul.

1 Corinthians 6:12 "Everything is permissible for me"--but not everything is beneficial. "Everything is permissible for me"--but I will not be mastered by anything. NIV

What I'm saying is that along with the identity beliefs and corresponding negative emotions that need to be dealt with, is the breaking down of associations, and if necessary, detoxing from addictive chemicals. In the case of wanting to break down the habit of having nuts following my lunch, I would fool my memory and associative process by telling myself that I will eat them later in the day. There is no prompt, cue, or trigger developed then, so it will be easy to resist, or the nuts may even be forgotten. This in a simple form is how we break down habits and associations.

Breaking with pressure points

Very often drug addicts form a clique because they identify with other people who have the same issues. This creates an environment where it becomes difficult to break away from the relationships that they have formed. They become encouraged by others in the group to continue with these substances. It's not merely the drugs that they have in common, but more probably they understand each other's rejection. So, it can become like a 'brotherhood' of addicts that needs to be broken with in the process of overcoming the bondage. Moving away from the 'us' and 'them' environment, along with the ready availability of temptations can be a vital part of the rehabilitation process.

Mental disorders produced by drugs or medications

What we're talking about here, are mental issues that people did not suffer from before the person was exposed to substances or medications. This could occur because of the pharmacological action of the substance on brain chemistry, or because the substance lowers the ability to hold down existing issues that have been suppressed to some degree. Some of these include chemically induced:

Bipolar or connected disorders, anxiety or depressive disorders, sleep disorders, OCD, sexual dysfunction, neurocognitive disorder, and psychotic problems.

As a generalization people who misuse substances have altered brain chemistry and function which distorts their thinking, judgement, perceptions, personality, decisions, and subsequently their behaviour. Clearly the more regularly and long-term substances are misused, the greater these changes will be, and they can remain even after the effects of the substance have worn off.

Different substances have a different action on the chemistry of the body, and produce different feelings and symptoms. People who abuse substances develop an intense desire or craving for the feelings of pleasure, intoxication, peace, euphoria, heightened sense of perception, or elevated states that are the result of exposure to the substance.

Other components that may need to be dealt with

<u>Conclusions</u>. Many people come to believe that there is no life without the substance making them feel better, or happier, or numbing out the other feelings and issues around their lives.

<u>Chemical cycles</u>. The actions on the body from the drugs may need to be dealt with by detoxing and/or displacement of some kind. Displacement is where, rather than leaving a void with nothing in it, you substitute the chemical with something that is good for you. This would be like instead of having a chocolate biscuit, you have a carrot or a handful of beans.

<u>The will</u>. It cannot be overstated how important a one-time decision to walk out of addictive bondage can be. Clearly, if the emotional driver is still in place, you may not want to let go of the substance.

<u>Spiritual factors</u>. At times there is a demonic element with addictive problems. Created order as an ideal, is a sound mind with a full grasp reality. So, when a person deliberately chooses withdrawal from life and going into unreality through an altered state, they are cooperating with, and following a spiritual entity other than God. So, deceptive spirits of unreality may be present when trying to break down substance misuse. Help may be needed, with spiritual authority exercised. At times we hear wonderful stories and instances of people who at conversion, or after prayer, just totally lose interest in their drug. These appear to be to some extent isolated cases that are not predictable, although they are amazing and we thank God for them. These may also be times where this occurs because a spirit has moved off.

<u>Generational substance problems</u>. Often people inherit a weakness for abuse of particular drugs and chemicals. This is the sins of the fathers visiting (drawing them towards) the same substances that they used.

> *Psalm 51:5 Surely I was sinful at birth, sinful from the time my mother conceived me. NIV*

For those who struggle to believe the scriptures on this there is an area of science called 'Epigenetics.' It is an area of brain research that reveals that your habits are passed on to your children and grandchildren. The study states that we not only pass along the DNA sequence to our children, but we also pass epigenetic instructions to them. The epigenetic information sits above the genome that controls the programming of DNA. So, this is the physical outworking of a spiritual reality. As expected, it confirms what scripture has already said, that if we sin in an area, it will affect our children in the same area. We have often inherited a weakness that we need to be set free from, and it can be infecting our offspring with the same problems.

CHAPTER TWENTY TWO
Schizophrenia

What is Schizophrenia?
People with Schizophrenia exhibit a distorted perception of reality. This will many times include delusions and even hallucinations. It is considered to be a relatively rare chronic mental disorder, although some reports indicate that it could affect as much as one percent of the general population. In the past it was confused with dissociative disorders and was termed 'split personality.' Today there is a distinction between the two conditions and it is no longer regarded in this way.

Although it can occur at any age, it reportedly develops in men in their late teens or early 20's, and in women in their late 20's. Nearly 50% of people suffering with Schizophrenia have other co-occurring mental issues. Statistics indicate that if you have this disorder, you are 2 to 3 times more likely to die early. This includes around 5% of sufferers dying by suicide, which in part is why it is considered one of the most serious mental health issues. Reportedly you have a 10% higher likelihood of developing this illness if it is in the immediate family, for example a parent or sibling. This points to a potential generational transfer of some kind. We'll take that up further at the end of observations made on case histories at the end of this study.

Symptoms that categorize Schizophrenia
Early signs and common symptoms that someone may be suffering from with this disorder are as follows: withdrawal and isolation from;

family, friends or groups that the person may have been connected with. Sleep problems, being easily irritated, loss of ability to concentrate or focus on tasks and pay attention, an inability to understand concepts or information, confusion, all of which could lead to poor decision making. There is a breaking down in thought and emotion, and this can present as inappropriate behaviour in a given situation. The preceding symptoms could exist for other reasons.

Where you see withdrawal the most common reasons are:
- massive insecurity in regards to people, and their motives. This most commonly proceeds from abuse of some kind.
- extreme low self-image where you want to hide your perceived weaknesses
- fear of rejection. Abuse is rejection of your person, and now you fear it happening again. If that is a potential problem in reality, then unreality and withdrawal appear to be a preferable option.

Additional symptoms that identify this disorder include items that you would not find in the general population such as; delusional thinking, (believing something to be true when there is no evidence.) This could include not being aware of their symptoms, abnormal or disorganized thought processes or ways of thinking, unsettled body movements or adopting strange postures, and hallucinations. (This is when your mind creates pictures or experiences that seem real, and could include sensory experiences such as seeing, hearing or smelling things that others are not aware of.)

Other factors that you would expect to be present with this disorder include:

Disordered speech as a result of disorganized thought processes, and moving quickly from one topic to another. Impulsivity, socially withdrawn, a diminished ability to experience pleasure, with a corresponding loss of interest in life. Additionally, sufferers will usually have either an absence of emotion, or an unusual emotional reaction to circumstances or situations.

The use of recreational drugs or prescription medication which facilitate escape, withdrawal, unreality and insanity can be implicated. (Insanity, is to not be sane, whole or sound in mind.) Someone who previously naturally maintained the walls of their personality and resisted unreality, now escapes into it.

Professor John Nash, famous for his story being depicted in the movie; 'A Beautiful Mind', suffered from Schizophrenia. He has been often quoted as saying, "People are always selling the idea that people with mental illness are suffering. I think madness can be an escape. If things are not so good, you maybe want to imagine something better." This is perhaps an indication of why the use of the imagination is distorted in an attempt to escape from the persons perceived reality.

The use of drugs obviously enables that process of moving into an altered state disposed to unreality to take place more easily. I read an article a number of years ago from a study saying that users of Cannabis are 700% more likely to develop Schizophrenia than the general populace. The question has to be asked, why do some people who don't have the same emotional issues, and so don't consequently have the same predisposition to wanting to escape from their perceived reality, use the drug for decades simply for pleasure and do not get this disorder? Clearly, the answer is that they don't have the same kind of identity damage as those with mental illness. (That said they will still suffer some kind of cognitive impairment!)

Along with most other mental disorders the health care professionals and scientists consider that the exact cause of Schizophrenia is unknown. Perhaps we can turn to a publicised account of a celebrity who suffered from Schizophrenia to confirm our own insights into the disorder.

As well as John Nash, another celebrity sufferer of Schizophrenia is American stand-up comedian and actor Darrell Hammond. He is known for publicly discussing the subject of mental health and abuse, having himself been diagnosed with schizophrenia and other mental disorders. His story is a good illustration of the types of roots and beginnings that you're likely to find behind Schizophrenia.

Where does Schizophrenia come from?
A case history such as that of T.V. personality Darrell Hammond is consistent with the types of backgrounds that I've encountered in cases of schizophrenia that I have dealt with. His story has been shared publicly through various forms of media, and I cite here an article written by Niki Swift. The piece was titled "The Tragic real-life story of Darrell Hammond." It can be seen in full on the internet.

Reportedly as a child 'his mother tortured him with hammers, knives, and electrical outlets. He repressed the memories of his mother's abuse for much of his life, well into his adult years.' In his own words; "I was a victim of systematic and lengthy brutality," he told CNN in 2011. "My mom did some things which have cost me dearly." As he recalled in his memoir (via ABC News), "I am getting into the car to go somewhere with my mother. 'Wait,' she says, holding the door open. 'Put your hand there.' When I do, she slams the door."

You can imagine how through the critical times of forming *identity* you would probably come to conclusions such as; 'I'm hated, unlovable, unimportant, don't matter, worthy of punishment' and so on. As children we have a tendency to interpret ourselves as being the reason that things are happening. This is well demonstrated when he recalls a previously repressed memory of an abusive event. "I remember the floor being red and me bleeding, in a vague sense ... I thought it was my fault," he said. "I mean, can you imagine the desperation of a child who chooses to believe that he did this to himself just so he doesn't have to consider the idea that his mother did it or his parents did it?"

In a situation such as this, to accept that it wasn't his fault would be to accept that he truly wasn't lovable or acceptable by his mother. In all probability allowing himself to believe that it was his fault, that he was the bad one, was behind the self-harming, self-punishing behaviour such as cutting reported as being present later in life. There was also drug and alcohol abuse, which is generally an attempt to 'numb out' mental and emotional turmoil and pain.

The article shared that Darrell Hammond self-harmed for decades. 'He started cutting when he began having flashbacks to his childhood trauma, which he often visualized as the colour red, and he would self-harm as a way to soothe his mind.'

'Darrell Hammond was diagnosed with an array of mental disorders, including bipolar disorder, manic depression, and schizophrenia. "I was on as many as seven medications at one time," he said. "Doctors didn't know what to do with me."' The story shared that; 'Darrell Hammond suffered years of debilitating PTSD as a result of his childhood traumas.'

The story further revealed that his father was an alcoholic World War II veteran.

'Darrell Hammond's father, Max, did not engage in the same kind of physical abuse as his mother. But as a World War II veteran, he was an alcoholic who suffered from "dreams of Nazis and dismembered corpses," Hammond told CNN in 2011, adding, "and it was frightening to be around that." "My father said on his deathbed, his last words, 'I let my anger be more important to me than my children,'" Hammond remembered. "'There was nothing as important to me. It was the only thing that was important to me.'"

Commonly if a person's reality is horrifying, abusive, or not something that they can't mentally deal with, they will choose unreality as a means of coping. If key caregivers are frightening and can't be trusted to care, love and protect, then a person begins to relate with, and have the same expectations of other authority figures or key people in a similar way. For Darrell, this could likely have been exacerbated by also being sexually abused by the family housekeeper.

'Hammond said he suffered from misdiagnoses for years, until he came under the care of Dr. Nabil Kotbi at the psychiatric facility, The Plains, in 2010, crediting the doctor for helping him realize the psychological roots of his mental health issues. "**You are this way because of something that happened to you**," Hammond remembers Kotbi telling him in the 2018 documentary Cracked Up (via CNN). Kotbi's therapy helped Hammond **grasp the extent of his childhood trauma and understand the way it impacted his brain**. "People were approaching me as if mental illness was an airborne virus, **as if this had come from nowhere** and a bunch of drugs would fix it," Hammond told The Columbus Dispatch. "That's the way it went for a long time.'" (emphasis mine)

Let me share one further noteworthy quotation from the article. Remembering that vital to mental order and emotional health is having significance, value, and worth programmed into the *identity beliefs* that you hold in your *heart*.

'Also speaking on the podcast was Cracked Up director Michelle Esrick, who connected Hammond's memories of his sexual abuse with one interpretation of trauma offered in the documentary. "I remember when I interviewed Dr. Bessel Van der Kolk who's in the film, and I asked him what's the definition of trauma?" she revealed. "And I thought he was going to say, when you're hit this many times or when you're sexually abused this many times. And he said, **when you are not seen or known, that is the trauma**. That's it. **When you're not seen or known**.'" (emphasis mine)

When as a child you have these conditions while you are forming your *identity*, you can easily come to the conclusion that you're 'nothing,' 'nobody.' This is a gut-wrenching interpretation of your characteristics that becomes a *heart belief* about <u>self</u> that cannot be removed without the ministry of the Holy Spirit. The result is extreme deep brokenness and broken heartedness. When you add in abuses of various kinds that program you that you're not lovable or acceptable, your reality is unacceptable. The following scriptures describe the outworking of *negative heart beliefs*, in regards to *identity*, that break down the human personality.

> *Proverbs 15:13 A merry **heart** makes a cheerful countenance, But by sorrow of the **heart** the spirit is broken. NKJV (Emphasis mine)*
>
> *Proverbs 17:22 A merry heart does good, like medicine, But a broken spirit dries the bones. NKJV*
>
> *Proverbs 18:14 The spirit of a man will sustain him in sickness, But who can bear a broken spirit? NKJV*

His story would be typical of the Schizophrenic cases that I've personally dealt with. I'm not proposing that I'm an expert on Schizophrenia. What we are proficient at is dealing with root cause negative *heart beliefs*, regardless of the fruit that they produce. As we can see, these same root beliefs, sourced in different memory events, can present and be implicated in more than one co-occurring disorder diagnosis.

Physical implications

Scientists have noted on imaging tests that there are abnormalities in some brain structures, along with imbalances and or low levels of certain brain chemicals, hormones and neurotransmitters. They are not sure why this is exactly. As we have already explained, with people who have suffered childhood abuses of some kind, the chicken always comes before the egg. We know this because once the chicken is dealt with in ministry, the egg, or result of the chicken, consistently disappears as well.

The use of drugs that produce altered states will contribute to these imbalances, as the pharmacological action on the body often precipitates an over release of hormones. These hormones stores may take considerable time to replenish. For example, dopamine has many actions and activities in the body, working both as a hormone and a neurotransmitter. As we have just noted from Proverbs 17:22 '*a broken spirit dries the bones.*' Immune system cells are made and multiplied in the bone marrow, so the marrow drying out can be implicated in a number of physical problems, and may be an indicator as to why people with this disorder are 2 to 3 times more likely to die prematurely.

Types of Schizophrenia

Although categorizing Schizophrenia into 5 subtypes was discarded in 2013, in order to make our study as complete as possible we will look at them briefly here.

Paranoid Schizophrenia: This is the most prevalent type of Schizophrenia. Because this is an accepted symptom of the disorder even though it may be predominant it is no longer considered a subtype. (Paranoia is a mental condition identified by thoughts producing fear or intense anxiety. These often relate to delusions of being persecuted, an exaggerated sense of self-importance, unnecessary jealousy, perceived threats or even conspiracies.) In saying that, paranoia is not present with every case of Schizophrenia, and can occur for other reasons such as the use of drugs or additional causes for a person to lose perspective of reality.

Disorganized or Hebephrenic: This diagnosis was applied to people who had disorganized behaviour or speech, but were not delusional or did not hallucinate.

Residual: This was characterized by people who were diagnosed with symptoms early in life, but who did not exhibit them later.

Catatonic: This term was applied to those who were unable to speak or were mute, or those who fell into a stupor or catatonic state. People who fell under this subtype were also noted to at times be defiant, rebellious and refuse to follow instructions. As you've seen recently in the case history that we presented, there can be a significant amount of unfairness and injustice in how a child is treated. A predictable universal response to injustice is rebellion, and it is typically directed towards authority figures, because these types of key figures were the original source of the unfairness in formative memories. In the rationale of the *heart* then, they are not to be trusted or submitted to.

Undifferentiated: This subtype was used when a person showed more than one predominant symptom.

Other reasons for symptoms that appear similar to Schizophrenia
Prescription medications, illegal or recreational drug use, other mental disorders with shared symptoms.

Childhood Schizophrenia

Although less common, this disorder can develop or be observed earlier in life. To be considered childhood schizophrenia the symptoms will have appeared prior to 13 years of age. Perhaps one reason that it is less commonly diagnosed is that it shares common signs with other mental health disorders such as: depression, bipolar, and attention deficit disorders. Common childhood symptoms are issues such as: sleep problems, paranoia, (as unusual fears or anxiety), emotionally unstable, sudden reactions or behaviour changes, cognitive deterioration, hallucinations.

Bipolar as opposed to Schizophrenia

These two disorders have overlapping symptoms and characteristics. Some people may in fact have both illnesses co-occurring. In order to make a distinction we'll list some of the differences.

Although people with Bipolar may also experience delusional thinking or hallucinate, unlike Schizophrenics they most likely will not have disorganized thought or speech. Bipolar people will tend to shift moods from mania to depressive, and are most likely to be delusional in the manic phase.

When psychosis (a state where thought and emotions are impaired in such a way that contact is broken with reality) occurs in schizophrenia it does not appear along with the manic state.

Differences between Schizophrenia and psychosis

Psychosis is considered to be a serious mental disorder where thought and emotions are impaired to the point that a person loses touch with, or breaks with reality. During an episode this can include delusions, (false beliefs, or believing things that aren't true), hearing voices, hallucinations, (seeing or hearing things that other people do not see or hear.) Psychosis can be confused with Schizophrenia, although by some it is considered to be a symptom associated with several other mental disorders as well as Schizophrenia. One reason that some consider it to at times be a disorder in itself, is because it can occur in isolation in people not presenting with other symptoms or mental issues. Not everyone with schizophrenia will have psychotic episodes.

Additional considerations associated with Schizophrenia

People suffering with this disorder will often experience anxiety, depression, phobic fears, relational, and family issues. Along with these problems, they may be disposed towards reactive behaviours, such as the misuse of alcohol or drugs in an attempt to mask their negative emotions. They may also be prone to self-harming to punish themselves for the perceived shortcomings that they hold about their worth and identity. They may become suicidal. This is probably because of hopelessness in regards to these inner beliefs, and consequent negative feelings about these never being able to be resolved.

For some people this disorder is cyclic with symptoms subsiding and then returning at a later time.

Causes
Abuse
Recent research indicates the connection between sexual, physical, or emotional abuse, and schizophrenia. This is consistent with case histories that have been recorded. These studies indicate that the critical time where this affects a person is during early childhood. As we have already pointed out these times are critical in terms of the formation of *identity*, and what is perceived to be true as we form an image of ourselves. Later abuses or stressors can 'trigger' these existing beliefs and produce an episode.

Stress
Studies indicate that stress is a potential 'trigger' for schizophrenia. In my opinion the type of stress involved is to do with states of insecurity that are present in people with this disorder as a result of past abuses. Any major changes, particularly in relationships can 'set off' the appearance of symptoms of the disorder.

Additionally, scientists, researchers and mental health professionals have identified that one element of the disorder can come from dysfunctional relationships with parents, siblings, or authority figures. These are often the source of the abuses. I recall one lady with this disorder who had suppressed memories of sexual abuses by her brothers. As the memory pictures began to return, she would close her session for day; saying that she had to get used to the idea of the contents of the events. She would come in the following week prepared to face the memories, accept what she had believed, and then receive truth.

Observations indicate that you will have a much higher likelihood of developing this disorder if it is pre-existing in the family line. People who abuse have generally been abused themselves, so it's not surprising when this disorder passes through generations.

One young man that I worked with would when triggered become insane, choosing unreality when he became insecure about life. This insecurity was triggered particularly by the absence of those he had learnt to trust. Clearly it is not God's order to leave reality and choose an insane, or unsound mind over a sound one. The result was that in this case there was a spirit of insanity that was involved in the schism. Once again there had been considerable abuse, of an incestuous nature, along with violence early in life involved in this case history.

Some of those that I've ministered to have come from interstate and we've only been able to do one or two sessions, not a full course of ministry, so even though there were changes I don't know of the final outcomes with these people. One case was a local lady, a believer but not a church goer because her husband was anti-Christian. She had significant breakthroughs and reported major changes in her condition.

Final thoughts

As we've pointed out from the beginning, brokenness in identity is still the key to restoration. I'm not setting myself up as an authority on this disorder. However, in most of the cases that I've dealt with there had been sexual abuse, and it was fairly specific in that it was often acted out by a member of the immediate family. Additionally, in many of the cases that I've dealt with in younger people, there has been drug use, multiple sexual partners, regular visits to psychiatric wards, and indications of generational mental illness. There have also often been demonic issues that need to be dealt with.

For this reason, my recommendation would be that you need an experienced, balanced, and well-trained ministry team when dealing with these kinds of problems. You will need a support group, and a knowledge that the ministry time will be a journey, not a single event.

As we've already discussed, it's not God's order to leave reality, whether by emotional overload, or by choice through the use of drugs. Once there is a breach in the personality of this type it can give place to a spirit that you could label as a 'spirit of withdrawal,' 'unreality,' or 'insanity.' Once invited, chosen, and installed, a demon can lock you into unreality. Even a drug such as marijuana can increase the risk of developing psychosis by 5 times, producing symptoms such as: paranoia, hallucinations, and delusions, even if only used in small doses. Repeated use amplifies the likelihood of complications.

This can also be the case in other disorders such as bipolar, dissociative states, and even autism.

Some Christian commentators consider mental disorders under the Old Testament law to be the result of a curse coming from occult activity, or sin, in departing from the Lord in the family line. We can certainly observe that incestuous activity in the family line, for example, will produce a curse.

> *Deuteronomy 27:22 'Cursed is anyone who has sexual intercourse with his sister, whether she is the daughter of his father or his mother.' And all the people will reply, 'Amen.' NLT*

The fact that mental disorder even exists is the outworking of ignoring the ways of God, whether as individuals, or as a corporate society.

> *Deuteronomy 28:28 "The LORD will strike you with madness and blindness and confusion of heart. NKJV*

The word translated 'madness,' also can be translated as 'craziness.' The NIV renders it confusion of mind, which is still relevant, even though the Hebrew word is heart. Because as we now understand, the outworking of negative *heart beliefs* is the distortion of thinking and consequent lack of wholeness in the mind, emotions, and finally body. I take confusion of mind or heart to mean that you cannot think clearly and get your thoughts in order.

> *Deuteronomy 28:28 The LORD will afflict you with madness, blindness and confusion of mind. NIV*

We thank God that He dealt with the law and the curse on our behalf, and so now all can be healed and set free. Ministry of the type that we're suggesting to the *broken heart*, is I believe the appropriation of Galatians 3:13, where Jesus became a curse for us, in order for us to no longer carry the results of sins coming to us through our family line. Jesus already paid for it, but it is facilitated and received through faith and the ministry of the Holy Spirit.

> *Galatians 3:13-14 Christ redeemed us from the curse of the law by becoming a curse for us, for it is written: "Cursed is everyone who is hung on a tree." 14 He redeemed us in order that the blessing given to Abraham might come to the Gentiles through Christ Jesus, so that <u>by faith</u> we might receive <u>the promise of the Spirit</u>. NIV (emphasis mine)*

CHAPTER TWENTY THREE

Neurodevelopmental Disorders

Brain development

This group of disorders is categorized by what is considered damage to, and altered development of, the function and wholeness of the central nervous system while in the womb, or the first few years after birth. Along with this there can be brain development disorders which affect learning, motor skills, language, as well as affecting non-verbal communication and/or sensory processes. Additionally, neurodevelopment disorders are implicated in how the brain functions and impacts a child's behaviour, along with memory, and may result in mental retardation, dyslexia, ADHD, and Autism.

These disorders, abbreviated as ND's, share some common characteristics: brain development is disrupted, they first appear in early childhood, and they neither get worse or better. The most common ND's are Autism Spectrum disorder (ASD), Attention Deficit Hyperactivity disorder (ADHD), and intellectual disabilities. There are often co-occurring mental disorders that appear along with each other.

They are usually observed in early development before school is commenced. Children suffering from ND's typically present with impairments in social skills, academic and learning problems, problems with intelligence, and an inability to regulate emotion. These children may have deficits that could be limited to particular areas, or they may exhibit more severe and general limitations and present with additional disorders. An example of this would be children with ASD commonly also have some kind of intellectual disorder.

In general, the rates of these ND's such as ASD are increasing sharply across the world. Scientists and researchers acknowledge that they have a limited understanding of what causes these disorders and why they develop. Although there are other types of ND's along with other co-occurring mental health issues which we'll detail at the end of the research, we'll mainly focus here on ASD having already covered ADHD in an earlier study. Perhaps a key is in the fact that these other problems co-exist. This may give us some insights into what could be behind them. (Perhaps there is a generational propensity? It certainly is a developmental problem, so what were the dynamics that interfered with proper development?)

Autism Spectrum Disorders (ASD'S)
Most people are familiar with the Neurodevelopmental disorder autism. The term 'autism' has been in use for around 100 years. It reportedly comes from the Greek word 'autos' which means 'self.' This then describes a state or condition where a person becomes an isolated *self*, withdrawn from social interaction. One study indicated that in 1975 the incidence of autism was 1 in 5,000. By 1985 it had become 1 in 2,500, 1995 1 in 500, 2001 1 in 250, and by 2012 1 in 88, and at the time of writing it is reportedly now around 1 child in 59. It normally appears during the first 2-3 years of life, and is 3-4 times more common in boys than girls.

Autism Spectrum Disorder (ASD) is characterized by repetitive patterns of behaviour, problems with social interaction and communication beginning in early childhood. It affects quality of life and acceptance of self. (Let me say here that the normal reason for withdrawal and independence from others is fear of rejection. This is generally the result of previously having suffered rejection/s of some kind. If you are independent of others, then using this as compensating behaviour, there is now no need to fear being rejected again by them. So, it follows that if there is insecurity about being accepted, then the way that a person would resolve this is to withdraw from others. Why this occurs and where and how it began in these children is the question.)

'Spectrum' is applied to cover the diversity of levels of disability, impairments of skills and abilities, and variety of symptoms. Some people with ASD require a high level of support, whereas on the other end of the scale are those who are able to function in everyday life. What is termed High functioning autism is considered the first level or mildest form. For example, today Asperger's syndrome fits into the ASD category, where they have some impairment of social skills and interpreting emotional cues, but they require very little support. They may actually at times be more intelligent than others, and have skills in music, science or mathematics.

At the other end of the spectrum we see non-verbal autism, which affects around 40% of children, and could include intellectual disability or other impairment of some kind.

ASD can be confused with, or co-exist with ADHD because in both cases the child may be overactive, have difficulties staying focussed and paying attention, suffer meltdowns, not understand social appropriateness, not be self-aware, and consequently be found impinging on other people's personal space.

Because ASD affects social interaction, the person can appear awkward or be inappropriate in dealing with other people. Reportedly the brain of someone suffering from ASD responds differently to sights, smells, and sounds than the average person. I recall one case that I dealt with where the child observed a small registration label change on the family vehicle. Although seemingly oblivious to the bigger picture of life, the details in the small world that he had come to live in were readily observable. Other things that people would normally not pay much attention to were heightened in his immediate sensory world, such as almost an ecstasy from bath or shower water running on him.

As we have discussed ASD varies in symptoms and severity from case to case. People suffering from ASD are still individuals with varying backgrounds and environments, so although they may share some common characteristics, they are all different.

Common ASD Characteristics
People with ASD are categorized due to the presence of a number the following issues: They have difficulty with interacting socially and relationally, with expressing and understanding emotion, picking up social cues or understanding facial expression. At times they can be void of their own facial expressions or speak in a monotone voice, struggle with eye contact, and exhibit communication problems, including being able to interact in conversation, or explaining what they're wanting.

A lot of children with ASD present with repetitive behaviour and patterns such as rocking, shaking a rag, clapping, spinning around, unusual blinking, making unusual noises. In my experience/opinion these are used to trigger the pattern of withdrawal away from reality, and/or interaction with others…..preferring to be alone, and be left to themselves.

These children, who seem to suffer significant insecurity for some reason, (Belief driven?) feel secure within a lot of structure and repetition. They gravitate towards routine, which if deviated from can produce a violent reaction, and/or anger, which we could term a tantrum. In extreme cases, they may for example become distraught with changes to routine patterns such as driving to school a different way, or an unscheduled stop, or even changing what they would normally have for breakfast. So, we could summarize this as exhibiting obsessive behaviour which is driven by insecurity and anxiety. Additionally, they may become upset in new environments or places where there is a lot of activity and stimulation.

It seems as though because their world is to some extent reduced to self and their immediate environment, they may become focussed on objects. For example, a fixation on certain toys. This could also include heightened sensory function such as responses to light movement, or as I recently described the feeling of water running on them in the bath or shower, and so on. Another side to this can be a disconnection from other senses, and an unawareness of things like hot and cold weather. Because of their heightened focus on senses, they can be upset by certain noises, smells or tastes, the appearance of things, and even have reactions to certain chemicals.

Early warning signs of ASD can be readily accessed on the internet. Some of these in a baby or very small child include: Lack of eye contact when feeding your child, no acknowledgement or response to their name, reacting to or not wanting to be touched, wanting to isolate and be alone, preferring rigid routines with responses to any changes. (To here, this fits with being massively insecure in relationships, and would in a normal setting be the result of fear of rejection as we've already described.) Other signs include delays in speech and communication skills, learning abilities inhibited, and repetitive movements.

Although many people with ASD have normal intelligence, a lot of people have mild or considerable mental impairment. It is considered that in general they are more prone to other mental illnesses and physical conditions. I will list here some of the simultaneously, or co-occurring mental disorders that may be present:

Anxiety disorders, Bipolar, depression, epilepsy, OCD, gender dysphoria, psychosis, schizophrenia, sleep disorders, ADHD, substance abuse, and in between 25 to 70% of cases, intellectual disability.

The fact that these other disorders can be coexisting, suggests that possibly the origins of these conditions will at times share some elements. Because ASD is a Neurodevelopmental disorder, we would expect that its origins could have their source prenatally, or we would say in the womb. This means that it could begin because of things that happen whilst developing in the womb. Additionally, it could indicate some kind of generationally based process and transference. Whereas many other disorders that we've studied involve abuses even though there may be a generational element or prenatal beginning. Research indicates that ASD is not the result of bad parenting, vaccines or other such factors.

Causes of ASD
Scientists consider that both genetic elements, (for Christians generational factors), and environmental dynamics are likely to be implicated in ASD. As a generalization it is more common to acquire ASD if it's in the family. Again, this could be because of the presence of people with ASD in influential roles, which creates an environment for this condition to be propagated. Or, because of spiritual transference through the generation line. These factors are considered to possibly produce disruptions in normal brain development and growth.

ASD is more often present in children born prematurely. As already stated, it is proven that it is not a disorder that is the result parenting practices. Some theories include the possibility of certain drugs interfering with prenatal development.

One study indicated that single parent families had a higher incidence of ASD. Being deprived of other securities in the family was cited as another possibility. This certainly adds up with being one possible reason for insecurity, particularly if the father left, or was uncommitted to the child during pregnancy. Or if the mother was against the father in rebellion for some reason. Any of these prenatal or early post-natal influences may be a potential source of rejection that leads to rebellion. Further study of actual case histories is certainly required.

It is well documented that ND's run-in families. A Father could present with mild Autism and the son may have ADHD. His sister could have an intellectual or learning disability. This certainly suggests that these problems share the same causative issues.

Dr. Henry W. Wright in his national best-selling book, 'A More Excellent Way,' made the following observations. "Our initial investigation has to do with a neurological breakdown coming out of rejection and rebellion." These emotional and reactive issues have certainly been present with cases that we've been exposed to. He goes on to say; "The entrance points, considering the young ages of autistic children, are some things we are not sure about." He cites contact from a lady with an autistic son, which adds some additional elements to behaviour common with the disorder.

"I had a call from Pennsylvania recently from a lady we have been working with. Her autistic son is now cutting himself. This is self-hatred and brings a new component into this disease. I believe autism is a result of rejection. The other components of autism involve rebellion and anger." His comments are certainly consistent with cases that we've seen where there is often rebellion, outward anger, and anger against self, evidenced by self-harming behaviour, such as the child banging their head against a wall. Etc. etc.

Art Mathias in his publication titled, 'In His Own Image,' writes the following statements based on his own research. "Autism is a developmental disorder that is characterized by impaired development in communication, behaviour and social interactions. Serotonin dysfunction and immune abnormalities play a role in autism." His research makes sense given that Serotonin is reportedly produced by the human body when you like and accept yourself. It is diminished in the body if you reject yourself, and so Serotonin dysfunction certainly fits the emotional profile. Art goes on to write his summation of why he believes that the disorder is present as follows:

"Spiritual/Emotional Strongholds: Inherited deaf and dumb spirit (coming out of matriarchal control,) rebellion, and self-rejection."

Once again, in my own experience I can confirm the presence of these observations. I have previously made comments on autism in our training manual, titled; 'SOHAF School Of Healing And Freedom Comprehensive Manual,' and I'll add them to our study here.

"I have had exposure to a number of other people suffering from autism in a general setting. In a number of those cases I have noted an observable spirit of rebellion in their fathers. By this I mean that their rebellion was demonic in nature from a spirit inside, as opposed to the pressure to be rebellious from the outside of our beings that we all have, or have had elements of. At the same time, I have seen other cases where this is not obvious in either parent but seems to be evident further up the family line.

I am certainly not suggesting any kind of standardization based on the few cases that I know of, but simply offer what I have seen in case it helps anyone understand their own loved ones. I have also heard testimonies of autism symptoms improving and reducing through the prayer of faith. Other Christian commentators have also observed the rebellion and self-rejection issues present with Autism. As we have previously pointed out, a result of rejection can be withdrawal as a countermeasure to extreme fear of rejection, along with self-rejection.

At times the withdrawal from relationships is so extreme that the speech or ability to communicate is also not functioning. Some consider this to be an inherited deaf and dumb spirit stemming from Matriarchal control. They consider this ungodly order in the household to be the root cause of the problem. In addition to fathers with rebellion problems I have certainly observed some controlling women and role reversal in the generation lines of children suffering with these problems. Some report changes as these spiritual issues are dealt with."

CHAPTER TWENTY FOUR
Conclusion and Summary

Over the years I have come to realize that everything begins with a thought. As we've stated emotions come from thoughts, and these thoughts and emotions conclude in the body through chemical and electrical actions. So, disease, in part is often the result of our inner thinking. Mental, emotional, relational and spiritual issues also proceed from these inner thoughts and beliefs. This could be expanded out to world events that occur because of the thoughts and beliefs of those who lead our world. The Bible has said it, and the evidence is that it is true that the centre piece in influencing the world, along with our personal lives, is our hearts, individual and collective.

> Proverbs 4:23 Above all else, guard your heart, for it affects everything you do. NLT

Having provided Part 2 as a diagnostic aid to specific disorders, my recommendation would be to review the ministry model that I have presented in Part 1. Chapter 10. This could be supplemented by other Manuals and books that I have written which invariably include the 'Truth Encounters' ministry.

Revision and Recap
In order to be equipped in this area, having studied Part 1, you will need to be able to answer the following questions:

1. As you begin to minister to people struggling with mental disorder what is the main thing that you are looking for?
   Answer – You are trying to identify root heart beliefs that the person generally is not consciously aware that they believe.

2. What will these beliefs relate to?
   Answer – these will mostly be in regard to perception of identity and beliefs about SELF. At times these will be beliefs connected to certain situations or circumstances.

3. How do you begin a ministry session?
   *Answer – A) We make sure that the person understands the ministry process.
   B) We listen to their story and note self-beliefs that may be evident.
   C) We ask about their issues, or current troubling events.*

4. How do we find what these beliefs are?
   *Answer – A) we have the person embrace thoughts and feelings and look for matching memory events in early childhood. Pre ten years old. (If there are no memories it may have a prenatal origin, or there could be suppression or disassociation)
   B) We ask questions to help them identify what they believe.*

Note: Experience is the best teacher. Someone can drive you to a location across a city many times, and as a passenger you still won't remember how to get there. But generally, if you make the journey once driving yourself you know the way. Ministry is the same. The best way to know what to do is make the journey...even if you make a few wrong turns.

My hope is that this book is just the beginning of many taking up the work, and being committed to bringing the good news to those struggling with mental disorder. God's intention has been, and is always, abundance of life, righteousness, peace and joy in the Holy Spirit.

Other Resources

1. YOU WILL INDEED BE SET FREE
This book is an excerpt from the publication HEALING AND FREEDOM THROUGH TRUTH ENCOUNTERS which explains the basis of how to be healed and set free through a 'Truth Encounter'.

2. HEALING AND FREEDOM THROUGH TRUTH ENCOUNTERS
This detailed publication includes the contents of YOU WILL INDEED BE SET FREE, along with considerable other information to help those wishing to minister or gain further understanding.

3. SCHOOL OF HEALING AND FREEDOM Comprehensive Training Manual
This Manual contains all of the materials contained in the books in a study format, as well as other Units relating to bringing freedom, healing and wholeness.

4. SCHOOL OF HEALING AND FREEDOM Basic Seminar Manual
This is the simplified version of the Comprehensive manual for those attending Schools or seminars.

5. PREPARING FOR A 'TRUTH ENCOUNTER'
This booklet is designed as a handout to help position those coming for a 'Truth Encounters' ministry session to understand and receive their breakthrough.

All resources can be purchased through most major book retailers in the U.K and the U.S.A. and Australia.

In Africa purchases can be made through, CLC booklink Kenya, Jumia, Amazon Africa

Further details about the 418Centre ministry and resources can be found on our website: www.418centre.org

www.ingramcontent.com/pod-product-compliance
Lightning Source LLC
Chambersburg PA
CBHW050308010526
44107CB00055B/2146